LES AMOURS J.

THESE JAUNDICED LOVES

for Brian & Liz

with many thanks

Chris

also by Christopher Pilling

*

Snakes & Girls
(New Poets Award, University of Leeds School of English Press, 1970)

In All the Spaces On All the Lines
(Phoenix Pamphlet Poets, Manchester, 1971)

Foreign Bodies (Flambard Press, Newcastle upon Tyne, 1992)

Cross Your Legs and Wish (Redbeck Press, Bradford, 1994)

These Jaundiced Loves

A translation of

TRISTAN CORBIÈRE'S
Les Amours Jaunes

by

CHRISTOPHER PILLING

Christopher Pilling

PETERLOO POETS

First published in 1995
by Peterloo Poets
2 Kelly Gardens, Calstock, Cornwall PL18 9SA, U.K.

A catalogue record for this book is available
from the British Library

ISBN 1-871471-55 9

Printed in Great Britain by
Latimer Trend & Company Ltd, Plymouth

Acknowledgements:

Earlier versions of some of these translations appeared in *Phoenix 13* (1975), *Peterloo Anthology No. 1* (Peterloo Poets, 1979) and *The Oxford Book of Verse in English Translation* (Oxford University Press, 1980). My thanks to the editors: Harry Chambers and Charles Tomlinson.

Also thanks to the many friends consulted over the years, in particular Gérald Fontaine. And for reactions to my English versions I am indebted to Sylvia's ear and intuition.

For my children: Mark, Zoë and Ceri.

À l'auteur du **Négrier.**
T.C.

To the author of **Le Négrier.**
T.C.

To the memory of the authors of the translator.

C'est une chose délicieuse que d'écrire, que de ne plus être soi, mais de circuler dans toute la création dont on parle. Aujourd'hui par exemple, homme et femme tout ensemble, amant et maîtresse à la fois, je me suis promené à cheval dans une forêt par un après-midi d'automne sous les feuilles jaunes, et j'étais les chevaux, les feuilles, le vent, les paroles qu'on se disait et le soleil rouge qui faisaient s'entrefermer leurs paupières noyées d'amour.

Gustave Flaubert.

A little life of Tristan Corbière 1845-1875

1845 July 18. Birth of Edouard-Joachim Corbière (who was to call himself Tristan) at Coat-Congar in Ploujean, near Morlaix in Finistère, Brittany. His mother, Marie-Angélique-Aspasie Puyo was then 18; his father, (Jean-Antoine-René-) Édouard Corbière, 52, had had an outstanding career as sailor, freethinking journalist and author of maritime adventures. 'Tristan' spent a happy childhood at Le Launay, very near Coat-Congar.

1850 Birth of his sister (Marie-)Lucie.

1855 Birth of his brother Edmond.
Publication of the 4th edition of *Le Négrier*, his father's most famous novel, considerably revised since the first edition of 1832. This edition had a considerable influence on him.

1859 From having been taught at the local school in Morlaix by a Monsieur Bourgeois, he was sent to boarding school: the Lycée Impérial de Saint-Brieuc. He did well at French, but especially Latin, winning prizes for translation and verse. He kept copies of *Le Négrier* among his treasures in a yellow tuck-box in his desk, to give to certain favoured teachers. Wrote home regularly, separate letters to mother and father and sometimes Lucie.

1860 Wrote a comic poem on his history teacher's hat. Drew caricatures. Suffered from chilblains on his hands and rheumatoid arthritis. In August transferred for health reasons to the Lycée at Nantes where he lived with his doctor uncle, Jules Chenantais, who could keep an eye on him.

1862 First signs of TB. A bad attack of rheumatism meant he had to abandon his studies and he did not sit the *baccalauréat*. His mother took him to Provence. Little improvement, despite other trips to Cannes and Luchon. Back in Brittany he read widely, drew, played practical jokes on Morlaix folk and wrote about them in satirical verse full of word-play.

1863 On uncle's advice went to live by the sea, in the family's holiday house in Roscoff. Free and easy existence. Met Breton sailors who nicknamed him *An Ankou* (the Breton figure of Death) because of his sickly if not skeletal appearance. Went out in his boat, *Le Négrier*, the sea the wilder the better! Always wanted to be a sailor like his father. Ate frequently at Le Gad's *pension*, where he met a group of Parisian artists.

1864-68 More hoaxes and practical jokes; Roscovites were not enamoured. Much reading and boating. Wrote *Gens de Mer* and *Armor*. Little is known of this period.

1869-70 From December until March 1870 travelled in Italy with the Breton artist Jean-Louis Hamon: Naples, Castellamare, Sorrento. Met the artist Jean Benner in Capri, where he spent 2½ months. Signed Pagano Hotel register adding *"far niente, pittore-poëta etc."* Enjoyed dressing up for carnival and masked ball. Some if not all of the poems set in Italy (in *Raccrocs*) were written on this trip. Went to Rome and saw *"autre curiosité — le pape; ... j'aurais pu le toucher et lui donner ma main à embrasser."* *(I could have touched him and given him my hand to kiss.)* Poked fun at the first Vatican Council on the infallibility of the Pope. Returned to Morlaix with a bishop's mitre and cope, and blessed the good people of Morlaix from the balcony. Hence to Roscoff again.

1871 In the Spring Count Rodolphe de Battine and his actress friend Armida-Josefina Cuchiani came to stay at Le Gad's. He befriended them and may have been enamoured of Armida. He took them out in *Le Négrier*, then later on the yacht he christened *Le Tristan*. Rodolphe, who had been wounded near Le Mans, would have spoken of the horrors of life at Conlie. After hearing more of Conlie from his brother-in-law Aimé Vacher, a volunteer, he wrote *La Pastorale de Conlie*. *La Rapsode Foraine* was probably written this year after he'd been to the *pardon* of Sainte-Anne-la-Palud on August 27th. Rodolphe and Armida left for Paris in October.

1872 In the Spring he too went to Paris and took a room in the Cité Gaillard, Monmartre, near Armida, and met up with the poet Gustave Mathieu and his artist friends again. Moved to 10 Rue Frochot. Mother sent the rent, 300 francs a month. Went with the couple to Capri. Considered changing his name to Mazzzeppa *(sic)*. Then back to Brittany (Douarnenez) with them in June, then back to Paris. Wrote numerous poems; drew caricatures often sending up the *Communards*. These drawings were collected for publication under the title *Le Peuple Souverain*, but are lost.

1873 *La Vie Parisienne* published 9 of his poems in 6 different isssues. His only collection *Les Amours Jaunes* was brought out in August by Glady Frères, at the author's expense. 10 years later some of these poems would be brought from obscurity by Verlaine, who chose Corbière as the first of his first trio of *Poètes Maudits*, along with Rimbaud and Mallarmé.

1874 Lack of success did not stop him writing. He 'improved' several of *Les Amours Jaunes* and wrote new poems. Stayed at Rodolphe's Château des Aiguesbelles, in La Sarthe. Then spent summer in Roscoff with the couple. *La Vie Parisienne* published his 2 prose pieces: *Casino des Trépassés* and *l'Américaine*. Despite poor health he went back to Paris in November. On the morning of December 20th, he was discovered inanimate on the floor of his flat, dressed for dancing. Friends took him to the Dubois hospital; he wrote to his parents: *" ... Je suis à Dubois dont on fait les cercueils ..."* (I'm at *Wood hospital you get coffins out of*).

1875 His mother took him back home to Quai de Léon, Morlaix on January 6th. He died on March 1st, without the last rites, *"célibataire ... sans profession ..."* *(bachelor ... unemployed ...)* His father, who was now director of a steam-boat company and had been made *chevalier de la Légion d'honneur,* died in September, aged 82; his mother not until 1891. Father and son are buried side by side in the family vault at Saint-Martin-des-Champs, Morlaix.

Painting of Ali Baba by Tristan Corbière.
(Bibliothèque Municipale de Morlaix)

Postface masquerading as a preface

In Bed 22, in Broussais hospital, in 1887, Paul Verlaine wrote: 'Bring me Corbière, if possible.'[1] On a winter night four years earlier he had asked Léo Trézenik and Charles Morice to read him the whole of *Les Amours Jaunes*, his curiosity whetted by a few quotations. 'From the beginning to the end, Verlaine did not stop laughing,' wrote Morice, 'and in the most moving and poignant passages his laugh actually interrupted us; it was laughter mixed with tears.'[2] It was almost as if Tristan Corbière foresaw what his verse might cause if anyone took the trouble to read him, when he wrote:

> ... If my lines have made you laugh,
> Come and cry;
> come and laugh, if they have made you cry ...

Here, in *Le Poète Contumace (The Poet by Default)*, he is writing a letter to his will o' the wisp of a Muse he claims to have buried and lost; he writes it though in inspired verse, cussed to the last. No wonder Verlaine chose him as the first of his *Poètes Maudits*. It was Verlaine's essay with a small selection of Corbière's poems which, when published in book form in 1884[3], alongside Rimbaud and Mallarmé, rescued him from near oblivion. His only collection *Les Amours Jaunes* had appeared (and only 490 copies at that) in August 1873 at the author's expense — or rather his father's — from a relatively new, small-scale publisher[4] of a strange assortment of books, this being only the second volume of poems. A handsome edition and quite expensive at 7fr. 50c., Anatole France's *Vers Dorés*[5] and Victor Hugo's *La Légende des Siècles*[6] selling for 3fr. 50c. in the same year. It received three reviews, one of which was in a Belgian art magazine[7]. There the critic winced at *une débauche de mots (a riot of words)*. 'The words dance a saraband, you are carried along despite yourself, and if later in the cold light of reason, you try to make sense of them, complete emptiness.' The reviewer in *L'Artiste*[8] considered him more down-to-earth in his realism than Courbet and Manet and thought mothers should forbid their daughters to read him. The one in *La Renaissance Littéraire et Artistique*[9] saw some merit in the collection but, quoting the masochistic *Poète, en dépit de ses vers (Poet, despite his verse)* from *Épitaphe*, took Corbière to task in forthright terms: '... all the rules of poetry, rhyme and rhythm are too often laid aside. If the author considers them useless constraints, why didn't he write in prose?' He did write two very fine prose pieces: *Casino des Trépassés* and *L'Américaine*, but his verse shows that he was distinctly aware of prosody and the effects that could be achieved by slight dislocations of form and metre. The reviewers' sweeping censure is wide of the mark. In fact, as *1 Sonnet* and *Un Jeune Qui S'en Va* show, his preoccupation with the writing and reading of poetry, the techniques and rationale, was a matter of life and death to him.

The Muse then, in her different embodiments, was a life-(and death)-force. And embodiments is a crucial word, for Tristan Corbière is sure to have heard his name as Triste en corps bière (Sad in body: coffin), having written over his door in Paris: TRISTE EN TOUS LIEUX (SAD EVERYWHERE) and imagined a *Corbillard (Hearse)* carrying his *âme (soul, spirit)* up to the graveyard because *Vivre notre métier — ça tue ... (To live one's calling is the killing part ...) (Convoi du Pauvre)*.

Corbière was to die (from rheumatism and pneumonia, as the admissions register of La Maison Dubois records[10]) less than two years later, at the age of 29. His mother brought him from the hospital in Paris to the family house in Morlaix and he asked for his room to be filled with heather. In *Le Poète Contumace* again he comforts himself with what he calls his harvests:

> .... the golden flowers of the broom —
> .... my large pine-woods for logs
> My heather from Armor ... — piled high on the fire-dogs.

He had put these in his verse and now he would die with an even more visible reminder of his native province, Armor — the ancient name for Brittany. Heather lasting, and Armor too, for he had given it new life in among his yellow loves *(amours jaunes)*: In *Cris d'Aveugle (Blind Man's Cries)* in the *Armor* section there appeared in his mind's eye: *Landes jaunes d'Armor (You yellow heathland of Armor)*.

His love for Brittany then was not jaundiced, far from it, but his great admiration for her sailors — very evident in the *Gens de Mer (Seafarers)* section — was that of a sailor manqué, and his Breton poems in *Armor* are love poems, even though, or perhaps because, they dwell on sinister landscapes, animated by toads, a Washerwoman laundering for the dead, Death himself with his *wheelbarrow* (listen, can you hear it squeaking? it needs more than a drop of oil, as certain critics have more than hinted about Corbière's verse), a blind man and a poor beggar (but a welcome guest at any farm), and the disconcerting figure of Want (or is she Misery? or both?) at the *Pardon* of Saint Anne. Saint-Anne-de-la-Palud may eventually succour all pilgrims who call on her but what are we to make of Saint Tupetu, a stranger to the Vatican, who will decide by the spin of a roulette wheel whether you'll live or die?

As Corbière decides that his own death is vital if his Muse is to cradle him in her arms — *la poésie est: ... mourir! (poetry is: ... dying!)* he writes in *Un Jeune Qui S'en Va* — he has his epitaph early on, before the *Jaundiced Loves* appear. Most of his poems then follow death, not in any morbid sense, for he is very much alive in his verses and reverses, seeing himself in an attic or on the street, in bed or at sea, in mirrors, pigeonholes and portholes — perhaps unwittingly sometimes — as the Hunchback Bitor, a sucking Juvenal, the Wandering Jew, a serenader beneath a balcony, a duellist, a plunderer of wreckage, a pariah, a lover in a lighthouse and even a mongrel. (He called his own dog Tristan.) All embodiments. As in sympathetic magic, there are affinities between these selves and himself which allow him to change and speak out in ways he couldn't if he were just acting or playing possum. The Absent Woman he dreams of will only appear in post-mortems too, for She *(Elle)* is a Shade, a wish-fulfilment, a bitch, a mare to be ridden bare-back, a bareback circus rider, himself as a woman, a woman even. She's a cicada too, borrowed from La Fontaine, whirring her presence; in fact she's the next-door neighbour who, because he conjures her up, will readily lend him a living and breathing rhyme so long as he sings. Hence the need for this translation to rhyme as fully as it can, to give it a chance of singing.

After *La Fin (The End)*, there is another life and Corbière will prove it in poems with lines that keep coming back, life-renewing rondels where he is a child again with an incredible future and no call to worry about the physical and spiritual deformities he attributed to himself in his earthly existence, where 'I am ugly; she won't want me' and 'She doesn't want me; I must be ugly' were two sides of his only coin. In these *Rondels pour Après (Rondels for Afterwards)* the Muse, almost a death's-head, will finally flit down to him, with no more sound than a hawk-moth, and he can take flight. She will ensure there's no-one in his coffin, despite what flat-footed bourgeois may presume, for he, as poet, is by then a bestrider of beams, an unhooker of stars, a light-fingered comber of comets ... Will o' the wisps will leap from his eye sockets (which once held the eyes of a toad) and it's his laughter you'll hear (behind you? by your side? beside yourself?), and this laughter will be distinctly earthy.

Corbière aimed to translate himself beyond death. But he is 'all mixed-up', not knowing which side of the grave he is on. Writing your epitaph as though you were dead would be to look back on your life with a certain finality, but in doing so you would need to relive it a little. The more you say, and if like Corbière you say it with telling paradoxes and wit (however much at your own expense), the more you are likely to bring your life to life. Here, in this earlier version of *Épitaphe*[11], Corbière does just that. Far from passé, he meets himself at the lych-gate:

Epitaph
for
Tristan Joachim-Edouard Corbière, philosopher,
down-and-out, still-born

A pure adulterous mish-mash:
Man of fortune short of cash,
Bounding energy on the wane,
Liberty with an ankle-sprain.
Heart-felt feelings, no soul though —
Friends, yes, but companion, no,

An intellect who'd no idea,
Lover no girl would come near,
Weary bones unable to rest.
Virtues in him were faults at best,
Blasé at heart with passions rife.
Dead, but not recovered from life,
Wrecker of life who'd missed the boat
By giving his hang-ups plenty of rope;
Head swimming, body high and dried,
Denying the future, living in hope,
Waiting to come to life, he died
And lived, taking death in his stride.

There is a significant order to the names in the title. He has put his Christian names Édouard-Joachim backwards and begun with the name he adopted about 1863, when, because of his poor health and on his uncle doctor's advice, he went to live on his own in the family's summer residence close to the sea in Roscoff. He told the painter Lafenestre that he had taken the name Tristan from his brother. He actually had two brothers, neither of whom was called Tristan. Alexis-Edmond only lived to be 5 and Edmond, who would have been 7 or 8 at the time of Édouard junior's move to Roscoff, was nicknamed affectionately *le gros monmon* and *Gouronnec* in letters home from boarding school (1859-62). His *brother* then must have been the Tristan of Celtic legend and like him Corbière was transported (if only in imagination) to Penmarc'h, a point on the south coast of Brittany, where Tristan of Lyonesse awaited his beloved Isolde. *Le Poète Contumace*, supposedly written in Penmarc'h, has the Poet writing to the *L'Absente (The Absent One (fem.))*. He is both ecstatic and disillusioned. Not only will his Isolde never come, but he tears up his letter to her with a laugh. The little pieces of paper go floating off into the mist, like so many seagulls, like so many unrequited love poems.

The *Epitaph* above has him dying to live. In the French there are only three main verbs: were (he was plural), died and lived (in that order). In this version he has denied himself any soul, but when we come to the longer *Epitaph*, after the bitter Paris sonnets, he includes a soul of sorts as an item he has to dispose of in his will, however mock it may be: *De l'âme et pas de violon (some soul and no violin)*. The word *âme* has a second sense allowing a typical play on words: it's a sound-post, which in a violin is the the short post under the bridge connecting the belly to the back of the instrument and allowing the treble notes to resonate more. Although the bow has been called the soul of the instrument, without which a violin must remain a mute *objet d'art* (unless the fingers are brought in to play), the sound-post is an inner necessity. Without it, a violin would be, not so much dead wood, but slightly off-key, planguorous[12] rather than languorous. But here of course there is not even a violin. The 'poetic', the mellifluous is taboo — the violin standing for the kind of verse Lamartine let gush, or more kindly, penned in perfect cadences.

Perfection is one thing, genius another. 'The impeccable ones,' wrote Verlaine, 'are wooden, wooden, and again wooden.' 'Corbière,' he goes on, 'was flesh and blood, to the point of looking foolish. His verse is living, laughing ...'[13] No, Corbière's verse is not wooden. He is, by writing it, up on stage, a century before rock-guitar-smashers, smashing a violin, but having something to offer in its place at one and the same time, being self-denigratory and parading his own originality. When, in *Petit Mort pour Rire*, the poet's coffin is an empty violin case, he will be in the theatre, in the brothel, in church or the graveyard, often at sea, playing odd tunes on comb and paper. Tunes that can be jarring, at odds with the 'poetic' ones of most of his contemporaries. Laforgue would call him 'an unseizable smoke-dried corsair, bold in his raids'[14]; no sailor manqué here.

In *Pauvre Garçon (Poor Boy)* the poet is referred to by *La Bête féroce (the Savage Beast)* as: *quel instrument rétif à jouer! (such a tricky instrument to play!)*. His tune was performed inside his head *(son petit air de tête)* and, because of its self-deprecating notes, it came out as out of tune: *Ses vers faux furent ses seuls vrais (His false lines were his only true ones* or *His out of tune lines were his only tuneful ones) (Épitaphe)*. But before he could sing these out loud, he needed someone or something to spark them off — so he called on the neighbour, in the dedicatory parody *Le Poète et la Cigale (The Poet and the Cicada)*, pleading hunger, hunger for a rhyme and the rhyme he wanted may have appeared a small matter to a constantly singing cicada but for the poet it would be the be-all and end-all. He gave the neighbour the name Marcelle and asked to borrow her better half, i.e. *elle*.

Marcelle has been assumed all too often to be a name invented for the actress Armida-Josefina Cuchiani. She came to stay in Roscoff in 1871 with her lover Count Rodolphe de Battine, who had been invalided out from the army division stationed in the mud of Conlie. They put up at the hotel where Corbière dined and he befriended them. Now Armida may have been one aspect of the Eternal Feminine in his jaundiced loves and could well be Hermine and Mina in *Après la Pluie* since her stage name was Herminie. She may be behind the theatrical imagery in the Paris poems. He could well have felt as intensely about her as Michel Dansel speculates in *Tristan Corbière: Thématique de l'Inspiration*[15]. Her initials: A-J. C could even have played a small part in the choice of title for a section or the whole collection of poems: A(mours)-J(aunes) C(orbière)!

The Poet leaves Marcelle after the introductory poem, only to return to her in the valedictory one. Into the book proper he takes what she has loaned: the rhyme -*elle* and all it signifies, leaving the other half: *Marc* out in the wings. The Tristan of legend brought Isolde (variously known as Iseut, Yseut or Yseult la Blonde) for his uncle, King Mark (*Le Roi Marc*) to marry, but the power of the love potion they took by accident is such that they remain lovers after the wedding. Because of their mutual passion Tristan and Yseut *(elle)* undergo hardships, a modicum of guilt, and exile from society until they are obliged to separate. Finally, as Tristan lies

v

wounded and dying in Brittany, he is told a lie: that Yseut, the only one who can cure him, has not sailed from Cornwall to bring him back to life. He dies, thinking she has failed him. The parallels between the legend and the personae of *Les Amours Jaunes* are quite striking.

Corbière was creating his own *état légendaire (legendary state)* as he dubs it in *The Poet by Default*, creating himself in his verse. Writing because he didn't know how to die *(manque de savoir-mourir)*. He could do the dying in verse: simultaneously *killing himself with ardour (Il se tua d'ardeur)* or just *dying through idleness (ou mourut de paresse)* in order to live as a legend. These quotations are from *Épitaphe*, placed so early that most of *Les Amours Jaunes* reads like a posthumous work. "*Je rime, donc je vis ...*" ("*I rhyme therefore I live ...*") he will announce, then put the tin lid on things in *Un Jeune Qui S'en Va* with: *Métier! métier de mourir ... (What a calling! A call to death ...)* and *Métier: se rimer finir (My career: rhyming out of breath! ...)* He rhymes himself to death! The very title *Un Jeune Qui S'en Va* is two-edged: *A Young Man Going to Glory*.

Tristan of Léonois *(Lyonesse)* was one of the first heroes in literature to die for the love of a woman; his love for Yseut was passionate and fated. Tristan Corbière's loves were too; he had wounds that only *She (Elle)* could cure. Suffering from 'le mal d'amour', Tristan from Léonois hid in the Château de Karhaix, Tristan from Léon in his *borgne tourelle* at Penmarc'h *(Le Poète Contumace)* where a swallow alights and where the golden broom and golden eyes of the owls could bring to mind the golden hair in the swallow's beak which was of course Yseut's. And the *Belles nuits pour l'orgie à la tour! (Lovely nights for the orgy in the tower!)* might be a quotation from Alexandre Dumas père, but, taken along with a line from *Femme: Lui dont la triste image est debout sur ma couche (He whose sad image is standing on my litter)* and almost giving us his name (Corbière signed himself Trist. when *L'Américaine* was printed in *La Vie Parisienne* and Trist(an) on the hotel register of the Pagano Hotel, Capri), can remind us of the leap from Tristan's bed to the royal bed and the incriminating blood from his wound could account for the late change of *jour sali (sullied day)* to *drap sali (sullied sheet)* in *Femme*. He imagines that, were he the Devil, *de quel bond/Je serais sur toi, la Donzelle! (how I'd bound onto you, my Filly!)* in Act II of *Grand Opéra*, where, incidentally, linen whiter than a lily, the boundary stone where Tristan the leper is to stand and the mire the horses sink in, have their echoes in *lys, borne,* and *fange*. Could the leap by the Lascar in *La Goutte* be an echo of this leap? He is certainly rewarded with a kiss! Or perhaps it's closer to Tristan's leap from the chapel window.

If some of these links seem rather tenuous, there are other and stronger ones. King Marc offered his nephew Tristan his throne. Why else would Tristan Corbière exclaim: *Ne m'offrez pas un trône! (Don't offer me a throne)* in *Bohème de Chic (Swish Bohemia)*? The final verses of this poem find him sleeping with the Muse, who is blond like Yseut (if she isn't drunk!), under a one-star sky, and laughing like a mad woman when

>   ... ta chair fraîche colle
>   Contre mon cuir lépreux

(... your clear skin sticks to my leprous hide). Yseut is given to the hundred lepers to have in their hovels — Marc being persuaded by their leader that it's a fate worse than death for 'There is such lust in us the very clothes stick to our bodies.' Tristan saves her from this, and then later dresses as a leper himself at Yseut's instigation so that she can call him to be her ass *(âne),* ride him over the swamp and claim that the only men to have been between her thighs are her husband and this leper.

The clearest echo of the Tristan and Yseut tale is in *Femme (Woman)* — the *Elle* poem par excellence, where he gives the platform to Woman herself. She announces: — *Je suis reine: Qu'il soit lépreux! (— I am queen: Let him be leper!).* In the original, Tristan took the knocks and abuse (and the gifts) for his own ends, the loving of Yseut. In *Femme* he is ugly and she is beautiful enough for them both together, but he is egging her on by playing hard to get, she doesn't love him, but wants to kiss him (like Judas) for loving her! Love is in italics, to be spat in his face. A jaundiced love, if ever there was one. He is a *mal aimé* well before Apollinaire's *Chanson du Mal-Aimé.* He seems to thrive on such masochism. Ugliness despite which there can be love of a sort was one of the appealing things about the assumption of the name Tristan and the dropping of Édouard, a Christian name that carried too many Christian expectations and too great a reminder of his father's career. Could he hear his father's voice when King Marc opposed Tristan's going off in an open boat, to sail at the whim of the waves, without oars or sail, to seek a cure for his wound? Tristan Corbière was only too keen to go on dare-devil outings in his cutter *Le Négrier.* Could he hear his father's refusal when he asked Marc to make him a knight to take on Morholt single-handed? Could he hear his father's objection to him having a horse when Tristan rode back to Marc with Yseut? Tristan suffered much, but all for love. And now his namesake would.

To appropriate Tristan's name was to take on the *idea* of his attributes: a well-built handsome lover, a weather-beaten sailor, a fine horseman and hunter, a dragon-killer with his tongue in his sock, and a musician who composed lays for Yseut. But, perhaps more than anything, it was the fact (as far as legends can have facts) that Tristan was happy to take on disguises to gain his ends that gave Tristan Corbière the sense of brotherhood. To have Yseut he became a beggar, a leper, a fool. And Tristan Corbière saw himself as an ugly toad, but there was a light in his eye. That light is the light of inspiration. *Je me sens un rayon,* he says when he picks up his stub of pencil *(Un Jeune Qui S'en Va).* Sunlight reaches him through his rags, moonlight through his hat. His lighthouse *est jauni/Et pose juste pour la lune/Comme un grand I. (has turned yellow/and poses like a capital I, just/for the moon — so!).* The male virgin of the lighthouse *(Le Phare)* is lunatic, meeting a vestal in the blaze of the lamp. Tristan is a lunar figure and one of the archetypes of Yseut, the Irish Grainné, comes from the word for sun. Jean Markale[16] points out that if Yseut la Blonde represents the sun and Tristan the moon (the sun being feminine and the moon masculine in Celtic languages) their love is impossible. *Marc'h* (the Breton for horse) represents the horseman who carries off light and the soul to the other world, a figure of darkness and death, terrible, vengeful, especially towards Tristan! As well as the possibility of love, there is the final impossibility — Tristan Corbière must sleep for it, die for it, and return her to Marc.

Tristan offers his apologies to Marcelle for his shameful monster of a book, *these jaundiced loves*, the work of a disillusioned poet whose Muse, inebriated, has rolled down from cloud nine onto scraps of paper and tinselry. His Muse without Marc was airborne for a while. Wings *(ailes)* are a homophone for *elle* and Tristan the poet could have them on his feet *(Guitare)*, or he might get carried away on them (Pegasus in *1 Sonnet*), or be shorn of them (the toad of *Le Crapaud*, that nightingale of the mud), or simply rhyme them *(aile* or *ailes* appear 11 times as a rhyme, just beating beautiful *(belle)* and faithful *(fidèle)*). The words ending in [εl] at the rhyme occur more times than there are poems in the collection! The final poem where [εl] rhymes appear, just before he returns to Marcelle, are in Rondel, a verse-form with repeated lines like a ritornello but in a totally different tone. After death now the poet is a mini-Prometheus, stealing, not fire from heaven, but sparks *(étincelles)* and evoking damselflies, brilliant hovering insects like dragonflies, which fold their transparent wings when at rest, and immortelles, those papery everlasting flowers which retain their shape and colour when dried. Here Love has wings. All that's missing is a real live woman, one of those *(celles)* who kept saying Never and in the same breath Always. So he lies in the dark, dead asleep, buoyed by hope, a mere *fleurette blême (deathly-pale small flower)*. (The other Tristan's mother was called Blanchefleur and she died in childbirth which is why her son was given a name full of sadness.) Finally he has to return to his generous neighbour Marcelle in *La Cigale et le Poète*, where the penultimate rhymes are *Marcelle* and *elle*. Right at the very end is 'now' *(maintenant)* but it has to look back for its rhyme with a ghost *(revenant)*. Marc and his Yseut are together again, which for Tristan is not perfection (*On n'est pas parfait*) but deep down he respects their marriage. He almost rubbed himself out *(c'est à blanc)*, or at least crossed himself out *(je suis là — mais comme une rature)* in *Le Poète Contumace*, and now here he is, in Marcelle's words, going for a song: *c'est tout comme .../Si vous chantiez ...!* (the phrase '*c'est comme si on chantait*' meaning it's useless). It is Marc and Yseut (I chose this spelling of her name without the l, because she is the [εl]) reunited as Marcelle who mortify him with *Écrivain public banal! (Scribe of the poor man's Iliad!)*. Tristan is only starting to sing now he's a dead and legendary lover but he can only be that because, like Bitor, he had known love, known it in writing *These Jaundiced Loves*. A ghostly self can still be heard singing, like the one on the quay in *Le Bossu Bitor*:

> Quelque novice seul, resté mélancolique,
> Se chante son pays avec une musique ...

His song may seem to be an adulterous affair, or betrayal, to those who wish Poetry to retain a capital P, it may sound to them like an air that is out of tune, sharp or flat. The betraying love still lasts as the song of yellow loves will sing on. In the arms of a death's-head Muse *Les Amours Jaunes* are for reviving, re-reading — *post mortem homo tristan est.*

Re-reading then, we can take another look, this time perhaps on a sleepless night. There are too many hints of the Tristan story in *Insomnie* for it not to have the legend behind it. Marc is known as the Cuckold King and this poem is in the *Les Amours Jaunes* section, yellow the colour of cuckoldry. Here is the *philtre amoureux, (the love potion)*, here Insomnia, for it's She he invites to come to rest in his hovel, licks him like a dog (Husdant discovering her master in the forest?), squeezes him between her knees and leaves him, neck outstretched, dying of thirst. Tristan, as leper, appeals for drinks to quench the fire in his body *(il ressent dans son corps une si grande brûlure)* then appeals to King Arthur for clothes by claiming to be unlike all other lepers and freezing! Tristan Corbière asks Insomnia whether she's Buridan's ass *(l'âne en peine)* in torment because she can't decide what she wants and tells her her kiss of fire leaves a cold taste of red-hot iron. *Ton baiser de feu/Laisse un goût froidi de fer rouge ...* . When Marc was convinced of Yseut's adultery, he made her swear she was faithful by the ordeal of holding a red-hot iron. Here Insomnia is one of Tristan's mistresses; he wants Her to sleep with him for a while, a reminder of Tristan's words about Yseut to the Hermit Ogrin: *Because of her I cannot sleep or doze.* No wonder one of the longest poems in *Les Amours Jaunes* is his *Litanie du Sommeil*. Insomnia is a time when he can think of the riches Sleep has to offer; it is, like love, an 'état de déséquilibre, d'angoisse mêlée d'agréable vertige.'[17]

The first line of *Le Naufrageur* sounds like Yseut protesting her innocence: *Si ce n'était pas vrai — Que je crève!* To Marc she says: *Even if I'm to die now I shall tell you the whole truth, not a single word shall be false.* She protests too much. And *Le Naufrageur* is a little beyond the realm of truth in his details about himself and his parents:

> Moi ...
> Oiseau de malheur à poil roux! ...

and

> Mon père était un vieux saltin
> Ma mère était une vieille *morgate*.

which are as outlandish as the answers the fool Picous (i.e. Tristan in disguise) gives when Marc asks: *Who was your father? A walrus. By whom did he have you? A whale. A whale that lives in the sea like a siren!*

So it was the disguises that Tristan wore, the personae adopted, changing his voice and his very appearance, that would have endeared him to Tristan Corbière. And the not inconsiderable having of a mistress. On a self-portrait, Tristan Corbière wrote his assumed name backwards, in mirror-writing. Reversing the two syllables of his name, Tristan called himself Tantris before he sailed to Brittany, wore torn clothes, blacked his face and pretended to be a minstrel. The hideously ugly buffoon sang an inspired tune. The tantrist is a dead man in life, for he has experienced his own death in advance. Tristan needed to disguise himself to go to Ireland for Yseut and played the harp for the Irish king. He composed a melancholy lay for Yseut to sing. Tristan Corbière needed to dress up too and in all sorts of garb, just as he liked to dress up in real life — as a Breton sailor, as a bishop, for the carnival on Capri — just for fun, *pour épater les bourgeois,* or just to show off. He dressed up in a motley array of verse forms, with words culled from here, there and nearly everywhere, from different ages and registers, taking some by the scruff of the neck, slipping others in by sleight of hand, easing awkward customers into a well-stocked avant-garde music shop where he sits cross-legged on the counter, playing the 'lines' he has to offer for all he's worth, as if his life depended on it.

Listen. He has shoed cicadas, in a lullaby to a dead child *(Mirliton: Kazoo),* so he can ride off on song. As a 15 year old in a letter home from boarding school to his mother, he was dying to ride off on his own horse, bareback and without a bridle if necessary. 'I'll break my neck just to show you, just to infuriate you. I'm only saying that for a joke,' he adds, 'because you won't stop me riding in the wood at Coat-Congar, will you?'[18]. It's not known for sure whether he was allowed to have the horse he called *'mon cheval'* or even ride it. He'd been told it was too frisky and his *'tu ne sais pas comme je suis bon cavalier'* would almost certainly have fallen on deaf ears. He could gallop through his school prep.[19] then and later climb in the saddle of a poem and ride off on it, become a *chevaucheur de rayons (a bestrider of beams).* To have a cicada as mount is to have a child-size feminine Pegasus and she appears just before he returns to the personified cicada, Marcelle. He dismisses the possibility of being an adequate horseman on a real live horse in *À Ma Jument Souris, (je ne suis pas cavalier ...)* though he does ride before he's thrown: it's his way of having a mistress, the cropper he comes *(la culbute!)* having an undisguised sexual sense. *Marc* (him again!) meaning horse, it's hardly surprising that young Tristan Corbière can't stay on in the saddle *(selle)*! His horse had to be in imagination and saddle-less; otherwise he would be straying into Marc (Mar — selle). It was all very well to borrow his wife but not part of the man himself, who could come crashing down on him like the cloud over his lighthouse: *Caracole et s'abat la nue,/Comme un cheval,* even though he would stay erect.

Instead, like his boat, he could ride the waves (even here it's a thing of the past, his boat *Le Négrier,* having been sold):

Nous n'irons plus sur la vague lascive
Nous gîter en fringuant!

remembering the excitement of

... tous les crins au vent, nos chaloupeuses!
Ces vierges à sabords!
Te patinant dans nos courses mousseuses! ...

One particular verse in *Le Naufrageur* is quite hallucinatory, combining mares, the sea, Brittany, death (if only in the laugh of a death-rattle) — all incarnations of the essential feminine he has borrowed — the whole scene an equestrian orgy:

L'enfer fait l'amour. — Je ris comme un mort —
Sautez sous le *Hû!* ... le *Hû* des rafales,
Sur les *noirs taureaux sourds, blanches cavales!*
Votre écume à moi, *cavales d'Armor!*
Et vos crins au vent! ... — Je ris comme un mort —

He could have horse and woman then and both with nostrils fuming *(naseaux fumants ...)* for the time of a poem as in *Déjeuner de soleil,* whose title is revealing, meaning something transient as well as shot through with sunlight. Here the token lover *(Arthur)* is riding out for an encounter in the Bois de Boulogne and feels the burgeoning of nature to such a degree he senses he could be a poet, just like Byron. Byron, apparently, is the name of his horse! A horse called Byron brings to mind Byron's poem Mazeppa (1819), the tale of a page who was caught *flagrante delicto* in adultery, and strapped, naked and tarred, to an unbridled horse which galloped off through the Russian steppes back to the deserts of its native Ukraine. And this page became a Cossack *hetman.* Jean Vacher-Corbière tells us of a visiting card Corbière had had printed with the name MAZZZEPPA *(sic)* CORBIÈRE[20].

With Mazeppa though, even with three z's (for sleep?), there was no other half: *ma moitié: c'est une femme* ... and, although he adds: *une femme que je n'ai pas,* it is clear She is essential. In the heart of his writing at least. She is *la Bête féroce* and just as the Savage Beast played the poet, and called the tune, it was Tristan Corbière who played the tunes. He played with words. And he played *la vielle* (the hurdy-gurdy), a running into one another of *vie* (life) and *elle.*

L'éternel féminin as he calls it in *Féminin singulier,* Goethe's *Ewig-Weibliche*[21], is not only *Yseut a la crine bloie*[22] *(with a blond mane). L'Absente* in *Le Poète Contumace* is as much Brittany herself. In *Au Vieux Roscoff* She is the town, that *vieille fille-à-matelots* (old sailors' concubine). She is the Sea, another face of Death: *la Mort change de face:/La Mer! ... (La Fin).* You can sleep with Her, drown in Her! *On dirait le ventre amoureux/D'une fille de joie en rut, à moitié soûle* ... .

La poésie veut quelque chose d'énorme, de barbare et de sauvage, wrote Diderot[23], in an age when poetry was singularly unable to rise to his challenge. Here, well over a century later, was a poetry with something of the enormity, barbarity and savagery Diderot was calling for. Outspoken, intense, the poems have, in Randall Jarrell's words 'a rude, laconic strength, a hammering and reckless wit, they work themselves up (with an ingenuity that would shame any Devil) into the blankest and most sardonic exaggeration .... The prevailing irony that blows through his poems is neither Byronic nor Laforguian, but something far more complicated, since it does not replace an idealistic or sentimental attitude with a "disillusioned" one but mocks at part of each and accepts part of each; and the mockery and acceptance are fused, sometimes, in one incandescent phrase — are transfigured, sometimes, by a cruel and magical tenderness.'[24] And, to quote Ezra Pound, one of Corbière's earliest champions: 'He is more real than the realists because he still recognises that force of romance which is a quite real and ineradicable part of our life.'[25]

The poet's eye view

In *Writers' France*, published as recently as 1989[26], John Ardagh states with conviction: 'Brittany has no Yeats or Joyce'. But even if he doesn't rate Tristan Corbière their equal, he could at least have mentioned him, especially as some of his finest poems, like *Au Vieux Roscoff* and *La Rapsode Foraine et Le Pardon de Sainte-Anne* are set in Brittany and others laud Breton sailors. There have been lone voices extolling his work for over a century now, and if lone voices are heard together they make a chorus of approval. It would be a typesetter's nightmare to make them simultaneous on the page, so I shall select the words of a dozen poets (including two who have already spoken) and let them sing his praises solo, with Jean Richepin acting as refrain. Even earlier than 1876 when he published *La Chanson des Gueux*[27], Richepin must surely have immersed himself in *Les Amours Jaunes*.

Ezra Pound: Corbière seems to me the greatest poet of the period. After Gautier France produced three chief and admirable poets: Tristan Corbière, Rimbaud and Laforgue[28]. If a man is too lazy to read the brief works of these four poets, he cannot hope to understand writing, verse writing, prose writing, any writing. If Corbière invented no process he at any rate restored French verse to the vigour of Villon and to an intensity that no Frenchman has touched during the intervening four centuries[29].

Jean Richepin: "Salut Maître!"[30]

Francis Carco: Villon, Verlaine et Rimbaud forment avec Tristan Corbière une sorte de même génie, à la fois trouble et conscient, inquiet, plaintif et révolté qu'on définira toujours mal, mais dont rien n'altérera la prodigieuse expression.[31]

Jean Richepin: "Salut Maître!"

T.S. Eliot: Rimbaud, Corbière and Laforgue were for us the masters more than any English poet of their time[32]. The poet must become more and more comprehensive, more allusive, more indirect, in order to force, to dislocate if necessary, language into his meaning. Hence we get something which looks very much like the conceit — we get, in fact, a method curiously similar to that of the 'metaphysical poets' similar also in its use of obscure words and of simple phrasing. Jules Laforgue, (really inferior to Corbière at his best[34]) and Tristan Corbière in many of his poems, are nearer to the 'school of Donne' than any modern English poet[33].

Jean Richepin: "Salut Maître!"

Edgell Rickword: Corbière is a naked man among his carefully-tailored contemporaries. In 1873 the critics were no keener than usual to appreciate essentials. Corbière had the first qualification for the poet — a mind of his own. He never serves up a hash of elegant sentiments acquired at second-hand. Such is his naturalness, his spontaneity, that *Les Amours Jaunes* is as varied in mood as the days of one's life. His studied self-depreciation, his *blague*, his brutal audacity and ridiculous foolery, do not for long obscure the impatient compassion of which his sarcasms and tangled ironies are the reflex.[35]

Jean Richepin: "Salut Maître!"

Yvor Winters: *La Rapsode Foraine* and *Cris d'Aveugle* are probably superior to any French verse of the nineteenth century save the best of Baudelaire.[36]

Jean Richepin: "Salut Maître!"

André Breton: Toute la mer, a-t-on dit, mais surtout celle des récifs nocturnes, la femme fatale, et non seulement toute la mer, mais toute la campagne — tel est le palimpseste que recouvre l'écriture en éclairs et en ellipses de Corbière.[37]

Jean Richepin: "Salut Maître!"

Max Jacob: Corbière est plus qu'écrivain, il est poète quand ayant à définir des marins, il les appelle: "Ces anges mal léchés". Cela est la poésie. C'est le bon style du poète.[38]

Jean Richepin: "Salut Maître!"

Randall Jarrell: I heard of no celebration of his centenary, I know almost no one who reads him; but there are not many men who have written poems as good as his. Certainly no poet of half his greatness is so undervalued and unread. Corbière's range is bewildering. The neurotic self-dramatising self-analysis of some of the dramatic monologues is quite as good as anything of the sort in Eliot — whom Corbière of course influenced. Corbière is far too serious a poet to be solemn; what he says he means; but he says it in a series of astonishingly colloquial and idiomatic exclamations — his speech, often, is a sort of living contradiction. Puns, mocking half-dead metaphors, parodied clichés, antitheses and paradoxes, idioms exploited on every level, are the seven-league crutches on which the poems bound wildly forward.[39]

Jean Richepin: "Salut Maître!"

Patrick Creagh: Corbière, despite himself, is one of our masters.[40]

Jean Richepin: "Salut Maître!"

Michael Hamburger: Corbière was truly modern not only because of the dilemma that was his constant theme, but in the tone and diction of his verse. The very thoroughness and daring of his self-exposures releases an energy whose vibrations are positive, though his theme isn't.[41]

Jean Richepin: "Salut Maître!"

Elizabeth Bishop: If you haven't read Corbière, do, by all means. He is really a marvellous poet.[42]

Jean Richepin: "Salut Maître!"

John Berryman: I wish I versed with his bite.[43]

Jean Richepin: "Salut Maître!"

'Corbière's qualities ought to have played a far larger part in the development of modern poetry than they usually have', wrote Martin Turnell; and, reviewing the translations of four notable French poets from this century, René Char, Yves Bonnefoy, Henri Michaux and Philippe Jaccottet, Malcolm Bowie seems to agree: 'The alarming thing is not just that the contingencies of urban living have been jettisoned nor that the ordinary expanse of a human day is never measured out in teaspoons or cycle clips, but that so little attention is paid to the ways in which human beings attend to one another. People do not detain each other for a closer look; they do not listen to each other much; little rage or tenderness or desire flows between them ...'[44]. Poetry then has too often turned in on itself, retreating to 'citadels of fine art (where) solitary self-sealed declamation or vatic utterance' is the order of the day. There is nothing oracular and aloof about Tristan Corbière. He takes risks, even the risk Bowie warns against in the work of Bonnefoy: 'Too much *ars moriendi*, and vitality in the form of brute poetic sensation will begin to ebb away.'[45] And here Tristan Corbière is, still vital, fully alive and kicking.

The translation:

Having 'yellow' in the title in English would have emphasised cowardice, which is just present in Corbière's *'jaune'*, but other more significant connotations, like betrayal *(Judas)*, cuckoldry *(peint en jaune)*, jealousy *(Sir Bob)*, exclusion *(le Juif errant)*, social ignominy *(Paria)*, yellow fever *(au Mexique)*, the complexion of the sickly or dying *(le teint jaune)* would be overshadowed. It is not for nothing that *corpora lutea* (yellow body) has come to be applied to a person considered so expendable as to be a fit object for experimentation, regardless of consequences. And there are other yellows in French which wouldn't occur to an English reader, because they are part of a set expression. *Un rire jaune* is a forced or sickly smile, *un conte jaune* a very tall story, *en faire une jaunisse* is to be piqued, *voir jaune* is to see things with a jaundiced eye. A few like *un drap jaune:* a wild and dangerous sea (it appears in *L'Américaine*), *une colère jaune:* violent anger *(colère* coming from the Greek for bile), which can apply to the wind and waves, would even sound foreign to modern French ears. And then there are the yellows from earlier literature which Corbière would have read (he has quite frequent literary allusions) and which are lost on most English ears. Those in Baudelaire, for instance:

> Tout homme digne de ce nom
> A dans le cœur un Serpent jaune,
> Installé comme sur un trône,
> Qui, s'il dit: "Je veux!" répond: "Non!"

from *L'Avertisseur*[46] where spleen is paramount or, from what in many ways is a precursor of *Un Jeune Qui S'en Va: Les Phares*[47], where Rembrandt is *triste hôpital* and Puget[48]: *Grand cœur gonflé d'orgueil, homme débile et jaune* which links yellow with feebleness and overweening pride.

By not having 'yellow' I'm losing the positive resonances, which are certainly present in the title. The yellow gorse of Corbière's beloved Brittany, the flowering whin, however thin and wiry it is, the yellow virgin-wax round the chapel of Saint Anne, the light of the lighthouse and in the eye of the toad, the moonlight ... And the golds: the golden mane of the sun at Waking, the golden eyes of his owls, the golden heart and mouth of a wax effigy (here he is positively sacrilegious), the sun larding bitumen with gold for the oil painter and a chord with gold for the guitarist, *la ceinture dorée*, the golden belt where Bitor's pleased for his money to go and where Tristan is pleased to know he can return (round the waists of prostitutes who come to life in his verse and round his Brittany) ...

The proverb: *Tout paraît jaune à qui a la jaunisse* appears in Pope's *Essay on Criticism* as 'all looks yellow to the jaundic'd eye', the English and the French seeing things here in the same light. Tristan Corbière has a dog called Pope. Pope savaged his enemies. The dog is encouraged to do likewise, so as not to be treated like a dog. Both are gentlemen with a distinctly jaundiced view.

If I have taken certain liberties in this English coming-to-terms with a highly original eccentric, who was not averse to combining archaisms and colloquialisms, slang and sophisticated word-play, it was not for want of trying to stay as close as possible to the text. To render puns and rhyme, to translate the states of heart and mind, to give the feeling of living breathing verse, these have been my aims. For the results — sometimes in longer lines than the pentameter dear to English ears, Corbière being as fond of the Alexandrine as so many of his predecessors — take a deep breath and dive in. When you come up for air, you can clamber on the good boat Tristan, but beware, he's still rocking it!

The French text:

The edition of *Les Amours Jaunes* edited by Elisabeth Aragon & Claude Bonnin (Presses Universitaires du Mirail 1992 Université de Toulouse-Le Mirail) is closer to the first edition (Glady Frères 1873) than any other. It corrects the Pléiade edition here and there (Charles Cros/Tristan Corbière: *Œuvres complètes* edited by Pierre-Olivier Walzer, Gallimard 1970) and restores some of the spellings of the original even where these are incorrect, like *pelotte* and *clignotte*, justifying most with the claim that they are deliberate eye-rhymes, *gifflent* rhyming more convincingly with *sifflent*. This is quite persuasive until one encounters *casserolles* rhyming with *castagnoles*, his own version of the Spanish *castañuelas!* I have not kept these 'eye-rhymes'. I think Tristan's spelling and the compositors must be held accountable for not a few errors. I have retained unusual spellings where they have an intrinsic interest (this includes all foreign words), or were acceptable at the time. Bohème is given a grave accent when it applies, like Henri Murger's timely novel *Scènes de la Vie de Bohème*[49], to the Bohemian way of life in Paris and a circumflex for the country, Bohemia. As for punctuation, 'Corbière's system of hysterical punctuation' as Elizabeth Bishop called it[50], I have made a few alterations which I trust will improve ease of comprehension. For conversation, I have left dashes to introduce a fresh speaker, and where the original used inverted commas as well, I have tended to reduce their number for the sake of clarity. I have substituted *drap* for *jour* in the final line of *Femme*, as Corbière did in his personal copy. As well as the two editions of *Les Amours Jaunes* already mentioned, I have consulted others, especially the 1973 nrf Poésie/Gallimard one edited by Jean-Louis Lalanne and two edited by Michel Dansel, the 1975 selection (Nouveaux Classiques Larousse) and the 1982 facsimile of the 1891 Léon Vanier edition (S.A.R.L. SOS Manuscrits).

Notes:

1. Small wonder when he had written: '*ce vertigineux livre des Amours Jaunes de ce stupéfiant Corbière*' in his essay on Mallarmé in *Les Poètes Maudits*, Léon Vanier, 1884.
2. Charles Morice: *Tristan Corbière*, Albert Messein, 1912, p.22.
3. Paul Verlaine: ibid.
4. Glady Frères.
5. Anatole France: *Vers Dorés*, Lemerre, 1873.
6. Victor Hugo: *La Légende des Siècles*,1873.
7. E.V.: *L'Art Universel*, 1st November 1873.
8. M. de Vaucelle: *L'Artiste*, 1st November 1873.
9. Anon.: *La Renaissance Littéraire et Artistique*, 26th October 1873.
10. His mother put his death down to pneumonia, brought on, he told her, by going out into the bitter cold of Paris streets in vain attempts to freeze his illness out. A thesis by Dr Vincent Le Berre (*Essai d'Approche de la Pathologie de Tristan Corbière*, Faculté de Médecine de Brest, Université de Bretagne Occidentale, 1988) suggests that the likeliest cause of death was a breakdown of the auto-immune system, probably with a secondary bacterial infection, which could well have been tubercular.
11. This *Épitaphe* was printed in the second edition of *Les Amours Jaunes* (Vanier 1891).
12. Corbière invented the verb *plangorer* for *À une Demoiselle* and *Litanie du Sommeil* (l.127)
13. Paul Verlaine: ibid.
14. Jules Laforgue: *Une Étude sur Corbière*, in *Mélanges Posthumes*, Mercure de France, 1903.
15. Michel Dansel: *Tristan Corbière: Thématique de l'Inspiration*, L'Âge d'Homme, Lausanne 1985.
16. Jean Markale: *L'Épopée Celtique en Bretagne*, Payot, 1971.
17. Elisabeth Aragon & Claude Bonnin, *Les Amours Jaunes*, Presses Universitaires du Mirail, 1992, p.241.
18. Letter of 10th July 1860 from Saint-Brieuc: Tristan Corbière: *Œuvres Complètes*, Gallimard 1970, p.1048.
19. Letter of 10th May 1860 from Saint Brieuc: Tristan Corbière: ibid. p.1032.
20. J.Vacher-Corbière: *Portrait de Famille: Tristan Corbière*, Regain, Monte Carlo, 1955, p.55.
21. Johann Wolfgang von Goethe: *Faust II*, 1831.
22. Béroul: *Le Roman de Tristan*, c.1160.
23. Denis Diderot: *Discours sur la poésie dramatique*, 1750. He adds: *En général, plus un peuple est civilisé, poli, moins ses mœurs sont poétiques; tout s'affaiblit en s'adoucissant.*
24. Randall Jarrell: *A Verse Chronicle* in *Poetry & the Age*, 1953.
25. Ezra Pound: *Poetra*, 1913.

26. Jean Richepin: La Chanson des Gueux, 1876, nouvelle édition, Bibliothèque Charpentier, Eugène Fasquelle, 1915.
27. John Ardagh: *Writers' France, A Regional Panorama*, Hamish Hamilton, 1989.
28. Ezra Pound: *Make It New*, Faber & Faber, 1934.
29. Ezra Pound: *Literary Essays of Ezra Pound*, Faber & Faber, 1954.
30. Jean Richepin: from a speech made in Morlaix, 1912.
31. Francis Carco: *Corbière, Villon, Verlaine et Rimbaud*, Les Marches de Provence, août-sept.1912.
32. T.S. Eliot: *Lettre d'Angleterre*, La Nouvelle Revue Française, Nov.1923.
33. T.S. Eliot: *The Metaphysical Poets*, 1921.
34. T.S. Eliot: from a letter to Mary Hutchinson, July 1919, *The Letters of T.S. Eliot* Vol.1 1898-1922, p.317.
35. Edgell Rickword: *Tristan Corbière 1945-1975*, New Statesman, 1923, then in *Essays and Opinions 1921-31*, Carcanet, 1974, p.98-104.
36. Yvor Winters: *Primitivism and Decadence*, 1937, p.55.
37. André Breton: *Anthologie de l'Humour Noir*, 1939.
38. Max Jacob: *Conseils à Un Jeune Poète*, Gallimard, 1945 & 1972, p.23-4.
39. Randall Jarrell: ibid.
40. Patrick Creagh: *A Picture of Tristan*, Heinemann, 1965.
41. Michael Hamburger: *The Truth of Poetry, Tensions in Modern Poetry from Baudelaire to the 1960s*, Weidenfeld & Nicolson, 1969.
42. Elizabeth Bishop: Letter to Carley Dawson, Oct 1st 1948 in *One Art* — Letters selected & edited by Robert Giroux, Chatto & Windus, 1994.
43. John Berryman: *Love & Fame*, 1971, p.7.
44. Malcolm Bowie: The Times Literary Supplement, January 27 1995.
45. Malcolm Bowie: ibid.
46. Charles Baudelaire: *L'Avertisseur* in *Nouvelles Fleurs du Mal*. Corbière would have read it in *Le Parnasse Contemporain*, 1866.
47. Charles Baudelaire: *Les Phares:* in *Spleen et Idéal, Les Fleurs du Mal*, 1857.
48. Pierre Puget (1620-94), sculptor, born in Marseilles but worked mainly in Italy; helped decorate the Pitti Palace; brought the Baroque style to France.
49. Henry Murger: *Scènes de la Vie de Bohème* first appeared in *Le Corsaire*, 1848, then as *La Vie de Bohème*, 1849.
50. Elizabeth Bishop: ibid.

Table des Titres/Contents

ARMOR / ARMOR

GENS DE MER / SEAFARERS

RONDELS POUR APRÈS / RONDELS FOR AFTERWARDS

À MARCELLE / TO MARCELLE

À Marcelle

Le Poète et la Cigale

Un poète ayant rimé,
                    IMPRIMÉ
Vit sa Muse dépourvue
De marraine, et presque nue:
Pas le plus petit morceau
De vers ... ou de vermisseau.
Il alla crier famine
Chez une blonde voisine,
La priant de lui prêter
Son petit nom pour rimer.
(C'était une rime en elle*)*
— Oh! je vous paîrai, Marcelle,
Avant l'août, foi d'animal!
Intérêt et principal. —
La voisine est très prêteuse,
C'est son plus joli défaut:
— Quoi: c'est tout ce qu'il vous faut?
Votre Muse est bien heureuse ...
Nuit et jour, à tout venant,
Rimez mon nom ... Qu'il vous plaise!
Et moi j'en serai fort aise.

Voyons: chantez maintenant.

To Marcelle

The Poet and the Cicada

A poet with rhymes new minted
            And PRINTED
Saw his Muse bereft
Of a godmother and left
Almost bare: with the thinnest veil
Of doggerel ... and a puppy dog's tail.
He went to cry his hunger
To a blonde who was his neighbour,
Imploring her to lend him
Her pet name as a rhyme.
(It was a rhyme in elle*)*
— Oh! I'll pay you back, Marcelle,
By August, as I'm an animal!
Both interest and principal. —
This neighbour, nothing daunted,
Lends readily — her prettiest foible:
— What: is that all you wanted?
Your Muse is soon contented ...
Night and day, for every comer, do
Rhyme my name ... May it please you!
And I shall be tickled pink.

Come on then: start to sing.

ÇA

THIS IS IT

Ça?

What? ...
— SHAKESPEARE.

Des essais? — Allons donc, je n'ai pas essayé!
Étude? — Fainéant je n'ai jamais pillé.
Volume? — Trop broché pour être relié ...
De la copie? — Hélas non, ce n'est pas payé!

Un poëme? — Merci, mais j'ai lavé ma lyre.
Un livre? — ... Un livre, encor, est une chose à lire! ...
Des papiers? — Non, non, Dieu merci, c'est cousu!
Album? — Ce n'est pas blanc, et c'est trop décousu.

Bouts-rimés? — Par quel bout? ... Et ce n'est pas joli!
Un ouvrage? — Ce n'est poli ni repoli.
Chansons? — Je voudrais bien, ô ma petite Muse! ...
Passe-temps? — Vous croyez, alors, que ça m'amuse?

— Vers? ... vous avez flué des vers ... — Non, c'est heurté.
— Ah, vous avez couru l'Originalité? ...
— Non ... c'est une drôlesse assez drôle, — *de rue* —
Qui court encor, sitôt qu'elle se sent courue.

— Du *chic* pur? — Et qui me donnera des ficelles!
— Du haut vol? Du haut mal? — Pas de râle, ni d'ailes!
— Chose à mettre à la porte? — ... Ou dans une maison
De tolérance. — Ou bien de correction? — Mais non!

— Bon, ce n'est pas classique? — À peine est-ce français!
— Amateur? — Ai-je l'air d'un monsieur à succès?
Est-ce vieux? — Ça n'a pas quarante ans de service ...
Est-ce jeune? — Avec l'âge, on guérit de ce vice.

... ÇA c'est naïvement une impudente *pose*;
C'est, ou ce n'est pas *ça*: rien ou quelque chose ...
— Un chef-d'œuvre? — Il se peut: je n'en ai jamais fait.
— Mais, est-ce du huron, du Gagne, ou du Musset?

This?

What? ...
— SHAKESPEARE.

Trial runs? — You must be joking, that assumes one tries!
Fair copy? — I'm far too idle to plagiarise.
A volume? — It's too skimped to ever need binding ...
Slip proof? — Sorry, I don't get paid for p.q. minding!

A poem? — Thanks, but I've hung out my lyre to dry.
A book? — A book's just another thing to edify! ...
Loose sheets? — No, thank God, it's all sewn up and pointed!
An album? — It isn't blank and it's too disjointed.

Rhymed odds and ends? — Beam ends? ... They're not a pretty sight!
Polished stuff? — It's not touched up, refined or polite.
Lays? — Now that's what I'd really like, my little Muse!
A diversion? — You think I'm that easy to amuse?

— Verse? ... you've let your lines run on ... — No, they jar and halt.
— Ah, so it's Originality you exalt? ...
— No ... it's *common* knowledge: a street-walker in haste
To take off the moment she feels she's being chased.

— Putting on the style? — And who'll give me strings to pull!
— High flying? Falling fits? — Look, no wings, no death-rattle!
— A *thing* to turn out of doors? — ... Or into a house
Of ill-repute. — Or reformatory? — Use your nous!

— Right, it's not in classical vein? — Its French is jaded!
— Amateur? — Do I look like someone who's made it?
Is it old? — It's not forty years since it broke the ice ...
Is it young? — With age one is broken of that vice.

... *THIS* is, artlessly though, impudent posturing;
It is, or it is not *this*: nothing or something ...
— A masterpiece? — May be: one's never come my way.
— But, is it Cheyenne, or Gagne-speak, or Musset?

15

— C'est du ... mais j'ai mis là mon humble nom d'auteur,
Et mon enfant n'a pas même un titre menteur.
C'est un coup de raccroc, juste ou faux, par hasard ...
L'Art ne me connaît pas. Je ne connais pas l'Art.

Préfecture de police, 20 mai 1873.

— It's ... but I've put my own name, albeit humble,
And my child's not foist with a title you've to rumble.
Bull's eye or no, it's a fluky throw of the dart ...
Art does not know me. I have no knowledge of Art.

Police headquarters, 20th May 1873.

Paris

Bâtard de Créole et Breton,
Il vint aussi là — fourmilière,
Bazar où rien n'est en pierre,
Où le soleil manque de ton.

— Courage! On fait queue ... Un planton
Vous pousse à la chaîne — derrière! —
... Incendie éteint, sans lumière;
Des seaux passent, vides ou non. —

Là, sa pauvre Muse pucelle
Fit le trottoir en *demoiselle*,
Ils disaient: Qu'est-ce qu'elle vend?

— Rien. — Elle restait là, stupide,
N'entendant pas sonner le vide
Et regardant passer le vent ...

Là: vivre à coups de fouet! — passer
En fiacre, en correctionnelle;
Repasser à la ritournelle,
Se dépasser, et trépasser! ...

— Non, petit, il faut commencer
Par être grand — simple ficelle —
Pauvre: remuer l'or à la pelle;
Obscur: un nom à tout casser! ...

Le coller chez les mastroquets,
Et l'apprendre à des perroquets
Qui le chantent ou qui le sifflent ...

— Musique! — C'est le paradis
Des mahomets et des houris,
Des dieux souteneurs qui se giflent!

Paris

Breton and a Creole's bastard child,
He came to where the sun lacks tone,
A bazaar where nothing's made of stone
Up on the hill whose ants run wild ...

— Grit your teeth! They're queueing! ... An O.D.
Shoves you into line — Take your turn! —
... With the fire put out, no flames burn;
Tin pails pass down the chain, empty

Or not. — Here, his poor virgin Muse
Walked the streets in well-heeled shoes,
— What's she selling? had but one reply:

— Nothing. — She looked vacant, standing
There, not hearing the emptiness ring,
Intent on watching the wind blow by ...

Living here: it's whiplash-style! — swish
By in cabs, be dressed down in dock,
Waltz in and sing for your supper, dish
On dish, and end up as a crock ! ...

— No, child, before you're very old
Begin being big — there's no catch —
If poor: by rolling in gold;
Obscure: a name that none can match! ...

Slap it up in public houses,
Teach it so every parrot knows
To squawk or whistle how it goes ...

— Strike up the band! — What ecstasies
For mahomets and their houris,
For *bully* gods who come to blows!

19

✧

"Je voudrais que la rose, — Dondaine!
Fût encore au rosier, — Dondé!"

Poète. — Après? ... il faut *la chose:*
Le Parnasse en escalier,
Les Dégoûteux, et la Chlorose,
Les Bedeaux, les Fous à lier ...

L'Incompris couche avec sa pose,
Sous le zinc d'un mancenillier;
Le Naïf *"voudrait que la rose,*
Dondé! fût encore au rosier!"

"La rose au rosier, Dondaine!"
— On a le pied fait à sa chaîne.
"La rose au rosier" ... — Trop tard! —

"La rose au rosier" ... — Nature!
— On est essayeur, pédicure,
Ou quelqu'autre chose dans l'art!

✧

J'aimais ... — Oh, ça n'est plus de vente!
Même il faut payer: dans le tas,
Pioche la femme! — Mon amante
M'avait dit: "Je n'oublîrai pas ..."

... J'avais une amante là-bas
Et son ombre pâle me hante
Parmi des senteurs de lilas ...
Peut-être Elle pleure ... — Eh bien: chante,

Pour toi tout seul, ta nostalgie,
Tes nuits blanches sans bougie ...
Tristes vers, tristes au matin! ...

"I would that the rose, — Tra la!
Were still on the rose-bush, — Tra lee!"

Poet. — So what? ... You perform *your trick*:
The Parnassians up their ladder,
The Sick at Heart, and the Greensick,
The Vergers, the stark staring Mad ...

The Misconstrued sleeps with his pose
In a manchineel's shade — in a bar:
The Simple Soul *"would that the rose*
Were still on the rose-bush, Tra la!"

"The rose on the rose-tree, Tra lee!"
— Your foot is made to fit its fetter.
"The rose on the rose-bush" ... — Can't be! —

"The rose on the rose-bush" ... — Nature's part!
— You're a chiropodist, a fitter,
Or something else in what's called art!

✧

I was in love ... — I'm out of luck
Now though! I've even got to pay:
Dig out a woman from the ruck!
— "I shan't forget ..." is what she'd say,

My sweetheart back home — lovestruck
I was and her pale shade keeps haunting
Me along with the scent of lilac...
Perhaps She's crying... — Oh well: sing

To yourself of your homesickness,
Your sleepless nights, all in darkness ...
Sad sad tunes, sad with the morning! ...

21

Mais ici: fouette-toi d'orgie!
Charge ta paupière rougie,
Et sors ton grand air de catin!

C'est la bohème, enfant: Renie
Ta lande et ton clocher à jour,
Les mornes de ta colonie
Et les *bamboulas* au tambour.

Chanson usée et bien finie,
Ta jeunesse ... Eh, c'est bon un jour! ...
Tiens: — C'est toujours neuf — calomnie
Tes pauvres amours ... et l'amour.

Évohé! ta coupe est remplie!
Jette le vin, garde la lie ...
Comme ça. — Nul n'a vu le tour.

Et qu'un jour le monsieur candide
De toi dise — Infect! Ah splendide! —
... Ou ne dise rien. — C'est plus court.

Évohé! fouaille la veine;
Évohé! misère: Éblouir!
En fille de joie, à la peine
Tombe, avec ce mot-là. — Jouir!

Rôde en la coulisse malsaine
Où vont les fruits mal secs moisir,
Moisir pour un quart-d'heure en scène ...
— *Voir les planches, et puis mourir!*

Va: tréteaux, lupanars, églises,
Cour des miracles, cour d'assises:
— Quarts-d'heure d'immortalité!

Here: it's whip yourself to orgy-pitch!
Shadow your reddened eyes, be witch
And put on such airs — of whoring!

This is Bohemia, child: Disown
The bluffs and heath of your *hickdom*,
Your belfry in open-work stone
And wild *bamboulas* to the drum.

Your youth, once in such good fettle,
Is a hackneyed song, through and through ...
It comes up fresh still, on its mettle —
Slander your poor amours ... love too.

Your cup is brimming! Evoe!
Keep the dregs ... That's it, throw away
The wine. — Nobody's seen that trick.

Then one day let the self's candid
Grown-up say — How vile! Ah splendid! —
... Or damn-all. — Which is twice as quick.

Evoe! lash the stroke of luck;
Evoe! hard graft it is: to dazzle!
Drop, like Hot-Pants on the razzle,
Overdoing it, with that word — Fuck!

Prowl in insalubrious slips, rage
Where soft fruit go to putrefy,
To have a short spell out on stage,
Mildewing ... — *See the boards and die!*

That's it: platforms, brothels, churches,
Courts for miracles or assizes:
— Two shakes of immortality!

Tu parais! c'est l'apothéose!!! ...
Et l'on te jette quelque chose:
— Fleur en papier, ou saleté. —

Donc, *la tramontane* est montée:
Tu croiras que c'est arrivé!
Cinq-cent-millième Prométhée,
Au roc de carton peint rivé.

Hélas: quel bon oiseau de proie,
Quel vautour, quel *Monsieur Vautour*
Viendra mordre à ton petit foie
Gras, truffé? ... pour quoi — Pour le four! ...

Four banal! ... — Adieu la curée! —
Ravalant ta rate rentrée,
Va, comme le pélican blanc,

En écorchant le chant du cygne,
Bec-jaune, te percer le flanc! ...
Devant un pêcheur à la ligne.

Tu ris. — Bien! — Fais de l'amertume,
Prends le pli, Méphisto blagueur.
De l'absinthe! et ta lèvre écume ...
Dis que cela vient de ton cœur.

Fais de toi ton œuvre posthume,
Châtre l'amour ... l'amour — longueur!
Ton poumon cicatrisé hume
Des miasmes de gloire, ô vainqueur!

You come on! it's the apotheosis!!! ...
And something's hurled at you for this:
— A paper flower, or obscenity. —

So, the omens being propitious:
You'll think what success can be scored!
Five hundred thousandth Prometheus
Riveted to rock of painted cardboard.

Heigh-ho: what kind predator will drop
In, what *Rapacious Landlord,* what vulture
Will come and peck your little liver
Pâté, truffle-stuffed? ... — Recipe for a flop!

Overdone! Spoils for review-hounds too!
Choking back the spleen you've repressed,
Like the white pelican, go west,

And, murdering the song of the swan,
Yellow-beaked fledgling, run yourself through! ...
Watched only by a week-end fisherman.

You laugh. — Good! — Now let rancour out;
Acquire the habit, wag Mephisto.
Absinth! and you're foaming at the mouth ...
Say it's your heart that's letting go.

Make yourself your posthumous work;
Castrate love ... love — that endless bore!
Your scarred lungs have begun to draw
Bad breaths of glory, O conqueror!

Assez, n'est-ce pas? va-t'en!

                        Laisse
Ta bourse — dernière maîtresse —
Ton revolver — dernier ami ...

Drôle de pistolet fini!
... Ou reste, et bois ton fond de vie,
Sur une nappe desservie ...

That'll do, won't it? Go! Round the bend,
Leaving your purse — last mistress/wife —
Your revolver — the final friend ...

Odd son of a gun shooting off!
... Or stay, and drink the lees of life,
Over a well-cleared tablecloth ...

Épitaphe

Sauf les amoureux commençans ou finis qui
veulent commencer par la fin il y a tant de choses
qui finissent par le commencement que le
commencement commence à finir par être la fin
la fin en sera que les amoureux et autres finiront
par commencer à recommencer par ce
commencement qui aura fini par n'être que la
fin retournée ce qui commencera par être égal à
l'éternité qui n'a ni fin ni commencement et
finira par être aussi finalement égal à la rotation
de la terre où l'on aura fini par ne distinguer plus
où commence la fin d'où finit le commencement
ce qui est toute fin de tout commencement égale à
tout commencement de toute fin ce qui est le
commencement final de l'infini défini par
l'indéfini — Égale une épitaphe égale une préface
et réciproquement.

Sagesse des nations.

Il se tua d'ardeur, ou mourut de paresse.
S'il vit, c'est par oubli; voici ce qu'il se laisse:

— Son seul regret fut de n'être pas sa maîtresse. —

Il ne naquit par aucun bout,
Fut toujours poussé vent-de-bout,
Et fut un arlequin-ragoût,
Mélange adultère de tout.

Du *je-ne-sais-quoi*. — Mais ne sachant où;
De l'or, — mais avec pas le sou;
Des nerfs, — sans nerf. Vigueur sans force;
De l'élan, — avec une entorse;
De l'âme, — et pas de violon;
De l'amour, — mais pire étalon.
— Trop de noms pour avoir un nom. —

Epitaph

> *Apart from lovers who are beginning or finished*
> *and want to begin at the end there are so many*
> *things which end at the beginning that the*
> *beginning begins to end by being the end the end*
> *of which will be that lovers and others will end by*
> *beginning to begin again with this beginning*
> *which will have ended by being nothing but the*
> *end reversed and that will begin by being equal to*
> *eternity which has neither end nor beginning and*
> *will end by being just as finally equal to the*
> *rotation of the earth whereupon one will have*
> *finished by no longer being able to distinguish*
> *where the end begins from where the beginning*
> *ends which is to say every end of every beginning*
> *equals every beginning of every end which is the*
> *final beginning of the infinite defined by the*
> *indefinite — An epitaph equalling a preface and*
> *vice versa.*
>
> Wisdom of the nations.

He killed himself with ardour, or died of idleness.
If he lives, it's an oversight; he leaves himself this:

— His one regret was not having been his mistress. —

He wasn't born, he just turned out,
With the wind in his teeth, brought about,
A motley left-overs goulash,
An all-in adulterous hash.

Some *je-ne-sais-quoi*. — But not knowing where;
A dash of gold, — but no copper to spare;
Some nerves, — losing their nerve. Might with no main;
A running jump, — with an ankle sprain;
Some soul, — with no sounding board;
Some heart, — but its G-string is flawed;
Some love, — a stud, more or less maimed.
— Too many names to have a name. —

Coureur d'idéal, — sans idée;
Rime riche, — et jamais rimée;
Sans avoir été, — revenu;
Se retrouvant partout perdu.

Poète, en dépit de ses vers;
Artiste sans art, — à l'envers,
Philosophe, — à tort à travers.

Un drôle sérieux, — pas drôle.
Acteur, il ne sut pas son rôle;
Peintre: il jouait de la musette;
Et musicien: de la palette.

Une tête! — mais pas de tête;
Trop fou pour savoir être bête;
Prenant pour un trait le mot *très*.
— Ses vers faux furent ses seuls vrais.

Oiseau rare — et de pacotille;
Très mâle ... et quelquefois très *fille*;
Capable de tout, — bon à rien;
Gâchant bien le mal, mal le bien.
Prodigue comme était l'enfant
Du Testament, — sans testament.
Brave, et souvent, par peur du plat,
Mettant ses deux pieds dans le plat.

Coloriste enragé, — mais blême;
Incompris ... — surtout de lui-même;
Il pleura, chanta juste faux;
— Et fut un défaut sans défauts.

Pursues an ideal, — with no idea,
A rhyme that's rich, — whose connection's not clear;
Without having been, — come back as a ghost,
He finds himself anywhere — lost.

Poet for now, but never in season;
Artless artist, — constructive treason;
Philosopher, — without rhyme or reason.

Poker-faced joker, — but not a card.
Actor — learning parts was too hard;
Painter: he would play the musette;
And musician: on the palette.

Headstrong! — but weak in the head;
Too far gone to be easily led;
Taking a tangent as a sign.
— With off-key notes for every key line.

Rare bird — a sorry bit of fluff;
Very *macho* ... but could give you the bluff:
Being very feminine and far from tough;
Fit for anything, — good as a dud;
Hatching the bad, botching the good.
Like the Prodigal Son, wilful,
— With nothing to leave in his will.
Daring, with cold feet, but skilful
At dragging his feet to a standstill
— For fear of the run of the mill.

Rabid colourist, — beyond the pale;
Misunderstood ... — by himself without fail;
Weepy, slightly out in his hummings;
— Was a goner with no shortcomings.

Ne fut *quelqu'un*, ni quelque chose,
Son naturel était la *pose*.
Pas poseur, — posant pour *l'unique*;
Trop naïf, étant trop cynique;
Ne croyant à rien, croyant tout.
— Son goût était dans le dégoût.

Trop cru, — parce qu'il fut trop cuit,
Ressemblant à rien moins qu'à lui,
Il s'amusa de son ennui,
Jusqu'à s'en réveiller la nuit.
Flâneur au large, — à la dérive,
Épave qui jamais n'arrive ...

Trop *Soi* pour se pouvoir souffrir,
L'esprit à sec et la tête ivre,
Fini, mais ne sachant finir,
Il mourut en s'attendant vivre
Et vécut, s'attendant mourir.

Ci-gît, — cœur sans cœur, mal planté,
Trop réussi, — comme *raté*.

Was not some *thing*, had no position,
The *pose* his natural disposition.
Not a poseur, — posing as *the unique* ...
Too naïve, — with a cynical streak;
Believing in nothing, took all on trust.
— With great gusto expressing disgust.

Too raw, — by being half-baked,
Oblivious of living when wide-awake,
Quite down-to-earth when on the shelf,
Looking like nothing on earth but himself;
World-weariness was his sole delight,
So much so it woke him at night.
Mooner in the offing, — cast adrift,
A wreck that never makes a shift ...

Too much *I* for him to suffer him,
Dried-up wits and head aswim,
Finished, but not knowing when to stop,
He died while his life was still a flop
And lived, expecting death on the hop.

Here lies, — a dry-eyed wet-nose, dogged by drought,
Too successful, — as a *wash-out.*

LES AMOURS JAUNES

THESE JAUNDICED LOVES

À l'Éternel Madame

Mannequin idéal, tête-de-turc du leurre,
Éternel Féminin! ... repasse tes fichus;
Et viens sur mes genoux, quand je marquerai l'heure,
Me montrer comme on fait chez vous, anges déchus.

Sois pire, et fais pour nous la joie à la malheure,
Piaffe d'un pied léger dans les sentiers ardus.
Damne-toi, pure idole! et ris! et chante! et pleure,
Amante! Et meurs d'amour! ... à nos moments perdus.

Fille de marbre! en rut! sois folâtre! ... et pensive.
Maîtresse, chair de moi! fais-toi vierge et lascive ...
Féroce, sainte, et bête, en me cherchant un cœur ...

Sois femelle de l'homme, et sers de Muse, ô femme,
Quand le poète brame en *Âme*, en *Lame*, en *Flamme!*
Puis — quand il ronflera — viens baiser ton Vainqueur!

To All Eternity Madam

Ideal dummy, whipping-girl lure who can deny,
Eternal Feminine! ... iron your muslin scarves;
And come on my lap, when it's high time to comply,
To show me, fallen angel, if you do things by halves.

Do worse: be our devilry at the devil's-shy,
Swift-footed, paw the ground on paths sheer hell to climb.
Damn yourself, pure idol! and laugh! and sing! and cry,
Paramour! And die for love! ... but in our spare time.

Marble jade! on heat! be frisky! ... and serious.
Mistress, flesh of mine! be chaste and lascivious ...
Barbaric, saintly, foolish, my heart's well-wisher ...

O woman, serve as Muse, and play the female part,
When the poet troats with *Heart*, with *Dart*, with *Smart*!
Then — when he's snoring — come and kiss your Vanquisher!

Féminin Singulier

Éternel Féminin de l'éternel Jocrisse!
Fais-nous sauter, pantins nous payons les décors!
Nous éclairons la rampe ... Et toi, dans la coulisse,
Tu peux faire au pompier le pur don de ton corps.

Fais claquer sur nos dos le fouet de ton caprice,
Couronne tes genoux! ... et nos têtes dix-cors;
Ris! montre tes dents! mais ... nous avons la police,
Et quelque chose en nous d'eunuque et de recors.

... Ah tu ne comprends pas? ... — Moi non plus — Fais la belle,
Tourne: nous sommes soûls! Et plats: Fais la cruelle!
Cravache ton pacha, ton humble serviteur! ...

Après, sache tomber! — mais tomber avec grâce —
Sur notre sable fin ne laisse pas de trace! ...
— C'est le métier de femme et de gladiateur. —

Feminine Singular

Eternal Feminine of the eternal Gull!
Make us, your puppets, leap — we're paying for the sets!
We turn on the footlights ... while you, to backstage pets
— Fireman with hosepipe? — give your body freely ... Trull!

Let the whip of your caprice be cracked on our backs,
Down and break your knees! ... and crown our ten-tined skull;
Laugh! and bare your teeth! but ... we have our protocol,
Something that smacks of eunuchs and the bailiff's hacks.

... Ah you don't understand? ... — Nor me — Be the belle
And keep spinning: we're drunk! And cowed: Be cruel as hell!
Horsewhip your humble servant, your one-tailed pasha!...

And then, know how to fall — but you must fall with grace —
On our fine-grained sand without leaving any trace! ...
— That's the role of woman and of buckle-swasher. —

Bohème de Chic

Ne m'offrez pas un trône!
À moi tout seul je fris,
Drôle, en ma sauce jaune
De *chic* et de mépris.

Que les bottes vernies
Pleuvent du paradis,
Avec des parapluies ...
Moi, va-nu-pieds, j'en ris!

— Plate époque râpée,
Où chacun a du bien;
Où, cuistre sans épée,
Le vaurien ne vaut rien!

Papa, — pou, mais honnête, —
M'a laissé quelques sous,
Dont j'ai fait quelque dette,
Pour me payer des poux!

Son habit, mis en perce,
M'a fait de beaux haillons
Que le soleil traverse;
Mes trous sont des rayons.

Dans mon chapeau, la lune
Brille à travers les trous,
Bête et vierge comme une
Pièce de cent sous!

— Gentilhomme! ... à trois queues:
Mon nom mal ramassé
Se perd à bien des lieues
Au diable du passé!

Swish Bohemia

— just tossed off —

No throne for me, or horse!
I fry alone with a nub
Of humour, in my yellow sauce
Panache with many a snub.

Let patent leather boots
Rain down from paradise,
With umbrellas — water proofs! —
Barefoot, I split my sides!

— Threadbare age, flat as a board,
When everyone is well-to-do;
When, big prick without a sword,
The good-for-nothing's no good too!

Dad, — tight-fisted but fair, —
Has left me a fistful of sous,
I've run up some debts here and there,
To pay for a life on the loose!

His coat, now that it's broached,
Has made me such handsome tatters
That, at the sun's approach,
Have sunbeams where it matters.

In my hat are many chinks
Which the moon frequents —
She's so daft and chaste you'd think
Her a *body* with no vents!

— Nobleman! ... with three tails:
My ill-gotten name got lost
— Or will do, the miles it trails —
To the devil of the past!

Mon blason, — pas bégueule,
Est, comme moi, faquin:
— *Nous bandons à la gueule,*
Fond troué d'arlequin. —

Je pose aux devantures
Où je lis: — DÉFENDU
DE POSER DES ORDURES —
Roide comme un pendu!

Et me plante sans gêne
Dans le plat du hasard,
Comme un couteau sans gaine
Dans un plat d'épinard.

Je lève haut la cuisse
Aux bornes que je voi:
Potence, pavé, suisse,
Fille, priape ou roi!

Quand, sans tambour ni flûte,
Un servile estafier
Au violon me culbute,
Je me sens libre et fier! ...

Et je laisse la vie
Pleuvoir sans me mouiller,
En attendant l'envie
De me faire empailler.

— Je dors sous ma calotte,
La calotte des cieux;
Et l'étoile pâlotte
Clignote entre mes yeux.

Ma Muse est grise ou blonde ...
Je l'aime et ne sais pas;
Elle est à tout le monde ...
Mais — moi seul — je la bats!

My coat of arms, — unbuttoned
Like me, is *one bound*
In your fesse: — *We're rampant*
On Harlequin's holey ground. —

A sign: NO DUMPING shows
Whenever I stand
Posing before shop-windows —
Stiff as any hanged man!

And then I stand at ease
In the lap of that bitch,
Chance, like a knife unsheathed
In a slap-dish of spinach.

I cock my leg in the air
At each bounder-stone I spot:
Gibbet, stone verge, verger,
King, priapus, *cocotte*!

When, not batting a drumstick,
Strong-Arm of the boot-licking crowd
Drums me into the nick,
Then I feel free and proud! ...

And I leave life to rain ...
Not getting my feet wet through,
Till it won't go against the grain
To be bedded in straw too.

— I sleep under my skull-cap,
The canopy of the skies;
And the wan star of my catnap
Twinkles between my eyes.

My Muse is blonde or gone grey ...
I love her and do not know;
She is, well ... anyone's lay ...
I'm the one who beats her though!

À moi ma Chair-de-poule!
À toi! Suis-je pas beau,
Quand mon baiser te roule
À cru dans mon manteau! ...

Je ris comme une folle
Et sens mal aux cheveux,
Quand ta chair fraîche colle
Contre mon cuir lépreux!

Jérusalem. — Octobre.

Be just mine, my Goose-flesh!
And yours! Aren't I handsomer
When my kisses — raw and fresh —
Roll you in my parka fur!

I keep laughing like Old Nick,
Go queasy and pop-eyed
To feel your clear skin stick
To my leprous hide!

Jerusalem. — October.

Gente Dame

Il n'est plus, ô ma Dame,
D'amour en cape, en lame,
    Que Vous! ...
De passion sans obstacle,
Mystère à grand spectacle,
    Que nous! ...

Depuis les *Tour de Nesle*
Et les *Château de Presle*,
    Temps frais,
Où l'on couchait en Seine
Les galants, pour leur peine ...
    — Après. —

Quand vous êtes *Frisette*,
Il n'est plus de grisette
    Que Toi! ...
Ni de rapin farouche,
Pur Rembrandt sans retouche,
    Que moi!

Qu'il attende, Marquise,
Au grand mur de l'église
    Flanqué,
Ton bon coupé vert-sombre,
Comme un bravo dans l'ombre,
    Masqué.

— À nous! — J'arme en croisière
Mon fiacre-corsaire,
    Au vent,
Bordant, comme une voile,
Le store qui nous voile:
    — Avant! ...

Gentle Lady

There is no longer, Lady,
Any love: style — cloak and blade,
  But You! ...
Any passion unimpeded,
Mystery play that's succeeded
  Like us two! ...

Since the *Towers of Nesle*
And the *Châteaux of Presle*
  It's been chill,
For every gallant's been laid
In the Seine if he outstayed ...
  Though not until ...

When you're acting *Frisette*
There's no other grisette
  But Thee! ...
Nor unlicked dauber-pup,
Pure Rembrandt, not touched up,
  But me!

Hard by the wall, Marchioness,
The wall of the church, no less,
  Let it wait,
Your bottle-green shandrydan,
Like a masked highwayman
  In the shade.

I'm fitting it out — Our cruiser! —
My hackney-carriage-corsair,
  To windward,
Hauling taut, like a sail-sheet,
The blind to veil our deeds:
  — Onward! ...

— Quartier-dolent — tourelle
Tout au haut de l'échelle ...
          Quel pas!
— Au sixième — Eh! madame,
C'est tomber, sur mon âme!
          Bien bas!

Au grenier poétique,
Où gîte le classique
          Printemps,
Viens courre, aventurière,
Ce lapin de gouttière:
          Vingt-ans!

Ange, viens pour ton hère
Jouer à la misère
          Des dieux!
Pauvre diable à ficelles,
Lui, joue avec tes ailes,
          Aux cieux!

Viens, Béatrix du Dante,
Mets dans ta main charmante
          Mon front ...
Ou passe, en bonne fille,
Fière au bras de ton drille,
          Le pont.

Demain, ô mâle amante,
Reviens-moi Bradamante!
          Muguet!
Eschôlier en fortune,
Narguant, de vers la brune,
          Le guet!

— The doldrums — What a hop:
To the turret at the ladder's top
    You'll be bound!
— The sixth floor, madam? — Oh!
The sixth is far too low,
    And going down ...

In the poetic garret
Where classic Spring is let
    Lodge and list,
Come and course, Miss Rantipole,
This gutter-rabbit, gutter-soul:
    Never-been-kissed!

Angel, come down for this lame squit
To play at the gods slumming it
    On cloud seven!
He, poor devil on strings,
Is busy fondling your wings
    In heaven!

Come, Dante's Beatrice, I'd
Let your gentle hand glide
    Over my brow ...
Or: pass to the other side,
Your man's arm round you, his *bride*,
    And you so proud.

He-mistress, come back groomed
Tomorrow as Bradamante! perfumed
    As a dandy!
Or as Villon, out to flout,
From nightfall on, the look-out
    — Red-handed!

1 *Sonnet*

AVEC LA MANIÈRE DE S'EN SERVIR

Réglons notre papier et formons bien nos lettres:

Vers filés à la main et d'un pied uniforme,
Emboîtant bien le pas, par quatre en peloton;
Qu'en marquant la césure, un des quatre s'endorme ...
Ça peut dormir debout comme soldats de plomb.

Sur le *railway* du Pinde est la ligne, la forme;
Aux fils du télégraphe: — on en suit quatre, en long;
À chaque pieu, la rime — exemple: *chloroforme.*
— Chaque vers est un fil, et la rime un jalon.

— Télégramme sacré — 20 mots. — Vite à mon aide ...
(Sonnet — c'est un sonnet —) ô Muse d'Archimède!
— La preuve d'un sonnet est par l'addition:

— Je pose 4 et 4 = 8! Alors je procède
En posant 3 et 3! — Tenons Pégase raide:
"Ô lyre! Ô délire! Ô ..." — Sonnet — Attention!

Pic de la Maladetta. — Août.

50

1 Sonnet

WITH DIRECTIONS FOR THE USE OF

Let us rule lines and form our letters clearly:

Lines drawn up by hand and with regular feet,
Falling into perfect step, by fours in a squad;
Marking the caesura, one could well fall asleep ...
They can sleep standing up like soldiers of lead.

The Pindus *railway* takes up the line, the form;
With telegraph wires: — there are four to a leg;
At every post, the rhyme — example: *chloroform.*
— Each line is a wire, and the rhyme a peg.

— Holy telegram — 20 words. — Quick, relief ...
(This must be a sonnet —) O Archimedes' Muse!
— The proof of a sonnet is in the brief:

— I lay down 4 and 4 = 8! Avoid invention
By adding 3 and 3! — Don't let Pegasus loose:
"O lyre! O delirium! O ..." — Sonnet — Attention!

Maladetta Peak. — August.

51

Sonnet à Sir Bob

Chien de femme légère, braque anglais pur sang.

Beau chien, quand je te vois caresser ta maîtresse,
Je grogne malgré moi — pourquoi? — Tu n'en sais rien ...
Je n'ai pas de maîtresse, et ... ne suis pas beau chien.

— *Bob! Bob!* — Oh! le fier nom à hurler d'allégresse! ...
Si je m'appelais *Bob* ... Elle dit Bob si bien! ...
Mais moi je ne suis pas *pur sang.* — Par maladresse,
On m'a fait *braque* aussi ... mâtiné de chrétien.

— Ô Bob! nous changerons, à la métempsycose:
Prends mon sonnet, moi ta sonnette à faveur rose;
Toi ma peau, moi ton poil — avec puces ou non ...

Et je serai *sir Bob* — Son seul amour fidèle!
Je mordrai les roquets, elle me mordrait, Elle! ...
Et j'aurai le collier portant Son petit nom.

Britisch channel. — 15 may.

52

Sonnet to Sir Bob

A fickle woman's dog, a thorough-bred English hound.

Handsome dog, when I see you nuzzle your mistress,
I growl despite myself — and why? — You're in a fog ...
— Well, it's all because, you see, I never caress,
I haven't a mistress, and ... am not a handsome dog.

— *Bob! Bob!* — A name to be proud of and howl for joy! ...
If only I were called *Bob* ... She says Bob so well! ...
But I'm no *thoroughbred* — just one of the *hoi polloi*
Whelped as a pointer ... crossed with a Christian: a mongrel.

— O Bob! we shall change at the metempsychosis:
You have my sonnet, your bell and pink favour for me:
You have my skin, me yours — with or without the fleas ...

And I shall be *sir Bob* — Her only devotee!
I'll snap at the pugs, She'll snap at me! ... I'll be tame
And wear a dog-collar bearing Her Christian name.

Britisch channel. — 15th May.

53

Steam-Boat

À une passagère.

En fumée elle est donc chassée
L'éternité, la traversée
Qui fit de Vous ma sœur d'un jour,
     Ma sœur d'amour! ...

Là-bas: cette mer incolore
Où ce qui fut Toi flotte encore ...
Ici: la terre, ton écueil,
     Tertre de deuil!

On t'espère là ... Va légère!
Qui te bercera, Passagère? ...
Ô passagère de mon cœur,
     Ton remorqueur! ...

Quel ménélas, sur son rivage,
Fait le pied? ... — Va, j'ai ton sillage ...
J'ai, — quand il est là voir venir, —
     Ton souvenir!

Il n'aura pas, lui, ma Peureuse,
Les sauts de ta gorge houleuse! ...
Tes sourcils salés de poudrain
     Pendant un grain!

Il ne t'aura pas: effrontée!
Par tes cheveux au vent fouettée! ...
Ni, durant les longs quarts de nuit,
     Ton doux ennui ...

Ni ma poésie où: — *Posée,*
Tu seras la mouette blessée,
Et moi le flot qu'elle rasa ...,
     Et cœtera.

Steam-Boat

To a fellow passenger.

In smoke then it is blown away
Eternity, the crossing
Which made You my sister for a day,
    My sister in loving! ...

Out there: that lack-lustre sea
Where what was You is still floating ...
Here: the land, your reef,
    Shoal of lamenting!

You're expected there ... O traveller,
Who will rock you once you depart? ...
Travel light-heartedly, Passenger
    Of my tug-boat heart! ...

What menelaus, on his shore,
Paces to and fro? ... — I have your wake ...
When he's there to see you come, it's your
    Memory I take!

My Timorous One, he shall not claim
Your heaving bosom's rise and fall! ...
Your eyebrows salted with spray
    During a squall!

He shall not have you: shameless wretch!
Skelped by your hair blowing free! ...
Nor, through each long night's watch,
    Your sweet ennui ...

Nor my poetry where: — *Laid low,*
You will be the wounded tern,
And I the billow she skimmed o'er ... ,
    Et cœtera.

— Le large, bête sans limite,
Me paraîtra bien grand, Petite,
Sans Toi! ... Rien n'est plus l'horizon
     Qu'une cloison.

Qu'elle va me sembler étroite!
Tout seul, la boîte à deux! ... la boîte
Où nous n'avions qu'un oreiller
     Pour sommeiller.

Déjà le soleil se fait sombre
Qui ne balance plus ton ombre,
Et la houle a fait un grand pli ...
     — Comme l'oubli! —

Ainsi déchantait sa fortune,
En vigie, au sec, dans la hune,
Par un soir frais, vers le matin,
     Un pilotin.

10' long. O.
40' lat. N.

— The open sea, that boundless creature,
Will seem huge when You have sped!
For me the horizon's reach
    Is a bulkhead.

It's going to seem so narrow!
All alone, the berth for two!
For sleep we only had one pillow
    And made do.

Already the sun's light is failing,
It no longer trims your shadow,
And the swell is not plain sailing ...
    — Like oblivion's O! —

Thus piping down about his fate,
High and dry, from the crow's nest,
Was a northo-rigger's mate,
    One raw night, going west ...

10' long. W.
40' lat. N.

Pudentiane

Attouchez, sans toucher. On est dévotieuse,
    Ni ne retient à son escient.
Mais On pâme d'horreur d'être: *luxurieuse*
    De corps et de consentement! ...

Et de chair ... de cette œuvre On est fort curieuse,
    Sauf le vendredi — seulement:
Le confesseur est maigre ... et l'extase pieuse
    En fait: *carême entièrement.*

    ... Une autre se donne. — Ici l'On se damne —
    C'est un tabernacle — ouvert — qu'on profane.
    Bénitier où le serpent est caché!

    Que l'Amour, ailleurs, comme un coq se chante ...
    CI-GÎT! la *pudeur-d'-attentat* le hante ...
    C'est la Pomme (cuite) en fleur de péché.

Rome. — 40 ans. — 15 août.

Lip-Server

Touch me, but no touching. One is holy-trustful,
Nor does not restrain wittingly.
But One faints with horror at becoming: *lustful*
Of body and consentingly! ...

In the flesh ... about this handye worke One's curious,
Except on Fridays — then solely:
The confessor's lean ... and One's raptures, being pious,
Ensure: *Lent entire and wholly.*

... Another gives herself. — Here One feels stained —
A tabernacle — open — and profaned.
A holy-water stoup the fell serpent's in!

Let Love, elsewhere, like a cock, be vaunting it ...
HERE LIES! *Decent assault* is haunting it ...
The Apple (done to a turn) in the bloom of sin.

Rome. — 40 years. — 15th August.

Après la Pluie

J'aime la petite pluie
    Qui s'essuie
D'un torchon de bleu troué!
J'aime l'amour et la brise,
    Quand ça frise ...
Et pas quand c'est secoué.

— Comme un parapluie en flèches,
    Tu te sèches,
Ô grand soleil! grand ouvert ...
À bientôt l'ombrelle verte
    Grand'ouverte!
Du printemps — été d'hiver. —

La passion c'est l'averse
    Qui traverse!
Mais la femme n'est qu'un grain:
Grain de beauté, de folie
    Ou de pluie ...
Grain d'orage — ou de serein. —

Dans un clair rayon de boue,
    Fait la roue,
La roue à grand appareil,
— Plume et queue — une Cocotte
    Qui barbote;
Vrai déjeuner de soleil!

— "Anne! ou qui que tu sois, chère ...
    Ou pas chère,
Dont on fait, à l'œil, les yeux ...
Hum ... Zoé! Nadjejda! Jane!
    Vois: je flâne,
Doublé d'or comme les cieux!

After the Rain

I love drizzle when and if
    It wipes its quiff
On a holey sky-blue clout!
I love love and the breeze,
    When it frizzes ...
And not when it's tossed about.

— Bare-ribbed, you start to get dried,
    Lofty sun, wide
Open like an umbrella ...
The green parasol of Spring
    Will be opening
Out soon — in Winter's Summer. —

Passion is the sudden burst
    And you're immersed!
But woman's just an April shower:
A beauty spot, a spot of rain
    Or a shade insane ...
A hint of thunder should skies lower!

In a limpid bed of ooze
    Struts a one whose
Plumes are fanned out for display:
A paddling *jay* who shows her tail,
    And, to regale,
A titbit that is here today ...

— "Anne! or whoever you are, dear ...
    Or not so dear,
Free for us to make sheep's eyes ...
Hm ... Zoë! Nadjejda! Jane!
    I'm in the vein,
Strolling, gold-lined like the skies!

"*English spoken?* — Espagnole? ...
      Batignolle? ...
Arbore le pavillon
Qui couvre ta marchandise,
      Ô marquise
D'Amaëgui! ... Frétillon! ...

"Nom de singe ou nom d'Archange?
      Ou mélange? ...
Petit nom à huit ressorts?
Nom qui ronfle, ou nom qui chante?
      Nom d'amante? ...
Ou nom à coucher dehors? ...

"Veux-tu, d'une amour fidelle,
      Éternelle!
Nous adorer pour ce soir? ...
Pour tes deux petites bottes
      Que tu crottes,
Prends mon cœur et le trottoir!

"N'es-tu pas doña Sabine?
      Carabine? ...
Dis: veux-tu le paradis
De l'Odéon? — traversée
      Insensée! ...
On emporte des radis." —

C'est alors que se dégaine
      La rengaine:
"Vous vous trompez ... Quel émoi! ...
Laissez-moi ... je suis honnête ...
      — Pas si bête!
— Pour qui me prends-tu? — Pour moi! ...

"*On parle français?* — You from Spain? ...
      Or Petticoat Lane? ...
Raise the awning — and the flag —
That covers your wares; or tease
      Me, *belle Marquise*
D'Amaëgui! ... Whose tail'll wag! ...

"Do you answer to: baboon,
      Archangel or quadroon? ...
A pet name bouncing on springs?
A kept mistress's bell-pull?
      A real mouthful? ...
A name that roars, a name that sings?

"Will you, with a love that's faithfull,
      And eternall!
Make this, our evening, compleat? ...
For each dainty laced bootee
      That you muddy,
Take my heart and to the street!

"Aren't you *the* Doña Sabine?
      La carabine? ...
On the look-out for paradise
In the gods, à la Old Vic?
      — Rough passage! ... I'm sick
For love ... and you fix the price." —

Then out of its sheath again
      Comes the refrain:
"You're so excited ... Leave me be!
You've got me wrong ... I'm an honest
      Girl ... — Who by some twist ...
— Who do you take me for? — Me! ...

"... Prendrais-tu pas quelque chose
        Qu'on arrose
Avec n'importe quoi ... du
Jus de perles dans des coupes
        D'or? ... Tu coupes! ...
Mais moi? Mina, me prends-tu?

" — Pourquoi pas? ça va sans dire!
        — Ô sourire! ...
Moi, par-dessus le marché! ...
Hermosa, tu m'as l'air franche
        De la hanche!
Un cuistre en serait fâché!

" — Mais je me nomme Aloïse ...
        — Héloïse!
Veux-tu, pour l'amour de l'art,
— Abeilard avant la lettre —
        Me permettre
D'être un peu ton Abeilard?"

. . . .
. . . .

Et, comme un grain blanc qui crève,
        Le doux rêve
S'est couché là, sans point noir ...
"Donne à ma lèvre apaisée,
        La rosée
D'un baiser levant — Bonsoir —

"C'est le chant de l'alouette,
        Juliette!
Et c'est le chant du dindon ...
Je te fais, comme l'aurore
        Qui te dore,
Un rond d'or sur l'édredon."

"... What would you say to a little
          Drink, your tipple
With a dash of ... let's think: the
Juice of pearls in golden cups? ...
          — My pick-me-ups! ...
— But Mina, will you take me?

" — Why not? it goes without saying!
          — Your hips are swaying ...
For me? ... I grin like a young Turk!
Hermosa, you look dandy,
          Not to say randy!
A wet blanket would be irked!

" — But my name is Aloïse ...
          — You mean Héloïse!
Will you, for the love of art,
— I'm Abelard in embryo —
          Now let me grow
To be a while your Abelard?"

. . . .
. . . .

The sweet dream has smoothed my frown
          And bedded down
— Like a breaking squall, it's white
Without a black spot or a cloud ...
          "Apply to my mouth
The dew of a kiss-rise — Goodnight —

"It's the song of the skylark,
          Juliet! and hark
At the cackle of the turkey-cock ...
Just as you're gilded by dawn,
          I shall coin
You a blob of gold on the bed-flock."

65

À Une Rose

Rose, rose-d'amour vannée,
        Jamais fanée,
Le rouge-fin est ta couleur,
        Ô fausse fleur!

Feuille où pondent les journalistes
        Un fait-divers,
Papier-Joseph, croquis d'artistes:
        — Chiffres ou vers —

Cœur de parfum, montant arôme
        Qui nous embaume ...
Et ferait même avec succès,
        Après décès;

Grise l'amour de ton haleine,
        Vapeur malsaine,
Vent de pastille-du-sérail,
        Hanté par l'ail!

Ton épingle, épine postiche,
        Chaque nuit fiche
Le hanneton-d'or, ton amant ...
Sensitive ouverte, arrosée
De fausses-perles de rosée,
        En diamant!

Chaque jour palpite à la colle
        De ta corolle
Un papillon-coquelicot,
        Pur calicot.

Rose-thé! ... — Dans le grog, peut-être! —
        Tu dois renaître
Jaune, sous le fard du tampon,
        Rose-pompon!

To a Rose

O Rose, exhausted rose-of-love,
    Never wilting,
Wine-red's the tint, false flower, of
    Your fine quilting!

Leaf where reporters lay — not eggs —
    But scraps of news;
Onion-skin where artists sketch:
    — Ciphers, haikus —

Heart of fragrance, whose rising scents
    Embalm our peace ...
And would do too to all intents
    After decease;

Befuddle love with your ozone,
    Unhealthy vapour,
Breath of rose-and-sandalwood cone,
    Garlic flavour!

Your pin, an artificial thorn,
    Each night sticks into
The gold rose-chafer, your *amor* ...
No sensitive plant's escaped
Fresh imitation pearls of dew,
    Diamond-shaped!

Each day on your corolla's glue
    There flutters though
A poppy-butterfly or two,
    Pure calico.

Tea-rose! ... — May be, in a toddy! —
    You must osmose
As yellow from your rouged body,
    Powder-puff-rose!

Vénus-Coton, née en pelote,
Un soir-matin,
Parmi l'écume ... que culotte
Le clan rapin!

Rose-mousseuse, sur toi pousse
Souvent la mousse
De l'Aï ... Du BOCK plus souvent
— À 30 C^{ent}.

— Un coup-de-soleil de la rampe!
Qui te retrempe;
Un coup de pouce à ton grand air
Sur fil-de-fer! ...

Va, gommeuse et gommée, ô rose
De couperose,
Fleurir les faux-cols et les cœurs,
Gilets vainqueurs!

Born on a clew, Venus-Cotton,
      One evening-morn,
In the foam ... well-thumbed by rotten
      Daubsters who spawn!

On you, bubbly, sparkling moss-rose,
      There often grows
The froth of Aÿ ... Or a head of BEER
      — It's not as dear.

— A touch of the footlights' sun! — Dutch
      Courage braces;
A twist of wire for the finishing touch:
      Your airs and graces! ...

Go, you stuck-up and sticky rose
      Of *acne rosacea*,
Make starched collars bloom, hearts appear
      As waistcoat heroes!

À la Mémoire de Zulma
VIERGE-FOLLE HORS BARRIÈRE
et d'un Louis

Bougival, 8 mai

Elle était riche de vingt ans,
Moi j'étais jeune de vingt francs,
Et nous fîmes bourse commune,
Placée, à fonds perdu, dans une
Infidèle nuit de printemps ...

La lune a fait un trou dedans,
Rond comme un écu de cinq francs,
Par où passa notre fortune:
Vingt ans! vingt francs! ... et puis la lune!

— En monnaie — hélas — les vingt francs!
En monnaie aussi les vingt ans!
Toujours de trous en trous de lune,
Et de bourse en bourse commune ...
— C'est à peu près même fortune!

. . . .

— Je la trouvai — bien des printemps,
Bien des vingt ans, bien des vingt francs,
Bien des trous et bien de la lune
Après — Toujours vierge et vingt ans,
Et ... colonelle à la Commune!

. . . .

— Puis après: la chasse aux passants,
Aux vingt sols, et plus aux vingt francs ...
Puis après: la fosse commune,
Nuit gratuite sans trou de lune.

Saint-Cloud. — Novembre.

70

To the Memory of Zulma
FOOLISH VIRGIN BEYOND THE PALE
and a Golden Louis

Bougival, May 8th.

She was rich: twenty in Spring,
I was a twenty franc *young thing*,
So, pooling our resources, we
Invested, with no security,
In one unfaithful Spring night fling ...

The moon shot a hole in it, a hole
As round as a silver obole,
And through it went our whole fortune:
Twenty Springs! twenty francs! ... and then the moon!

Oh it's small change now the twenty francs!
The twenty years are small change too!
There's always pitfalls in moonlit banks,
Pools of moonlight I now see through;
On moonlight flits there's money due;
Having shares in shared expenses
Is, more or less, to lose one's censes!

. . . .

— I found her — many a springtide,
Many score francs, years a-plenty,
Many a pitfall and much moonslide
Later — A virgin still, still twenty,
And ... a colonel on the Commune side!

. . . .

— Then later: dunning passers-by
For francs, not just centime bits ...
Later still: the paupers' grave, a night
Shot-free with no moonlight flits.

Saint-Cloud. — November.

71

Bonne Fortune
ET
Fortune

Odor della feminita.

Moi, je fais mon trottoir, quand la nature est belle,
Pour la passante qui, d'un petit air vainqueur,
Voudra bien crocheter, du bout de son ombrelle,
Un clin de ma prunelle ou la peau de mon cœur ...

Et je me crois content — pas trop! — mais il faut vivre:
Pour promener un peu sa faim, le gueux s'enivre ...

Un beau jour — quel métier! — je faisais, comme ça,
Ma croisière. — Métier! ... — Enfin, Elle passa
— Elle qui? — La Passante! Elle, avec son ombrelle!
Vrai valet de bourreau, je la frôlai ... — mais Elle

Me regarda tout bas, souriant en dessous,
Et ... me tendit sa main, et ...
                                          m'a donné deux sous.

Rue des Martyrs.

72

Good Fortune
AND
a Fortune

Odor della feminita.

I walk the streets, when all around is beautiful,
For the passer-by who, with her malapert art,
Will want to hook, with the tip of her parasol,
A bat of my eyelid or a beat of my heart ...

And I think I'm happy — but a lot goes in touting
When down-and-outs treat their hunger to an outing ...

One fine day — what a game! — I was out to ply,
On the off-chance, my trade! — At long last, She passed by
— Who? — The Passer-by! The One with the parasol!
Executioner's right-arm, I brushed against her ... Moll

Gave me a furtive glance, half-smiling admittance,
And ... stretching out her hand ...
                              handed me a pittance.

Martyrs Way.

À une Camarade

Que me veux-tu donc, femme trois fois fille? ...
Moi qui te croyais un si bon enfant!
— De l'amour? ... — Allons: cherche, apporte, pille!
M'aimer aussi, toi! ... moi qui t'aimais tant.

Oh! je t'aimais comme ... un lézard qui pèle
Aime le rayon qui cuit son sommeil ...
L'Amour entre nous vient battre de l'aile:
— Eh! qu'il s'ôte de devant mon soleil!

Mon amour, à moi, n'aime pas qu'on l'aime;
Mendiant, il a peur d'être écouté ...
C'est un lazzarone enfin, un bohème,
Déjeunant de jeûne et de liberté.

— Curiosité, bibelot, bricole? ...
C'est possible: il est rare — et c'est son bien —
Mais un bibelot cassé se recolle;
Et lui, décollé, ne vaudra plus rien! ...

Va, n'enfonçons pas la porte entr'ouverte
Sur un paradis déjà trop rendu!
Et gardons à la pomme, jadis verte,
Sa peau, sous son fard de fruit défendu.

Que nous sommes-nous donc fait l'un à l'autre? ...
— Rien ... — Peut-être alors que c'est pour cela;
— Quel a commencé? — Pas moi, bon apôtre!
Après, quel dira: c'est donc tout — voilà!

— Tous les deux, sans doute ... — Et toi, sois bien sûre
Que c'est encor moi le plus attrapé:
Car si, par erreur, ou par aventure,
Tu ne me trompais ... je serais trompé!

Just Good Friends

What do you want of me, thrice-virgin Mary? ...
Who thought you a goody-goody, or some such!
— Love? ... — But all you know is: go, fetch, tear him!
You, love me as well! ... who've loved you so much.

Oh! I've loved you like ... a lizard that's peeling
Loves the sunbeam that's baking it stupid ...
Love has come between us, flapping its wings;
— Hey there! just shift from my sunshine, Cupid!

My love doesn't like being loved, it's mine;
When it's begging, it's afraid to be heard ...
It's a *lazzarone*, a bohemian, fine
For breakfasting on fasts and the last word

In freedom. — Curio, knick-knack, kickshaw? ...
Could be: it is rare — and that's its asset —
But a broken trinket can be re-set;
And this, come unstuck, 's worth nothing any more! ...

Now then, let's not break down the doors which lead
Into an Eden already gone to seed!
And let's keep on the apple, that forbidden
Fruit, its skin, once green, that rouge has hidden.

What have we done to one another then? ...
— Nothing ... — Which, perhaps, is half the trouble;
— Who on earth began things? — Not me, great heaven!
Once it's over, which will prick the bubble?

— Both of us, I dare say ... — And please believe
I am still the one who is most smitten:
For if, by error, or the biter bitten,
You weren't deceiving me ... I'd be deceived!

75

Appelons cela: *l'amitié calmée*;
Puisque l'amour veut mettre son holà.
N'y croyons pas trop, chère mal-aimée ...
— C'est toujours trop vrai ces mensonges-là! —

Nous pourrons, au moins, ne pas nous maudire
— Si ça t'est égal — le quart-d'heure après.
Si nous en mourons — ce sera de rire ...
Moi qui l'aimais tant ton rire si frais!

Let's call it: *when-ardour-has-abated;*
Since love's wanting to cut things down to size.
Dear ill-beloved, such ideas are inflated ...
— They're always too close to the truth, those lies! —

At least we'll manage not to be chaffing
One another — alright? — a short while after.
If we die of it — it will be laughing ...
I did so love your refreshing laughter!

Un Jeune Qui S'en Va

Morire.

Oh le printemps! — Je voudrais paître! ...
C'est drôle, est-ce pas: Les mourants
Font toujours ouvrir leur fenêtre,
Jaloux de leur part de printemps!

Oh le printemps! Je veux écrire!
Donne-moi mon bout de crayon
— Mon bout de crayon, c'est ma lyre —
Et — là — je me sens un rayon.

Vite! ... j'ai vu, dans mon délire,
Venir me manger dans la main
La Gloire qui voulait me lire!
— La gloire n'attend pas demain. —

Sur ton bras, soutiens ton poète,
Toi, sa Muse, quand il chantait,
Son Sourire quand il mourait,
Et sa Fête ... quand c'était fête!

Sultane, apporte un peu ma pipe
Turque, incrustée en faux saphir,
Celle qui *va bien à mon type* ...
Et ris! — C'est fini de mourir;

Et viens sur mon lit de malade;
Empêche la mort d'y toucher,
D'emporter cet enfant maussade
Qui ne veut pas s'aller coucher.

Ne pleure donc plus, — je suis bête —
Vois: mon drap n'est pas un linceul ...
Je chantais cela pour moi seul ...
Le vide chante dans ma tête ...

A Young Man Going to Glory

Morire.

Oh 'tis Spring! — Put me out to graze! ...
It's odd, is it not: The dying
Always want their window raised,
Coveting their fair share of Spring!

Now it's Spring, I've a yen to write!
Hand me my stub of pencil, do,
— My pencil stub is my lyre too —
I see myself as a pencil of light.

Quick! ... in my raving, I have seen
Fame come up and start eating
From my hand, wanting to read me!
— And Fame can't be kept waiting. —

Bolster up your poet once more,
You, his Muse, when he used to sing,
His Smile, when he was at Death's door,
His Saint's Day ... when the saints marched in!

Sultana, bring my Turkish pipe,
Inlaid with imitation sapphire,
The one that really suits my type ...
And laugh! — Dying's no longer dire;

Come to my sick-bed now and stay
Death who's got it into his hood
To bear this peevish child away
Who doesn't want to lie down for good.

Don't cry any more, — I'm daft not dead —
See: my sheet is not a shroud ...
I was just singing in my head
To myself, but the void sings so loud ...

Retourne contre la muraille.
— Là — l'esquisse — un portrait de toi —
Malgré lui mon œil soûl travaille
Sur la toile … C'était de moi.

J'entends — bourdon de la fièvre —
Un chant de berceau me monter:
"J'entends le renard, le lièvre,
Le lièvre, le loup chanter."

… Va! nous aurons une chambrette
Bien fraîche, à papier bleu rayé;
Avec un vrai bon lit honnête
À nous, à rideaux … et payé!

Et nous irons dans la prairie
Pêcher à la ligne tous deux,
Ou bien *mourir pour la patrie!* …
— Tu sais, je fais ce que tu veux.

… Et nous aurons des robes neuves,
Nous serons riches à bâiller
Quand j'aurai revu *mes épreuves!*
— Pour vivre, il faut bien travailler …

— Non! mourir…
                    La vie était belle
Avec toi! mais rien ne va plus …
À moi le pompon d'immortelle
Des grands poètes que j'ai lus!

À moi, *Myosotis! Feuille morte*
De *Jeune malade à pas lent!*
Souvenir de soi … qu'on emporte
En croyant le laisser — souvent!

— Décès: Rolla: — l'Académie —
Murger, Baudelaire: — hôpital, —
Lamartine: — en perdant la vie
De sa fille, en strophes pas mal …

Turn to face the wall. — There — that sketch —
It's a portrait of you — Headstrong,
My drunken eye is apt to etch
In facets ... It was me all along.

I hear a lullaby in the air
— The bumble bee of fever crooning —
*"I can hear the fox, the hare,
The hare and the wolf a-tuning."*

... We shall have a little haven,
Clean, well-aired, with blue-striped paper;
And an alcove bed, a heaven
Of our own, curtained ... and paid for!

And we'll cross the fields together
When it's lovely fishing weather,
Or else *die for the fatherland!* ...
— You know, your wish is my command.

... And we shall have money to spend
On new clothes and a life of ease
When I've checked *my proofs* — all these!
— To live, you've to work to that end ...

— No! you've to die ...
                        Life is beautiful
With you! but I have lost the thread ...
I want the everlasting laurel
Sprig of the great poets I have read!

Be mine, *Forget-me-not! Dead leaf
Of Sick Youth, creeping like snail!*
Memory of oneself ... it's one's belief
One's quashing it, when one salts its tail!

— Deaths: Rolla: — the Academy —
Murger, Baudelaire: — hospital, —
Lamartine: — his daughter's memory
Penned in verse one can't belittle ...

Doux bedeau, pleureuse en lévite,
Harmonieux tronc des *moissonnés*,
Inventeur de la *larme écrite*,
Lacrymatoire d'abonnés! ...

Moreau — j'oubliais — Hégésippe,
Créateur de l'art-hôpital ...
Depuis, j'ai la phtisie en grippe;
Ce n'est plus même original.

— Escousse encor: mort en extase
De lui; mort phtisique d'orgueil.
— Gilbert: phtisie et paraphrase
Rentrée, en se pleurant *à l'œil.*

— Un autre incompris: Lacenaire,
Faisant des vers en amateur
Dans le goût anti-poitrinaire,
Avec Sanson pour éditeur.

— Lord Byron, gentleman-vampire,
Hystérique du ténébreux;
Anglais sec, cassé par son rire,
Son noble rire de lépreux.

— Hugo: l'Homme apocalyptique,
L'Homme-Ceci-tûra-cela,
Meurt, gardenational épique;
Il n'en reste qu'un — celui-là! —

... Puis un tas d'amants de la lune,
Guère plus morts qu'ils n'ont vécu,
Et changeant de fosse commune
Sans un discours, sans un écu!

J'en ai lus mourir! ... Et ce cygne
Sous le couteau du cuisinier:
— Chénier — ... Je me sens — mauvais signe! —
De la jalousie. — Ô métier!

Gentle verger, armchair keener,
Harmonious offertory,
Inventor of the *written tear*,
Subscribers' lachrymatory! ...

Moreau — Hégésippe — before I forget,
Creator of hospital-art ...
Phthisis is a pain in the neck
Since then, you can't take it to heart.

— Then there's Escousse: died in a wallow
Of self; consumptive death from pride.
— Gilbert: consumption and hollow
Paraphrase, with self-pity on the side.

— Another who has had the strain
Of verse: that maligned amateur,
Lacenaire, in anti-TB vein,
With the hangman as publisher.

— Lord Byron, gentleman vampire,
Hysteric of gloom — what broke
Him was his laugh, that dry English squire,
— His noble laugh a leper's croak.

— Hugo: apocalyptic Bard,
The-Press-will-stifle-the-Church Man.
Is dying, epic national guard,
The only one left in the van!

... Then a horde who fell for the moon,
Hardly deader than when alive,
From one grave to the next, they're soon
Too speechless and broke to survive.

I've read some corpses! ... And that swan,
Chénier, beneath the head-chef's knife ...
— Ominous! — What I feel coming on
Is jealousy. — Oh what a life!

Métier! Métier de mourir ...
Assez, j'ai fini mon étude.
Métier: se rimer finir! ...
C'est une affaire d'habitude.

Mais non, la poésie est: vivre,
Paresser encore, et souffrir
Pour toi, maîtresse! et pour mon livre;
Il est là qui dort
           — Non: mourir!

. . . .

Sentir sur ma lèvre appauvrie
Ton dernier baiser se gercer,
La mort dans tes bras me bercer ...
Me déshabiller de la vie! ...

Charenton. — Avril.

What a calling! A call to death ...
That will do: manuscript completed.
My career: rhyming out of breath! ...
Which happens when things get repeated.

No, no, poetry is: living,
Idling along, and suffering
For you, my love! and for my book;
It's sleeping now
                    — No: dying, look!

. . . .

Feeling your final kiss chapping
These impoverished lips of mine,
And death, in your arms, unwrapping
Me from life! and cradling my spine ...

Charenton Asylum. — April.

Insomnie

Insomnie, impalpable Bête!
N'as-tu d'amour que dans la tête?
Pour venir te pâmer à voir,
Sous ton mauvais œil, l'homme mordre
Ses draps, et dans l'ennui se tordre! ...
Sous ton œil de diamant noir.

Dis: pourquoi, durant la nuit blanche,
Pluvieuse comme un dimanche,
Venir nous lécher comme un chien:
Espérance ou Regret qui veille,
À notre palpitante oreille
Parler bas ... et ne dire rien?

Pourquoi, sur notre gorge aride,
Toujours pencher ta coupe vide
Et nous laisser le cou tendu,
Tantales, soiffeurs de chimère:
— Philtre amoureux ou lie amère,
Fraîche rosée ou plomb fondu! —

Insomnie, es-tu donc pas belle? ...
Eh pourquoi, lubrique pucelle,
Nous étreindre entre tes genoux?
Pourquoi râler sur notre bouche,
Pourquoi défaire notre couche,
Et ... ne pas coucher avec nous?

Pourquoi, Belle-de-nuit impure,
Ce masque noir sur ta figure? ...
— Pour intriguer les songes d'or? ...
N'es-tu pas l'amour dans l'espace,
Souffle de Messaline lasse,
Mais pas rassasiée encor!

Insomnia

Insomnia, impalpable Beast!
Is love only in your head, not breast?
That you are in raptures at the sight,
O evil eye, of man abrading
His sheets, tossing and turning, jaded
Under your black diamond eye?

Tell me: why, on a sleepless night,
That's as rainy as a Sunday,
Do you come and lick us like a dog:
As Hope or Regret that stays alight,
Whisper when you've nothing to say
And our ears do nothing but throb?

Why, above our throats that are parched,
Tilt your empty cup and leave us,
Tantaluses, our necks outstretched,
Ever athirst for chimeras:
— Love potion or bitter dregs,
Morning dew or molten lead! —

Are you not beautiful then? ... How
Could you, lubricious puss in boots,
Squeeze us tight between your knees!
Why the heavy breathing at our mouth,
Why the rumpling of our sheets,
And ... still not let us sleep with you?

And why, sullied Love-in-a-mist,
This black mask pulled over your face? ...
— So our golden dreams are mystified? ...
Aren't you Venus's mount in space,
Gasps from Messalina, so kissed
And weary, but still not satisfied!

Insomnie, es-tu l'Hystérie …
Es-tu l'orgue de barbarie
Qui moud l'*Hosannah* des Élus? …
— Ou n'es-tu pas l'éternel plectre,
Sur les nerfs des damnés-de-lettre,
Raclant leurs vers — qu'eux seuls ont lus.

Insomnie, es-tu l'âne en peine
De Buridan — ou le phalène
De l'enfer? — Ton baiser de feu
Laisse un goût froidi de fer rouge …
Oh! viens te poser dans mon bouge! …
Nous dormirons ensemble un peu.

Insomnia, are you Hysteria ...
Grinding out on your hurdy-gurdy
A *Hosanna* for the Elect?
— Or are you the eternal plectrum
On the nerves of the *poètes maudits*
Twanging lines — only read by them.

Insomnia, are you Buridan's ass
In a purgatory of dithering
— Or the moth of hell? — Your kiss
Of fire leaves a chill iron tang ...
Oh! come and settle in my hovel! ...
We'll *sleep* together for a while.

La Pipe au Poète

Je suis la Pipe d'un poète,
Sa nourrice, et: j'endors *sa Bête.*

Quand ses chimères éborgnées
Viennent se heurter à son front,
Je fume ... Et lui, dans son plafond,
Ne peut plus voir les araignées.

... Je lui fais un ciel, des nuages,
La mer, le désert, des mirages;
— Il laisse errer là son œil mort ...

Et, quand lourde devient la nue,
Il croit voir une ombre connue,
— Et je sens mon tuyau qu'il mord ...

— Un autre tourbillon délie
Son âme, son carcan, sa vie!
... Et je me sens m'éteindre. — Il dort —

. . . .

— Dors encor: la *Bête* est calmée,
File ton rêve jusqu'au bout ...
Mon Pauvre! ... la fumée est tout.
— S'il est vrai que tout est fumée ...

Paris. — Janvier.

90

The Poet's Pipe

I'm a poet's Pipe, his wet-nurse,
And: I lull the *Beast* in him to sleep.

When his one-eye-blind chimeras
Come bumping into his brow's keep,
I smoke ... On his ceiling spiders
Blur, and up there in his belfry
He can no longer see the bats.

... For him I can create a sky,
Clouds, sea, desert, mirages — that's
Where he lets it rove, his wall-eye ...

And, when the clouds weigh heavier,
He thinks he sees a familiar
Spirit, — And I feel him bite my pap ...

Another swirl of smoke releases
His soul, his choker, all he is!
... And I go out. — He's having a nap —

. . . .

— Sleep on: the *Beast* is calmed and yoked;
Spin out your pipe-dream to its end ...
Smoke is everything, my Poor Friend!
— If everything goes up in smoke ...

Paris. — January.

Le Crapaud

Un chant dans une nuit sans air ...
La lune plaque en métal clair
Les découpures du vert sombre.

... Un chant; comme un écho, tout vif
Enterré, là, sous le massif ...
— Ça se tait: Viens, c'est là, dans l'ombre ...

— Un crapaud! — Pourquoi cette peur,
Près de moi, ton soldat fidèle!
Vois-le, poète tondu, sans aile,
Rossignol de la boue ... — Horreur! —

... Il chante. — Horreur!! — Horreur pourquoi?
Vois-tu pas son œil de lumière ...
Non: il s'en va, froid, sous sa pierre.

. . . .

Bonsoir — ce crapaud-là c'est moi.

Ce soir, 20 Juillet.

The Toad

A song on an oppressive night ...
The moon is plating with bright
Metal the dark-green cut-outs it has made.

... A song; like an echo, so alive
Buried under bushes down the drive ...
— It's stopped: Look, he's there, in the shade ...

— A toad! — Why this fear and trembling
With me here, your faithful conscript!
See him, poet without wings, clipped
Nightingale of the mud ... — Revolting! —

... He's singing. — How horrible!! — If you're told
There's a light in his eye, won't you see ...
No: he's off under his stone, stone-cold.

. . . .

Goodnight — that toad down there is me.

This evening, 20th July.

Femme

La Bête féroce.

Lui — cet être faussé, mal aimé, mal souffert,
Mal haï — mauvais livre ... et pire: il m'intéresse. —
S'il est vide après tout ... Oh mon dieu, je le laisse,
   Comme un roman pauvre — entr'ouvert.

Cet homme est laid ... — Et moi, ne suis-je donc pas belle,
   Et belle encore pour nous deux! —
En suis-je donc enfin aux rêves de pucelle? ...
   — Je suis reine: Qu'il soit lépreux!

Où vais-je — femme! — Après ... suis-je donc pas légère
   Pour me relever d'un faux pas!
Est-ce donc Lui que j'aime! — Eh non! c'est son mystère ...
   Celui que peut-être Il n'a pas.

Plus Il m'évite, et plus et plus Il me poursuit ...
   Nous verrons ce dédain suprême.
Il est rare à croquer, celui-là qui me fuit! ...
   Il me fuit — Eh bien non! ... Pas même.

... Aurais-je ri pourtant! si, comme un galant homme,
   Il avait allumé ses feux ...
Comme Ève — femme aussi — qui n'aimait pas la Pomme,
   Je ne l'aime pas — et j'en veux! —

C'est innocent. — Et lui? ... Si l'arme était chargée ...
   — Et moi, j'aime les vilains jeux!
Et... l'on sait amuser, avec une dragée
   Haute, un animal ombrageux.

De quel droit ce regard, ce mauvais œil qui touche:
   Monsieur poserait le fatal?
Je suis myope, il est vrai ... Peut-être qu'il est louche;
   Je l'ai vu si peu — mais si mal. —

Woman

The Savage Beast

Him — that warped creature, out of tune, ill-loved, wished dead,
Ill-loathed — a chronic book ... and worse: he intrigues me. —
What if he's empty after all ... My god, I shall leave
        Him like a poor romance — half-read.

The man is ugly ... — Am I not beautiful then,
        Enough for us both together! —
Have I finally come to a virgin's dream of men? ...
        — I am queen: Let him be leper!

Where am I going — woman! — Aren't I light enough
        To pick myself up when I've stumbled!
So is it Him I love! — No! it's his enigma: bluff,
        Perhaps, to which I haven't tumbled.

The more He avoids me, the more he comes running ...
        We shall see this supreme disdain.
He looks good enough to eat, but he's not gunning
        For me now — Yes, he is! ... Again.

... And yet would I have laughed if he'd set his cap
        And kindled the flames of his passion ...
Like Eve — woman too — who didn't love the Apple,
        I don't love him — and want my ration! —

All innocent. — As for him? ... If the gun were loaded ...
        — As for me, I like shabby tricks!
And ... an animal that is easily goaded
        Will keep leaping up for titbits.

What right has he to glare, with a basilisk glint:
        Would Sir make out he's deadly?
I'm short-sighted, it's true ... He could well have a squint;
        I've seen so little of him — and badly. —

95

... Et si je le laissais se draper en quenouille,
        Seul dans sa honteuse fierté! ...
— Non. Je sens me ronger, comme ronge la rouille,
        Mon orgueil malade, irrité.

Allons donc! c'est écrit — n'est-ce pas — dans ma tête,
        En pattes-de-mouche d'enfer;
Écrit, sur cette page où — là — ma main s'arrête.
        — Main de femme et plume de fer. —

Oui! — Baiser de Judas — Lui cracher à la bouche
        Cet *amour!* — Il l'a mérité —
Lui dont la triste image est debout sur ma couche,
        Implacable de volupté.

Oh oui: coller ma langue à l'inerte sourire
        Qu'il porte là comme un faux pli!
Songe creux et malsain, repoussant ... qui m'attire!

        . . . .
        — Une nuit blanche ... un drap sali...

***

... Should I let him take himself in hand, offloading
        Alone his arrogant self-abuse? ...
— No. My inflamed self-esteem begins corroding,
        As rust corrodes, through lack of use.

And yet! it is written — is it not — in my head,
        In a spidery scrawl that's evil;
Written, on this page where — here — my hand stops dead.
        Woman's hand and iron quill. —

Correct! — A Judas kiss — This love of his, I could spit it
        In his face! — He's deserved my ire —
He whose sad image is standing on my *litter*,
        Implacable with desire.

But oh: to glue my tongue to the lifeless smile he
        Wears like a crease that isn't straight!
Sick anguishful thinking, that repels ... to beguile me!
        . . . .
        — A sleepless night ... a sullied sheet...

***

Duel aux Camélias

J'ai vu le soleil dur contre les touffes
Ferrailler. — J'ai vu deux fers soleiller,
Deux fers qui faisaient des parades bouffes;
Des merles en noir regardaient briller.

Un monsieur en linge arrangeait sa manche;
Blanc, il me semblait un gros camélia;
Une autre fleur rose était sur la branche,
Rose comme ... Et puis un fleuret plia.

— Je vois rouge ... Ah oui! c'est juste: on s'égorge —
... Un camélia blanc — là — comme Sa gorge ...
Un camélia jaune — ici — tout mâché ...

Amour mort, tombé de ma boutonnière.
— À moi, plaie ouverte et fleur printanière!
Camélia vivant, de sang panaché!

Veneris Dies 13****

98

Duel With Camellias

I've seen the harsh sun swashing at each blade
Of grass. — I've seen two sword blades flinting:
What comic thrusts and parries they have made!
Sombre blackbird seconds watched the glinting.

Arranging his sleeve, a gentleman in trim
Was white, resembling a plump camellia;
Another flower, pink, was out on a limb,
As pink as ... Then swish went a rapier!

— I see red ... Yes: throats being cut — you've guessed!
... A white camellia — there — like Her breast ...
A yellow camellia, — here — all tattered ...

Dead love, fallen from my buttonhole, pinked.
— With open sore and Spring flower I'll be prinked!
Living camellia, flecked and freaked with blood!

Veneris Dies 13 ***

Fleur d'Art

Oui — Quel art jaloux dans Ta fine histoire!
Quels bibelots chers! — Un bout de sonnet,
Un cœur gravé dans ta manière noire,
Des traits de canif à coups de stylet. —

Tout fier mon cœur porte à la boutonnière
Que tu lui taillas, un petit bouquet
D'immortelle rouge — Encor ta manière —
C'est du sang en fleur. Souvenir coquet.

Allons, pas de pleurs à notre mémoire!
— C'est la mâle-mort de l'amour ici —
Foin du myosotis, vieux sachet d'armoire!

Double femme, va! ... Qu'un âne te braie!
Si tu n'étais fausse, eh serais-tu vraie? ...
L'amour est un duel: — Bien touché! Merci.

***

Flower of Art

Mercutio: O, he is ... the very butcher of a silk button, a duellist, a duellist;
a gentleman of the very first house, — of the first and second cause: ah, the immortal
passado! the punto reverso! the hay!
Benvolio: The what?
— Romeo and Juliet

Yes — What jealous art in your *Marcellaise!*
What darling trinkets! — A few sonnet stabs,
A heart you engraved in your blackest phase,
Penknife etchings pricked out with stylet jabs. —

In its buttonhole you cut him for show
My heart proudly wears a little nosegay
Of red immortelles — More of your sword-play —
Blood in flower. A coquettish memento.

No, don't go shedding tears for us! — It's just
The death-blow to love through all the male ranks —
A fig for forget-me-nots, old cupboard-must!

You're a two-faced piece! ... May an ass bray you!
If you were not false, now would you be true? ...
Love is a duel: — The hay! — The what? — Thanks.

***

Pauvre Garçon

La Bête féroce.

Lui qui sifflait si haut son petit air de tête,
Était plat près de moi; je voyais qu'il cherchait ...
Et ne trouvait pas, et ... j'aimais le sentir bête,
Ce héros qui n'a pas su trouver qu'il m'aimait.

J'ai fait des ricochets sur son cœur en tempête.
Il regardait cela ... Vraiment, cela l'usait?...
Quel instrument rétif à jouer, qu'un poète! ...
J'en ai joué. Vraiment — moi — cela m'amusait.

Est-il mort? ... Ah — c'était, du reste, un garçon drôle.
Aurait-il donc trop pris au sérieux son rôle,
Sans me le dire ... au moins. — Car il est mort, de quoi? ...

Se serait-il laissé fluer de poésie ...
Serait-il mort *de chic*, de boire, ou de phtisie,
Ou, peut-être, après tout: de rien...
ou bien de Moi.

***

102

Poor Boy

The savage Beast.

He who piped so loud his little melody
Was flat beside me; I could see he was seeking ...
And not finding, and ... I liked to feel him weaken,
This hero unaware he was in love with me.

I played ducks and drakes on his tempestuous heart.
He would look on ... Now was that wearing him away? ...
A poet's such a tricky instrument to play!
And I've played some. For me it was fun from the start.

Is he dead? ... Ah — he was a most eccentric soul.
Could he have been in dead earnest about his role,
Without telling me ... at least. — What's your presumption?

Could he have had a haemorrhage of poetry ...
Could he have died of chichi, drink or consumption,
Or, perhaps, after all: of nothing ...
                                        or of Me.

***

103

Déclin

Comme il était bien, Lui, ce Jeune plein de sève!
Âpre à la vie *Ô Gué!* ... et si doux en son rêve.
Comme il portait sa tête ou la couchait gaîment!
Hume-vent à l'amour! ... qu'il passait tristement.

Oh comme il était Rien! ... — Aujourd'hui, sans rancune
Il a vu lui sourire, au retour, la Fortune;
Lui ne sourira plus que d'autrefois; il sait
Combien tout cela coûte et comment ça se fait.

Son cœur a pris du ventre et dit bonjour en prose.
Il est coté fort cher ... ce Dieu c'est quelque chose;
Il ne va plus les mains dans les poches tout nu ...

Dans sa gloire qu'il porte en paletot funèbre,
Vous le reconnaîtrez fini, banal, célèbre ...
Vous le reconnaîtrez, alors, cet inconnu.

On the Wane

He was really Something, this Young Man full of steam!
Hissing at life Tra la! ... soft-centred in his dream.
He carried his head high or laid it down gladly!
He'd had a whiff of love! ... and expelled it sadly.

Or rather, he was Nothing! ... — He's seen Fortune smile
On him today, on her way back, and not been riled;
He has smiles now only for things past; he's found out
How much everything costs and how things come about.

His lion-heart's grown a paunch and says hello in prose.
He's no longer hands-in-pockets and ... well ... exposed:
The sun shines out of him ... this God in a manger!

In his glory — worn like a graveside overcoat —
You will recognise him, a has-been of some note ...
You will recognise him then, this complete stranger.

Bonsoir

Et vous viendrez alors, imbécile caillette,
Taper dans ce miroir clignant qui se paillette
D'un éclis d'or, accroc de l'astre jaune, éteint.
Vous verrez un bijou dans cet éclat de tain.

Vous viendrez à cet homme, à son reflet mièvre
Sans chaleur ... Mais, au jour qu'il dardait la fièvre,
Vous n'avez rien senti, vous qui — midi passé —
Tombez dans ce rayon tombant qu'il a laissé.

Lui ne vous connaît plus, Vous, l'Ombre déjà vue,
Vous qu'il avait couchée en son ciel toute nue,
Quand il était un Dieu! ... Tout cela — n'en faut plus. —

Croyez — Mais lui n'a plus ce mirage qui leurre.
Pleurez — Mais il n'a plus cette corde qui pleure.
Ses chants ... — C'était d'un autre; il ne les a pas lus.

Goodnight

And so you will come, you featherbrain, fandangling
To take this winking mirror's fancy — it's spangling
With a golden shiver, a fleck of the yellow star
That's gone out. In the quicksilver you will see a spar.

You'll come to this man's simpering reflection, come
Though it's no warmth. But on the day his delirium
Flared, you felt nothing, you who — now noon has chimed —
Are falling in this falling beam that he has left behind.

He no longer knows You, the Shade he's seen before,
You he once bedded in his heaven in the raw,
When he was a God! ... Well, that's not on any more. —

Believe — But he's no mirage now to catch his eye.
Weep — But he's no more plangent notes with which to cry.
His songs ... were someone else's; he hasn't known the score.

Le Poète Contumace

Sur la côte d'ARMOR. — Un ancien vieux couvent,
Les vents se croyaient là dans un moulin-à-vent,
        Et les ânes de la contrée,
Au lierre râpé, venaient râper leurs dents
Contre un mur si troué que, pour entrer dedans,
        On n'aurait pu trouver l'entrée.

— Seul — mais toujours debout avec un rare aplomb,
Crénelé comme la mâchoire d'une vieille,
Son toit à coups-de-poing sur le coin de l'oreille,
Aux corneilles bayant, se tenait le donjon,

Fier toujours d'avoir eu, dans le temps, sa légende ...
Ce n'était plus qu'un nid à gens de contrebande,
Vagabonds de nuit, amoureux buissonniers,
Chiens errants, vieux rats, fraudeurs et douaniers.

— Aujourd'hui l'hôte était de la borgne tourelle,
Un Poète sauvage, avec un plomb dans l'aile,
Et tombé là parmi les antiques hiboux
Qui l'estimaient d'en haut. — Il respectait leurs trous, —
Lui, seul hibou payant, comme son *bail* le porte:
Pour vingt-cinq écus l'an, dont: remettre une porte. —

Pour les gens du pays, il ne les voyait pas:
Seulement, en passant, eux regardaient d'en bas,
        Se montrant du nez sa fenêtre;
Le curé se doutait que c'était un lépreux;
Et le maire disait: — Moi, qu'est-ce que j'y peux,
        C'est plutôt un Anglais ... un *Être*.

Les femmes avaient su — sans doute par les buses —
Qu'il *vivait en concubinage avec des Muses!* ...
Un hérétique enfin ... Quelque *Parisien*
De Paris ou d'ailleurs. — Hélas! on n'en sait rien. —
Il était invisible; et, comme *ses Donzelles*
Ne s'affichaient pas trop, on ne parla plus d'elles.

Poet by Default

On the ARMOR coast. — An old nunnery of yore
The winds took for a windmill, never blew through its like before,
        And the donkeys of thereabouts,
With the ivy threadbare, would rasp their teeth on a wall
So full of holes that to find one's way in is a very tall
        Order, which the way-in, which the way-out?

Still standing with extraordinary poise — alone —
Embattled like the jawbone of an ancient crone,
Its punch-drunk roof knocked askew above one ear,
Gaping at the ravens and the moon, stood the keep,

Proud still of having, once upon a time, a past steeped
In legend; but since — nothing more than the retreat
Of smugglers, truant sweethearts and benighted tramps,
Stray dogs and defrauders, low tidesmen and old rats.

— Nowadays the inmate of the one-eyed turret,
A lead-weight in his wings, was a wild and winged Poet,
Hard-hit and fallen there among the antique owls
Who appraised him from above. — He respected their holes, —
He, the only paying owl, as his lease declares: For
Twenty crowns a year, of which: a sum to replace a door. —

For the locals he had not even a passing glance:
But, as they passed, their noses pointed up askance
        At his dubitable features;
The parish priest presumed that he was a leper
And: — What can I do about it, the mayor kept on,
        He's probably an English ... creature.

The womenfolk had known — buzzards have their uses —
That he dwelt in concubinage with certain Muses! ...
In short, a heretic ... A Parisian
From Paris or elsewhere. — Let your imagination run. —
He was invisible; and as his *Hussies*
Didn't flaunt themselves unduly, gossip let them be.

— Lui, c'était simplement un long flâneur, sec, pâle;
Un ermite-amateur, chassé par la rafale ...
Il avait trop aimé les beaux pays malsains.
Condamné des huissiers, comme des médecins,
Il avait posé là, soûl et cherchant sa place
Pour mourir seul ou pour vivre par contumace ...

> Faisant, d'un à-peu-près d'artiste
> Un philosophe d'à peu près,
> Râleur de soleil ou de frais,
> En dehors de l'humaine piste.

Il lui restait encor un hamac, une vielle,
Un barbet qui dormait sous le nom de *Fidèle;*
Non moins fidèle était, triste et doux comme lui,
Un autre compagnon qui s'appelait l'Ennui.

Se mourant en sommeil, il se vivait en rêve.
Son rêve était le flot qui montait sur la grève,
> Le flot qui descendait;
Quelquefois, vaguement, il se prenait attendre ...
Attendre quoi ... le flot monter — le flot descendre —
> Ou l'Absente ... Qui sait?

Le sait-il bien lui-même? ... Au vent de sa guérite,
A-t-il donc oublié comme les morts vont vite,
Lui, ce viveur vécu, revenant égaré,
Cherche-t-il son follet, à lui, mal enterré?

— Certe, Elle n'est pas loin, celle après qui tu brames,
Ô Cerf de Saint Hubert! Mais ton front est sans flammes ...
N'apparais pas, mon vieux, triste et faux déterré ...
Fais le mort si tu peux ... Car Elle t'a pleuré!

— Est-ce qu'il pouvait, Lui! ... n'était-il pas poète ...
Immortel comme un autre? ... Et dans sa pauvre tête
Déménagée, encor il sentait que les vers
Hexamètres faisaient les cent pas de travers.

— He was simply a lanky dawdler, gaunt and pale;
A dilettante hermit blown in by the gale ...
He had loved too dearly beautiful unhealthy lands.
Condemned by writ-servers and doctors out of hand,
He had alighted there, drunk and seeking a vault
To die all alone or to live on by default ...

> Making, of an artist more or less,
> A philosopher loosely speaking,
> Grousing at sunshine and at showers,
> Beyond the pale and out of keeping.

He still had left a hammock, a hurdy-gurdy,
A dozy spaniel dubbed *Faithful*, fast asleep;
No less faithful, as sad, and mild to a degree,
Was another boon companion called Ennui.

Dying in his sleep, he came alive in dreamland.
His dream was the tide which ebbs down the strand,
> The tide which flows;
He might catch himself waiting, as though in a web,
Waiting for what... the tide to flow — the tide to ebb —
> Or the Absent Woman ... Who knows?

Does he really know himself? ... To windward of his mound,
Has he forgotten how quick the dead cover the ground,
This outpaced pace-setter, this strayed and haunted ghost,
Is he after his will o' the wisp he's buried but lost?

— She can't be far away, the One you're troating for,
O Hart of Saint Hubert! But your brow's no flames to draw ...
Do not appear unearthed, sad out of earth's safe keeping ...
Play posssum if you can ... For She has mourned you, weeping ...

— Could he though, Him! ... wasn't he a poet ... immortal
As the next man? ... And in his poor old noddle
That had taken leave of its senses, he sensed still
Hexameter lines to-ing and fro-ing through the mill.

— Manque de savoir-vivre extrême — il survivait —
Et — manque de savoir-mourir — il écrivait:

"C'est un être passé de cent lunes, ma Chère,
En ton cœur poétique, à l'état légendaire.
Je rime, donc je vis ... ne crains pas, c'est *à blanc.*
— Une coquille d'huître en rupture de banc! —
Oui, j'ai beau me palper: c'est moi! — Dernière faute —
En route pour les cieux — car ma niche est si haute! —
Je me suis demandé, prêt à prendre l'essor:
Tête ou pile ... — Et voilà — je me demande encor ...

"C'est à toi que je fis mes adieux à la vie,
À toi qui me pleuras, jusqu'à me faire envie
De rester me pleurer avec toi. Maintenant
C'est joué, je ne suis qu'un gâteux revenant,
En os et ... (j'allais dire en chair). — La chose est sûre
C'est bien moi, je suis là — mais comme une rature.

"Nous étions amateurs de curiosité:
Viens voir *le Bibelot.* — Moi j'en suis dégoûté. —
Dans mes dégoûts surtout, j'ai des goûts élégants;
Tu sais: j'avais lâché la Vie avec des gants;
L'*Autre* n'est pas même à prendre avec des pincettes ...
Je cherche au mannequin de nouvelles toilettes.

"Reviens m'aider: Tes yeux dans ces yeux-là! Ta lèvre
Sur cette lèvre! ... Et, là, ne sens-tu pas ma fièvre
— Ma *fièvre de Toi?* ... — Sous l'orbe est-il passé
L'arc-en-ciel au charbon par nos nuits laissé?
Et cette étoile? ... — Oh! va, ne cherche plus l'étoile
            Que tu voulais voir à mon front;
            Une araignée a fait sa toile
            Au même endroit — dans le plafond.

"Je suis un étranger. — Cela vaut mieux peut-être ...
— Eh bien! non, viens encor un peu me reconnaître;
Comme au bon saint Thomas, je veux te voir la foi,
Je veux te voir toucher la plaie et dire: — Toi! —

— Severe lack of *savoir-vivre* — he went on surviving —
And — lack of *savoir-mourir* — he went on writing:

"He's a sometime soul of a hundred moons, my Dear,
Gone to your poetic heart — the legend is not dead.
Je rime, donc je vis ... my rhymes are vacant, never fear.
— An oyster shell that's broken the bounds of its bed! —
Yes, in vain I pinch myself: it's me! — Final offence —
On the way to heaven — for my niche is high from hence! —
I have wondered: heads or tails ... ready to take wing ...
— And would you believe it — I am still wondering ...

"To you I said *au revoir* to life and *adieu*,
To you who mourned me, so much so that I had a
Hankering to stay and mourn me with you. Now, i'faith,
'Tis all one, I'm simply senile, bones, a wraith ...
(I was going to say flesh and blood). — What's beyond doubt,
Though, is: This is me, I am here — but ... crossed-out.

"We were sniffers-out of antiques and no sneezers:
Come and see the Curio. — I can't stomach paste. —
In my distastes I have such elegant taste;
I had let go of Life, you know, with my kid gloves;
The Other can't be had, not even with tweezers ...
I'll order for the dummy a new collar and cuffs.

"Come back and help me: Your eyes in these eyes! Your lips
On these lips! ... Now then, can't you feel the fever's grip
— My fever for You? ... Or has the coal-black rainbow
Left by our nights together passed under the globe?
And that star? ... — Oh no! search no longer for the star
You wished to see upon my brow;
A spider's spun its cobweb there —
Bats are flying in the belfry now.

"I am a stranger. — Which is perhaps just as well ...
— Well, not exactly! See if I still ring a bell;
Be like Doubting Thomas, who found his faith anew:
I want to see you touch the wound and say: — It's You! —

"Viens encor me finir — c'est très gai: De ta chambre
Tu verras mes moissons — Nous sommes en décembre —
Mes grands bois de sapin, les fleurs d'or des genêts,
Mes bruyères d'Armor ... — en tas sur les chenets.
Viens te gorger d'air pur — Ici j'ai de la brise
Si franche! ... que le bout de ma toiture en frise.
Le soleil est si doux ... — qu'il gèle tout le temps.
Le printemps ... — Le printemps n'est-ce pas tes vingt ans.
On n'attend plus que toi, vois: déjà l'hirondelle
Se pose ... en fer rouillé, clouée à ma tourelle. —
Et bientôt nous pourrons cueillir le champignon ...
Dans mon escalier que dore ... un lumignon.
Dans le mur qui verdoie existe une pervenche
Sèche. — ... Et puis nous irons à l'eau *faire* la planche
— Planches d'épave au sec — comme moi — sur ces plages.
La Mer roucoule sa *Berceuse pour naufrages;*
Barcarolle du soir ... pour les canards sauvages.

"En *Paul et Virginie*, et virginaux — veux-tu —
Nous nous mettrons au vert du paradis perdu ...
Ou *Robinson avec Vendredi* — c'est facile —
La pluie a déjà fait, de mon royaume, une île.

"Si pourtant, près de moi, tu crains la solitude,
Nous avons des amis, sans fard — Un braconnier;
Sans compter un caban bleu qui, par habitude,
Fait toujours les cent-pas et contient un douanier ...
Plus de clercs d'huissier! J'ai le clair de la lune,
Et des amis pierrots amoureux sans fortune.

— "Et nos nuits! ... *Belles nuits pour l'orgie à la tour!* ...
Nuits à la Roméo! — Jamais il ne fait jour. —
La Nature au réveil — réveil de déchaînée —
Secouant son drap blanc ... éteint ma cheminée.
Voici mes rossignols ... rossignols d'ouragans —
Gais comme des poinçons — sanglots de chats-huans!
Ma girouette dérouille en haut sa tyrolienne
Et l'on entend gémir ma porte éolienne,
Comme chez saint Antoine en sa tentation ...
Oh viens! joli Suppôt de la séduction!

"Come and finish me off — that's a laugh: From your room
You'll see my harvests, the golden flowers of the broom —
We're in December though — my large pine-woods for logs,
My heather from Armor ... — piled high on the fire-dogs.
Breathe your fill of pure air — Here I've such a steady
Breeze, that the edge of my roof is crimped already.
The sun is so mild ... — that it's freezing all the time.
Spring ... — Isn't Spring you at twenty and in your prime?
There's only you to come now: already the swallow
Alights ... as rusty iron, nailed to my folly. —
And soon we shall be able to gather mushrooms ...
From my staircase — where a stub of candle gilds the gloom.
In the green and mouldering wall there lives a dried
Periwinkle. — ... Then we'll swim on our backs and glide
— Planks of a ship run aground on these shores — like me.
Coo-cooing its *Lullaby for wrecks* is the Sea;
Evening barcarolle ... for the wild ducks flying free.

"Like *Paul et Virginie*, and virgins — if *you* please —
We'll put ourselves to grass when paradise lost's at hand ...
Or as Crusoe with Man Friday — that's done with ease —
Rain's already turned my kingdom to an island.

"But if, by my side, you fear solitude's approach,
We've friends who ... without beating about the bush, poach;
Not to mention a sailor-blue jacket round the lath
Who's wont to sentry-go along the beaten path ...
No more bailiff's men! I have moonlight for my coat,
And doting pierrot pals who've always missed the boat.

— "And our nights! ... *Lovely nights for the orgy in the tower!* ...
Nights à la Romeo! — Even watchmen forget the hour ...
Nature at the awakening — cutting loose from the briars —
Shaking out her white sheet ... extinguishes my fires.
Here, whistlers in hurricanes, are my nightingales —
As merry as marline-spikes — the sobs of long-eared owls!
My weathercock unrusts its yodel, its screaking,
And you can hear my aeolian gate a-creaking,
Like one Saint Anthony heard in his temptation ...
Oh come! enticing Minion of seduction!

— "Hop! les rats du grenier dansent des farandoles!
Les ardoises du toit roulent en castagnoles!
Les Folles-du-logis ...
                        Non, je 'ai plus de Folles!

... "Comme je revendrais ma dépouille à Satan
S'il me tentait avec un petit Revenant ...
— Toi — Je te vois partout, mais comme un voyant blême,
Je t'adore ... Et c'est pauvre: adorer ce qu'on aime!
Apparais, un poignard dans le cœur! — Ce sera,
Tu sais bien, comme dans *Inès de La Sierra* ...
— On frappe ... oh! c'est quelqu'un ...
                        Hélas! oui, c'est un rat.

— "Je rêvasse ... et toujours c'est *Toi.* Sur toute chose,
Comme un esprit follet, ton souvenir se pose:
Ma solitude — *Toi!* — Mes hiboux à l'œil d'or:
— *Toi!* — Ma girouette folle: Oh *Toi!* ... — Que sais-je encor ...
— *Toi:* mes volets ouvrant les bras dans la tempête ...
Une lointaine voix: c'est Ta chanson! — c'est fête! ...
Les rafales fouaillant Ton nom perdu — c'est bête —
C'est bête, mais c'est *Toi!* Mon cœur au grand ouvert
                Comme mes volets en pantenne,
                Bat, tout affolé sous l'haleine
                Des plus bizarres courants d'air.

"Tiens ... une ombre portée, un instant, est venue
Dessiner ton profil sur la muraille nue,
Et j'ai tourné la tête ... — Espoir ou souvenir —
Ma sœur Anne, à la tour, voyez-vous pas venir? ...
— Rien! — je vois... je vois, dans ma froide chambrette,
Mon lit capitonné de *satin de brouette*;
Et mon chien qui dort dessus — Pauvre animal —
... Et je ris... parce que ça me fait un peu mal.

"J'ai pris, pour t'appeler, ma vielle et ma lyre.
Mon cœur fait de l'esprit — le sot — pour se leurrer ...
Viens pleurer, si mes vers ont pu te faire rire;
                Viens rire, s'ils t'ont fait pleurer ...

— "Hey-hup! the attic rats are dancing farandoles!
The slates are clacking on the roof like castanolls!
Dame Fancy's lunatics ...
                         No, I've no more pretty Polls!

... "I'd sell my skin and bones back to Satan and roast
If only he would tempt me with a little Ghost ...
— You — I see you everywhere, but as a seer pale as doves,
I adore you ... A poor do: adoring what one loves!
Appear, a poniard in your heart! — Make no error,
It needs must be as in *Inès de la Sierra* ...
— There's a knock ... someone's come ...
                         Oh dear! yes, it's a rat.

— "I daydream ... and it's always *You*. Like an elfish sprite,
On everything the memories of you alight:
My solitude — *You!* — My owls with their golden eyes:
— *You!* — My mad weathercock: Oh *You!* ... — And more besides
— *You:* my shutters opening their arms to the storm ...
A distant voice: Your song! — Tune up rebec and shawm! ...
The squalls lathering Your lost name — it's cock-eyed —
It's foolish, but it's *You!* My heart, open wide and blown
          Like my shutters any-old-how,
          Is beating distractedly, now
          The oddest draughts make moan.

"Look there ... a shadow projected an instant, falls
And traces your profile on the naked wall,
So I have turned my head ... — Hope or remembrance thrumming
Sister Anne, in the tower, can't you see her coming? ...
— No! — I can see ... in my chamber cold and narrow,
My bed quilted with satin like any wheelbarrow;
And my dog sleeping on it — the poor animal —
... And I laugh ... because it hurts me a little.

"I have taken down my hurdy-gurdy and my lyre
To call you up. At its own expense, the mooncalf,
My heart is frivolous. If my lines have made you laugh,
Come and cry;
               come and laugh, if they have made you cry...

"Ce sera drôle ... Viens jouer à la misère,
D'après nature: — *Un cœur avec une chaumière.* —
... Il pleut dans mon foyer, il pleut dans mon cœur feu.
Viens! Ma chandelle est morte et je n'ai plus de feu ..."

*

Sa lampe se mourait. Il ouvrit la fenêtre.
Le soleil se levait. Il regarda sa lettre,
Rit et la déchira ... Les petits morceaux blancs,
Dans la brume, semblaient un vol de goëlands.

Penmarc'h — jour de Noël.

"It will be fun ... Let's play at pocket-with-a-hole,
True to life: — Love in a cottage — Love on the dole. —
... It's raining in my hearth, and what was once my heart.
Come! My candle is out and I haven't got a spark ... "

*

His lamp was dying down. He opened the window.
The sun was rising. He looked his letter over,
Laughed and tore it up ... The pieces of paper, white
And small in the morning mist, resembled gulls in flight.

Penmarc'h — Christmas Day.

SÉRÉNADE DES SÉRÉNADES

SERANADE OF SERENADES

Sonnet de Nuit

Ô croisée ensommeillée,
Dure à mes trente-six morts!
Vitre en diamant, éraillée
Par mes atroces accords!

Herse hérissant rouillée
Tes crocs où je pends et mords!
Oubliette verrouillée
Qui me renferme ... dehors!

Pour Toi, Bourreau que j'encense,
L'amour n'est donc que vengeance? ...
Ton balcon: gril à braiser? ...

Ton col: collier de garotte? ...
Eh bien! ouvre, Iscariote,
Ton judas pour un baiser!

Night Sonnet

O sleepy-leaded lattices,
Hard on my starstruck dead!
Diamond window panes, fretted
By my atrocious harmonies!

Rusted cusps of a herse:
Your fangs on which I hang and bite!
Bolted oubliette — perverse
In that it shuts me ... outside!

For You, Torturer, I burn;
Is love only nemesis? ...
Your balcony: a braising grill? ...

Your collar: a garotter's *frill*? ...
Well then! Iscariot, open
Your judas-hole for a kiss!

Guitare

Je sais rouler une amourette
   En cigarette,
Je sais rouler l'or et les plats!
Et les filles dans de beaux draps!

Ne crains pas de longueurs fidèles:
Pour mules mes pieds ont des ailes;
Voleur de nuit, hibou d'amour,
   M'envole au jour.

Connais-tu Psyché? — Non? — Mercure? ...
Cendrillon et son aventure?
— Non? — ... Eh bien! tout cela, c'est moi:
   Nul ne me voit.

Et je te laisserais bien fraîche
Comme un petit Jésus en crèche,
Avant le rayon indiscret ...
   — Je suis si laid! —

Je sais flamber en cigarette
   Une amourette,
Chiffonner et flamber les draps,
Mettre les filles dans les plats!

124

The same Old Song

with guitar accompaniment

I can roll an amourette
　　　In a cigarette,
I can spin gold coins and dishes!
And get girls in pretty fixes!

I won't vow long-winded things:
Instead of mules my feet have wings;
The owl of love, thief in the night,
　　　Flies me to daylight.

You know Psyche? — No? — Mercury? ...
Cinderella and her fairy g.?
— No? — ... Well! each is my story:
　　　No one can see me.

And I would leave you quite fresh
Like a sweet innocent in a crèche,
Before dawn peeps indiscreetly ...
　　　— I am so ugly! —

I can light up an amourette
　　　As a cigarette,
Rumple and singe the blanket,
Make girls put their foot in it!

Rescousse

Si ma guitare
Que je répare,
Trois fois barbare:
Kriss indien,

Cric de supplice,
Bois de justice,
Boîte à malice,
Ne fait pas bien ...

Si ma voix pire
Ne peut te dire
Mon doux martyre ...
— Métier de chien! —

Si mon cigare,
Viatique et phare,
Point ne t'égare;
— Feu de brûler ...

Si ma menace,
Trombe qui passe,
Manque de grâce;
— Muet de hurler ...

Si de mon âme
La mer en flamme
N'a pas de lame;
— Cuit de geler ...

Vais m'en aller!

S O S

If my guitar
That I unjar,
— It's thrice Tartar:
Malayan *kris*,

Strappado, stocks,
The scaffold's blocks,
Jack-in-the-box,
Does me no justice ...

If my refrain
Barks out in vain
Of my sweet bane ...
— A dog's life, this! —

If my cigar,
Last rite and star,
Won't lead you far;
— Let embers grill ...

If my wild threat,
A whirlwind fret,
Brings no regret;
— Let the dumb be shrill ...

If the sea on fire
With my desire
Is but a pyre;
— Let scorching chill ...

I'll go, I will!

Toit

Tiens non! J'attendrai tranquille,
    Planté sous le toit,
Qu'il me tombe quelque tuile,
    Souvenir de Toi!

J'ai tondu l'herbe, je lèche
    La pierre, — altéré
Comme *la Colique-sèche*
    De Miserere!

Je crèverai — Dieu me damne! —
Ton tympan ou la peau d'âne
    De mon bon tambour!

Dans ton boîtier, ô Fenêtre!
Calme et pure, gît peut-être …
    · · · · · · · · · · · · ·

    Un vieux monsieur sourd!

Roof

No, no! I shall wait sedately
    Underneath the roof
For a tile to fall on me,
    In memory of You!

I've cropped the grass, and I
    'm licking the stone,
Parched as I am like *the dry*
    Iliac Passion!

Christ! — I shall burst a vein
And split your membrane
    Or mine: my good drum!

There lies, perhaps, in your case,
O Window! quite calm and chaste ...
    . . . .

    A deaf old gentleman!

Litanie

Non ... Mon cœur te sent là, Petite,
Qui dors pour me laisser plus vite
Passer ma nuit, si longue encor,
Sur le pavé comme un rat mort ...

— Dors. La berceuse litanie
Sérénade jamais finie
Sur Ta lèvre reste poser
Comme une haleine de baiser:

— "Nénuphar du ciel! Blanche Étoile!
Tour ivoirine! Nef sans voile!
Vesper, amoris Aurora!"

Ah! je sais les répons mystiques
Pour le cantique des cantiques
Qu'on chante ... au Diable, Señora!

No ... My heart can sense you there, Little
Darling, sleeping to let me scrat
My night, still so long, much quicker
Out in the street like a dying rat ...

— Sleep on. The lullaby litany
Serenade that's never eclipsed
Like the breath of a kiss is free
To play on Your lips:

— "Nave with no veil! Nenuphar
Of Heaven! Ivorine Tower! White Star!
Vesper, amoris Aurora!"

Ah! I know each mystic response
To the song of songs — for the nonce
Intoned ... to the Devil, Señora!

131

Chapelet

À moi, grand chapelet! pour égrener mes plaintes,
Avec tous les AVE de Sa *Perfeccion,*
Son nom et tous les noms de ses Fêtes et Saintes ...
Du Mardi-gras jusqu'à la *Circoncicion:*

— *Navaja-Dolorès-y-Crucificcion!* ...
— Le Christ avait au moins son éponge d'absinthe ... —
Quand donc arriverai-je à ton *Ascencion!* ...
— Isaac Laquedem, prête-moi ta complainte.

— *O Todas-las-Santas!* Tes vitres sont pareilles,
Secundum ordinem, à ces fonds de bouteilles
Qu'on casse à coups de trique à la *Quasimodo* ...

Mais, ô *Quasimodo,* tu ne viens pas encore;
Pour casse-tête, hélas! je n'ai que ma mandore ...
— *Se habla español: Paraque ... raquando?* ...

Rosary

Help me, great rosary! to run through my complaints,
With all the AVES to Her *Perfeccion*,
Her name and all the names of her Feast-days and Saints ...
From Shrove Tuesday until the *Circoncicion*:

— *Navaja-Dolorès-y-Crucificcion!* ...
— At least Jesus Christ had his sponge of absinth ... —
When shall I be rising to your *Ascencion !* ...
— Isaac Laquedem, please lend me your lament.

— *O Todas-las-Santas!* Your stained-glass resembles,
Secundum ordinem, half-emptied bottles
They smash to smithereens when it's *Quasimodo* ...

But, O *Quasimodo*, you are slow to appear;
My mandora's my sole life-preserver, I fear ! ...
— *Se habla español: Paraque ... raquando?* ...

Elizir d'Amor

Tu ne me veux pas en rêve,
Tu m'auras en cauchemar!
T'écorchant au vif, sans trêve,
— Pour moi ... pour l'amour de l'art.

— Ouvre: je passerai vite,
Les nuits sont courtes, l'été ...
Mais ma musique est maudite,
Maudite en l'éternité!

J'assourdirai les recluses,
Éreintant à coups de pieux,
Les Neuf et les autres Muses ...
Et qui n'en iront que mieux! ...

Répéterai tous mes rôles
Borgnes — et d'aveugle aussi ...
D'ordinaire tous ces drôles
Ont assez bon *œil* ici:

— À genoux, haut Cavalier,
À pied, traînant ma rapière,
Je baise dans la poussière
Les traces de Ton soulier!

— Je viens, Pèlerin austère,
Capucin et Troubadour,
Dire mon bout de rosaire
Sur la viole d'amour.

— Bachelier de Salamanque,
Le plus simple et le dernier ...
Ce fonds jamais ne me manque:
— Tout vœux! et pas un denier! —

Elizir d'Amor

You don't want me in your dreams,
So I'll come up with nightmare schemes
To skin you alive, without a break,
For the love of art ... for my sake!

— Open up: I'll soon be gone,
The nights in summer are not long ...
But my music is accursed,
Cursed for ever is my verse!

I'll deafen the she-recluses,
And I'll give them lots of stick,
The Nine and the other Muses ...
Who'll be all the better for it ! ...

I'll rehearse all my roles: the one-
Eyed ones — and the blind ones too ...
They create quite an impression,
Such sights here usually do:

— Down on your knees, High Rider;
On foot, trailing my weapon,
I kiss in the dust your guiding
Footprints as you step on!

— I'm one of the Grey Friar breed,
Capuchin and Troubadour,
Come to tell each rosary bead
On the viola d'*amour*.

— Novice of Salamanca,
The simplest and last of many ...
I'm always my own banker
— Of wishes! and not one penny!

— Retapeur de casseroles,
Sale Gitan vagabond,
Je claque des castagnoles
Et chatouille le jambon ...

— Pas-de-loup, loup sur la face,
Moi chien-loup maraudeur,
J'erre en offrant de ma race:
— Pur-Don-Juan-du-Commandeur. —

Maîtresse peut me connaître,
Chien parmi les chiens perdus:
Abeilard n'est pas mon maître,
Alcibiade non plus!

— I'm a Toucher-up of saucepans,
A dirty vagabond Gypsy,
Clacking castanets when tipsy
And tickling the hams ...

— With wolf-loo mask and wolf-like tread,
I'm a marauding Alsatian,
I rove, offering a thoroughbred:
— The Commander's-Pure-Don-Juan. —

My Mistress knows me as poetaster;
Among stray dogs the one with fleas:
Abelard is not my master,
Nor is Alcibiades!

Vénerie

Ô Vénus, dans ta Vénerie,
Limier et piqueur à la fois,
Valet-de-chien et d'écurie,
J'ai vu l'Hallali, les Abois! ...

Que Diane aussi me sourie! ...
À cors, à cris, à pleine voix
Je fais le pied, je fais le bois;
Car on dit que: *bête varie* ...

— Un pied de biche: Le voici,
Cordon de sonnette sur rue;
— Bois de cerf: de la porte aussi;
— Et puis un pied: un pied-de-grue! ...

Ô Fauve après qui j'aboyais,
— Je suis fourbu, qu'on me relaie! —
Ô Bête! es-tu donc une laie?
. . . .
Bien moins sauvage te croyais!

Venery

O Venus, in your Venery,
As bloodhound and whipper-in for sport,
As ostler and as kennel-boy
I've witnessed the Bay, the Mort! ...

Smile on me too — would Diana could! ...
With horns, with cries voiced lustily
I go on foot, I beat the wood;
For it's said: *wild creatures vary* ...

— Here's a hind foot, in the thicket;
I'll pull it ... just see how it feels:
Stiff as the horns of a pricket
— I'm the buck, and kicking my heels! ...

O Fallow Deer, for you I've bayed,
— I've foundered, may I be relayed! —
Like a Paphian sow you ravage ...
. . . .
I had thought you much less savage!

Vendetta

Tu ne veux pas de mon âme
Que je jette à tour de bras:
Chère, tu me le payeras! ...
Sans rancune — je suis femme! —

Tu ne veux pas de ma peau:
Venimeux comme un jésuite,
Prends garde! ... je suis ensuite
Jésuite comme un crapaud,

Et plat comme la punaise,
Compagne que j'ai sur moi,
Pure ... mais, — ne te déplaise, —
Je te préférerais, Toi!

— Je suis encor, Ma très-Chère,
Serpent comme le Serpent
Froid, coulant, poisson rampant
Qui fit pécher ta grand'mère ...

Et tu ne vaux pas, Pécore,
Beaucoup plus qu'elle, je croi ...
Vaux-tu ma chanson encore? ...
Me vaux-tu seulement moi! ...

Vendetta

You don't want my soul and heart
I keep throwing up at you:
No hard feelings, dear — you'll smart
For this, though — I'm womanish too! —

You don't want my skin: I'll explode!
Virulent as a jesuit
I am, and then ... Just you watch it!
As jesuitical as a toad,

And contemptible as the bug
That's my intimate too —
She's pure, but, — and you can shrug, —
I'd really prefer Y.O.U.!

— What's more, I am, O Apple
Of my Eye, a snake like the sin-
Uous cold Serpent, the base eel
That coaxed your granny to sin ...

And you're not worth, you Popinjay,
Much more than she was, I ween ...
Are you even worth my lay? ...
Are you even worth me to me! ...

Heures

Aumône au malandrin en chasse!
Mauvais œil à l'œil assassin!
Fer contre fer au spadassin!
— Mon âme n'est pas en état de grâce! —

Je suis le fou de Pampelune,
J'ai peur du rire de la Lune,
Cafarde, avec son crêpe noir ...
Horreur! tout est donc sous un éteignoir.

J'entends comme un bruit de crécelle ...
C'est la male heure qui m'appelle.
Dans le creux des nuits tombe: un glas ... deux glas ...

J'ai compté plus de quatorze heures ...
L'heure est une larme — Tu pleures,
Mon cœur! ... Chante encor, va — Ne compte pas.

The Hours

Alms for the prowling highwayman!
The evil eye for looks that could kill!
Crossed swords for the duelling hooligan!
— My soul is not in a state of grace, or goodwill! —

I'm the madman, the Pamplona loon,
I fear the laughter of the Moon,
Hecate, in black crape ... O horrors!
With everything snuffed out, there'll be no tomorrows.

I can hear, like a sexton's rattle,
My evil hour come to do battle.
Into the hollow of night there falls: one knell ... two knells ...

I've counted more than fourteen striking ...
Each hour is a tear — You're *skriking*,
My heart! ... Please sing again — And stop counting those bells.

Chanson en Si

Si j'étais noble Faucon,
Tournoîrais sur ton balcon ...
— Taureau: foncerais ta porte ...
— Vampire: te boirais morte ...
      Te boirais!

— Geôlier: lèverais l'écrou ...
— Rat: ferais un petit trou ...
Si j'étais brise alizée,
Te mouillerais de rosée ...
      Roserais!

Si j'étais gros Confesseur,
Te fouaillerais, ô Ma Sœur!
Pour seconde pénitence
Te dirais ce que je pense ...
      Te dirais ...

Si j'étais un maigre Apôtre,
Dirais: "Donnez-vous l'un l'autre
Pour votre faim apaiser:
Le pain d'amour: Un baiser."
      Si j'étais! ...

Si j'étais Frère-quêteur,
Quêterais ton petit cœur
Pour Dieu le Fils et le Père,
L'Église leur Sainte Mère ...
      Quêterais!

Si j'étais Madone riche,
Jetterais bien, de ma niche,
Un regard, un sou béni
Pour le cantique fini ...
      Jetterais!

Song in May[b]

If I were a noble Falcon,
I'd wheel above your balcony ...
— Bull: I'd charge down your door ...
— Vampire: I'd drink from your corpse ...
     I'd drink you!

— Gaoler: I'd undraw the bolt ...
— Rat: I'd gnaw a small hole ...
If I were a steady trade breeze,
I'd wet you with dew-beads ...
     I'd dew you!

If I were a fat Confessor,
I'd horsewhip you, little Sister!
As second penance of a kind,
I'd tell you what's on my mind ...
     I'd tell you ...

If I were a lean Lay-brother,
I'd say: "Give to one another,
To allay your hungriness,
The bread of love: a kiss."
     I'd lay you! ...

If I were a mendicant Vicar,
I'd beg for your little ticker
For God the Son and the Father,
The Church their Holy Mother ...
     I'd beg you!

If I were a rich Madonna,
I'd toss a sou in honour
Of the canticle when it's over,
And a glance — from my alcove —
     I'd toss that too!

145

Si j'étais un vieux bedeau,
Mettrais un cierge au rideau ...
D'un goupillon d'eau bénite,
L'éteindrais, la vespre dite,
      L'éteindrais!

Si j'étais roide pendu,
Au ciel serais tout rendu:
Grimperais après ma corde,
Ancre de miséricorde,
      Grimperais!

Si j'étais femme ... Eh, la Belle,
Te ferais ma Colombelle ...
À la porte les galants
Pourraient se percer des flancs ...
      Te ferais ...

Enfant, si j'étais la duègne
Rossinante qui te peigne,
SEÑORA, si j'étais Toi ...
J'ouvrirais au pauvre Moi.
      — Ouvrirais! —

If I were an ancient beadle,
I'd light the veil with a candle ...
With a sprinkler of holy water
I'd douse it, after vespers,
            When I was through!

If I were hanged, about to stiffen
And abandon all to heaven,
I'd swarm up my rope, I'd clamber,
Anchor of mercy, sheet anchor,
            Not heave to!

If I were a woman, why, Love,
I'd make you my Turtle-dove ...
At your door the gallants
Could pierce each other's flanks ...
            I'd make you ...

Child, if I were the duenna
Rosinante dyeing you henna,
SEÑORA, if I were you, pardie ...
I'd open up to poor Me.
            — *I'd* open up to *You*!

Portes et Fenêtres

N'entends-tu pas? — Sang et guitare! —
Réponds! ... je damnerai plus fort.
Nulle ne m'a laissé, Barbare,
Aussi longtemps me crier mort!

Ni faire autant de purgatoire! ...
Tu ne vois ni n'entends mes pas,
Ton œil est clos, la nuit est noire:
Fais signe — Je ne verrai pas.

En enfer j'ai pavé ta rue.
Tous les damnés sont en émoi ...
Trop incomparable Inconnue!
Si tu n'es pas là ... préviens-moi!

À damner je n'ai plus d'alcades,
Je n'ai fait que me damner moi,
En serinant mes sérénades ...
— Il ne reste à damner que Toi!

Doors and Windows

You deaf? — Sitars and stigmata! —
Respond! ... I'll blast you to the sky.
No woman has left me, you Tartar,
To cry out so long that I'll die!

Or to be so stretched on the rack! ...
At my approach, what apathy!
Your eyes are shut, the night is black:
Were you to wave — I shouldn't see.

I've paved your road down in hell.
All the damned are in a tizzy ...
Faire Unknowne, too incomparable!
If you are not there ... apprise me!

With no more gaolers to upbraid,
Damn me's all I've managed to do
By tub-thumping my serenades ...
— It only remains to damn You!

Grand Opéra

Ier ACTE (*Vêpres*)

Dors sous le tabernacle, ô Figure de cire!
    Triple Châsse vierge et martyre,
    Derrière un verre, sous le plomb,
Et dans les siècles des siècles ... Comme c'est long!

Portes-tu ton cœur d'or sur ta robe lamée,
Ton âme veille-t-elle en la lampe allumée? ...

        Elle est éteinte
        Cette huile sainte ...
        Il est éteint
        Le sacristain! ...

L'orgue sacré, ses flots et ses bruits de rafale
Sous les voûtes, font-ils frissonner ton front pâle? ...

Dans ton éternité sais-tu la barbarie
De mon orgue infernal, *orgue de Barbarie?*

Du prêtre, sous l'autel, n'ouïs-tu pas les pas
Et le mot qu'à l'Hostie il murmure tout bas? ...

— Eh bien! moi j'attendrai que sur ton oreiller,
La trompette de Dieu vienne te réveiller!

. . . .

Châsse, ne sais-tu pas qu'en passant ta chapelle,
    De par le Pape, tout fidèle,
Évêque, publicain ou lépreux, a le droit
De t'entr'ouvrir sa plaie et d'en toucher ton doigt? ...
      À Saint-Jacques de Compostelle
J'en ai bien fait autant pour un bout de chandelle.

Grand Opera

ACT I *(Vespers)*

Sleep beneath the tabernacle, o waxwork Figure!
    Triple Reliquary, virgin and martyr,
    Laid in lead casing, behind a glass screen,
Down centuries on centuries ... How long it has been!

Do you wear your heart of gold on your lamé robe,
Does your soul keep vigil in the lighted globe? ...

       It's off the boil
       This holy oil ...
       He's quite undone
       Is the sacristan! ...

Does the sacred organ, with its swell and sounds of squall
Under the vault, make you go pale, your flesh crawl? ...

In your eternity do you watch the birdie
Of my infernal organ, my hurdy-gurdy?

When the priest is by the altar, are you deaf as a post
To his footfall and the murmured word to the Host? ...

— Well then! I shall wait for the trumpet of the Lord
To rouse you from your pillow of its own accord!

. . . .

O Casket, don't you know that as they pass your chapel,
    By leave of the Pope, the faithful,
Bishop, publican or leper — all are thought fit —
Can open up their wound to touch your finger with it? ...
    In Saint-Jacques de Compostelle
I have done as much on the strength of a candle.

À ce prix-là je dois baiser la blanche hostie
Qui scelle, sur ta bouche en or, ta chasteté
Close en odeur de sainteté
. . . .
Cordieu! Madame est donc sortie? ...

IIe ACTE (*Sabbat*).

Je suis un bon ange, ô bel Ange!
Pour te couvrir, doux gardien ...
La terre maudite me tient.
Ma plume a trempé dans la fange ...

Hâ! je ne bats plus que d'une aile! ...
Prions ... l'esprit du Diable est prompt ...
— Ah! si j'étais lui, de quel bond
Je serais sur toi, la Donzelle!

... Ma blanche couronne à ma tête
Déjà s'effeuille; la tempête
Dans mes mains a brisé mon lys ...

Par Belzébuth! contre la borne
Je viens de me rompre la corne!
. . . .
Comme les trucs sont démolis!

IIIe ACTE (*Sereno*)

Holà! ... je vois poindre un fanal oblique
        — Flamberge au vent, joli Muguet!
        Sangre Dios! rossons le guet! ...

Un bonhomme mélancolique
Chante: — Bonsoir Señor, Señor Caballero,
Sereno ... — Sereno toi-même!
Minuit: second jour de carême,
Prêtez-moi donc un cigaro ...

At that price I must kiss, upon the golden cleft
Of your lips, the white wafer that seals your chastity
    Shrined in the odour of sanctity
    . . . .
    Zounds! has Milady up and left? ...

ACT II *(Sabbath)*

    I'm an angel, O my Heart's Desire,
    Wanting to take you ... under my wing!
    This bally earth has me on a string.
    My quill has been dipped in the mire ...

    Agh! now one of my wings has clammed! ...
    Let us pray ... the Devil's quick to round ...
    — Ah! if I were him, how I'd bound
    Up on you, my Filly, my Dam!

    ... The white crown I wear is shedding
    Its petals already; the stiff wind
    In my hands has snapped my lily ...

    'Pon Beelzebub! here's the bourn
    On which I've just broken my horn!
    . . . .
    How such set-ups are knocked silly!

ACT III *(Sereno)*

Not so fast! ... I can see a lantern glow
    — Draw your sword, sweet Desperado!
    Sangre Dios! it's the watch ... for us to bastinado!

    There's a melacholy fellow
Singing: — Evening Señor, Señor Caballero ...
Sereno ... — *Sereno* yourself! Seein' as you're a gent.
    And it's midnight: the second day of Lent,
    Just lend me a fat *cigaro* ...

153

Gracia! La Vierge vous garde!
— La Vierge? ... grand merci, vieux! Je sens la moutarde! ...
— Par Saint-Joseph! Señor, que faites-vous ici? —
      — Mais ... pas grand'chose et toi, merci.

— C'est pour votre plaisir? ... — Je damne les alcades
    De Tolose au Guadalété!
— Il est un violon, là-bas sous les arcades ...
      — Çà: n'as-tu jamais arrêté
    Musset ... musset pour sérénade?

      — *Santos!* ... non, sur la promenade,
    Je n'ai jamais vu de mussets ...
      — Son page était en embuscade ...
— *Ah Carambah!* Monsieur est un señor Français
    Qui vient nous la faire à l'aubade? ...

Gracia! The Virgin protect you from all harms!
— The Virgin? ... that's great! now that I'm up in arms! ...
— By Saint-Joseph! What brings you here, Señor? —
      — Well ... not a lot, and you?
                                — Out for the day? ...
      — I'm out to blast every gaoler
From *Tolose* to the *Guadalété*!
— There's a jug-jug there, under the arcade ...
Gaol-birds can whistle, they won't fly away!
      — But then, have you never waylaid
Musset ... the bird for a serenade?

      — *Santos*! ... no, I've spotted, to date,
No *mussets* on parole or parade ...
      — His page has been lying in wait ...
— *Ah Carambah*! Is Monsieur then a French Señor
Waiting for sun-up to give us what-for? ...

Pièce à Carreaux

Ah! si Vous avez à Tolède
    Un vitrier
Qui vous forge un vitrail plus raide
    Qu'un bouclier! ...

À Tolède j'irai ma flamme
    Souffler, ce soir;
À Tolède tremper la lame
    De mon rasoir!

Si cela ne vous amadoue:
    Vais aiguiser,
Contre tous les cuirs de Cordoue,
    Mon dur baiser:

— Donc — À qui rompra: votre oreille,
    Ou bien mes vers!
Ma corde-à-boyaux sans pareille,
    Ou bien vos nerfs?

— À qui fendra: ma castagnette,
    Ou bien vos dents ...
L'Idole en grès, ou le Squelette
    Aux yeux dardants!

— À qui fondra: vous ou mes cierges,
    Ô plombs croisés! ...
En serez-vous beaucoup plus vierges,
    Carreaux cassés?

Et Vous qui faites la cornue,
    Ange là-bas! ...
En serez-vous un peu moins nue,
    Les habits bas?

Room With Lattice Windows

Ah! if You have in Toledo
    A glazier
Who can forge a lattice window
    That's stronger

Than a buckler! ... I shall, this evening
    In Toledo,
Fan my passion's flame, tempering
    My razor's blade!

If that won't draw you, I'll even
    Set to and sharpen
My blunt kiss on all Cordovan
    Leather: — Then

— What will split first? Your ear-drum
    Or my verse!
My unrivalled gut and plectrum
    Or your nerves?

— What will crack first? My castanet
    Or your teeth ...
The stone Idol or skeletal Pet-
    Cockatrice!

— What will melt first? You or my candles,
    You crossed lead cames! ...
Will it make you much more virginal
    With broken panes?

You raise the horns of my dilemma,
    Angel up there! ...
Will that make you less in the altogether
    When you're bare?

— Ouvre! fenêtre à guillotine:
    C'est le bourreau!
— Ouvre donc porte de cuisine!
    C'est Figaro.

... Je soupire, en vache espagnole,
    Ton numéro
Qui n'est, en français, Vierge molle!
    Qu'un grand ZÉRO.

Cadix. — Mai.

— Open! executioner- or
      Sash-window!
Or, better still, kitchen door!
      Here's Figaro.

... I sigh your number, butchering
      The lingo, phrased
In Spanish cow mood; in French, soft Virgin!
      It's ZERO grazed*.

Cadiz. — May.

* or glazed?

RACCROCS

FLUKES

Laisser-Courre

Musique de: ISAAC LAQUEDEM.

J'ai laissé la potence
Après tous les pendus,
Andouilles de naissance,
Maigres fruits défendus;
Les plumes aux canards
Et la queue aux renards ...

Au Diable aussi sa queue
Et ses cornes aussi,
Au ciel sa chose bleue
Et la Planète — ici —
Et puis tout: n'importe où
Dans le désert au clou.

J'ai laissé dans l'Espagne
Le reste et mon château;
Ailleurs, à la campagne,
Ma tête et son chapeau;
J'ai laissé mes souliers,
Sirènes, à vos pieds!

J'ai laissé par les mondes,
Parmi tous les frisons
Des chauves, brunes, blondes
Et rousses ... mes toisons.
Mon épée aux vaincus,
Ma maîtresse aux cocus ...

Aux portes les portières,
La portière au portier,
Le bouton aux rosières,
Les roses au rosier,
À l'huys les huissiers,
Créance aux créanciers ...

Letting Go

Music by: ISAAC LAQUEDEM

I have left the gibbet
To all those hanged by the neck,
Addlepates from the egg,
Skinny forbidden fruit;
All quills to the ducks
And my brush to the fox ...

Let the devil take his tail
And his horns as well,
The sky its blue you-know-what
And the Planet — this freak —
All the works; I've left the lot
On the hook up the creek.

I have left in Spain
My castle and what remains! ...
Elsewhere, at grass roots,
My head and its hat, complete;
I have left my boots
Sirens, at your feet.

I've left all over the world
Among the kiss-curls
Of blond, brunette, bald
And redhead ... my fleeces.
My sword to the cut-to-pieces,
My mistress to all cuckolds ...

To doorkeepers doors to keep,
Knockers to budding porters,
Rose-buds to Rose Queens,
Roses to be watered;
Bailiffs to bail out debtors,
All credit to my creditors ...

Dans mes veines ma veine,
Mon rayon au soleil,
Ma dégaine en sa gaine,
Mon lézard au sommeil;
J'ai laissé mes amours
Dans les tours, dans les fours ...

Et ma cotte de maille
Aux artichauts de fer
Qui sont à la muraille
Des jardins de l'Enfer;
Après chaque oripeau
J'ai laissé de ma peau.

J'ai laissé toute chose
Me retirer du nez
Des vers, en vers, en prose ...
Aux bornes, les bornés;
À tous les jeux partout
Des rois et de l'atout.

J'ai laissé la police
Captive en liberté,
J'ai laissé La Palisse
Dire la vérité ...
Laissé courre le sort
Et ce qui court encor.

J'ai laissé l'Espérance,
Vieillissant doucement,
Retomber en enfance,
Vierge folle sans dent.
J'ai laissé tous les Dieux,
J'ai laissé pire et mieux.

To my heart a lucky break,
My shafts to the sunlight,
To gaiters my awkward gait,
My lizard to sleep tight;
I have left my loved ones
To their havens, to their ovens ...

My coat of mail and the likes
On the clusters of spikes
That jut up from the wall
Round Hell's garden-stall;
On every tinsel trapping
I've left ribbons of my skin.

I've left everything rope
To worm things from my nose
In threads of verse or prose ...
To dopes I've left the dope;
To the down-in-the-dumps
A chance to come up trumps.

I have left the police
Footloose on the beat,
I have left La Palisse
To tell us the truth this week ...
Let slip the hounds of fate
And whatever couldn't wait.

I've left fond Hope dying
To grow old gracefully
And, foolish toothless virgin,
Sink back to infancy;
I've let all the Gods disperse,
I've left better and worse.

J'ai laissé bien tranquilles
Ceux qui ne l'étaient pas;
Aux pattes imbéciles
J'ai laissé tous les plats;
Aux poètes la foi ...
Puis me suis laissé moi.

Sous le temps, sans égides
M'a mal mené fort bien
La vie à grandes guides ...
Au bout des guides — rien —
... Laissé, blasé, passé,
Rien ne m'a rien laissé ...

I've left well alone
Those who weren't before;
I've left meat on the bone
For boneheads to paw;
To poets faith in fee ...
Then I've left me free.

In all weathers outriding,
Life set the pace, misleading
Me well — I'm under no wing —
At the reins' end — nothing —
... Left, blasé, an ex,
Nothing's left me nothing next ...

À Ma Jument Souris

Pas d'éperon ni de cravache,
N'est-ce pas, Maîtresse à poil gris ...
C'est bon à pousser une vache,
Pas une petite Souris.

Pas de mors à ta pauvre bouche:
Je t'aime, et ma cuisse te touche.
Pas de selle, pas d'étrier:
J'agace, du bout de ma botte,
Ta patte d'acier fin qui trotte.
Va: je ne suis pas cavalier ...

— Hurrah! c'est à nous la poussière!
J'ai la tête dans ta crinière,
Mes deux bras te font un collier.
— Hurrah! c'est à nous le hallier!

— Hurrah! c'est à nous la barrière!
— Je suis emballé: tu me tiens —
Hurrah! ... et le fossé derrière
Et la culbute! ... — Femme tiens!!

To My Mouse-Dun Mare

I've neither spurs nor riding-crop,
Bare-backed Mistress with coat so grey ...
All they're good for's pricking a
Jade not a Filly ... So gallop

With no bit in — my colt in the tooth:
I love you, my thighs to your flanks.
You've no saddle, no stirrups:
I prod with the tip of my boot —
You trot on your steel-hooved shanks.
I'm too raw for stirrup-cups ...

— Hurrah! we're raising the dust!
Into your mane my head is thrust,
My two arms make a collar for you.
— Hurrah! into the brake and through!

— Hurrah! we're over the fail-dike!
— I'm carried away: it's touch, and go —
Hurrah! ... past the ditch: tally-ho!
Then head over heels! ... — Woman alright!!

À la Douce Amie

Çà: badinons — J'ai ma cravache —
Prends ce mors, bijou d'acier gris;
— Tiens: ta dent joueuse le mâche ...
En serrant un peu: tu souris ...

— Han! ... C'est pour te faire la bouche ...
— V'lan! ... C'est pour chasser une mouche ...
Veux-tu sentir te chatouiller
L'éperon, honneur de ma botte? ...
— Et la *Folle du Logis* trotte ... —
Jouons à l'Amour-cavalier!

Porte-beau ta tête altière,
Laisse mes doigts dans ta crinière ...
J'aime voir ton beau col ployer! ...
Demain: je te donne un collier.

— Pourquoi regarder en arrière? ...
Ce n'est rien: c'est une étrivière ...
Une étrivière ... et — je te tiens!
. . . .
Et tu m'as aimé ... — rosse, tiens!

To My Tender-Mouthed Love

Come on: let's frisk — I've got my whip —
You wear this bit, this grey steel jewel;
— Hey: your playful teeth are champing it ...
By clenching a little: you smile ...

— Crack! ... That's so your teeth cut their eye ...
— Smack! ... That's to flick off a botfly ...
Now how would you like to feel a spur
Touch you up, my boot's point of honour? ...
— Round trots *Dame Fancy*, presiding ... —
Let's play at Cupid-out-riding!

Carry your head high, act urbane,
Let my fingers stay in your mane ...
I love to watch your sleek neck curve! ...
I'll give you the collar you deserve.

— Why look back? To see a tether? ...
It's nothing: this stirrup-leather
Lashing you ... and — me saddled too!
. . . .
And you've loved me ... — you jade, you screw!

À Mon Chien Pope

— GENTLEMAN-DOG FROM NEW-LAND —
mort d'une balle.

Toi: ne pas suivre en domestique,
Ni lécher en fille publique!
— Maître-philosophe cynique:
N'être pas traité comme un chien,
Chien! tu le veux — et tu fais bien.

— Toi: rester toi; ne pas connaître
Ton écuelle ni ton maître.
Ne jamais marcher sur les mains,
Chien! — c'est bon pour les humains.

... Pour l'amour — qu'à cela ne tienne:
Viole des chiens — Gare la Chienne!

Mords — Chien — et nul ne te mordra.
Emporte le morceau — Hurrah! —

Mais après, ne fais pas la bête;
S'il faut payer — paye — Et fais tête
Aux fouets qu'on te montrera.

— Pur ton sang! pur ton chic sauvage!
      — Hurler, nager —
Et, si l'on te fait enrager ...
        Enrage!

Île de Batz. — Octobre.

172

To My Dog Pope

— GENTLEMAN-DOG FROM NEW-LAND —
killed by a bullet.

Not to come to heel like a helot,
Not to lick a bone like a harlot!
— Master-sage and -cynic on the trot:
Not to be treated like a dog,
Dog! is your wish — you're all agog

To be yourself — You! — and not to know
Your master or your feeding-bowl.
Never to walk on your hands,
Dog! — that's only fit for humans.

... As for love — that needn't cause a hitch:
Assault dogs — Watch out for the Bitch!

Bite — Dog — then none will bite you.
Be mordant, bite off all you can chew —

But afterwards, don't act too dumb;
If you have to pay — pay — And come
At the whips that'll be cracked at you.

— You're a thoroughbred, feral style!
        — Howl and perspire —
And, if you're goaded to spit fire ...
        Go wild!

Isle of Batz. — October.

À un Juvenal de Lait

Incipe, parve puer, risu cognoscere ...

À grands coups d'avirons de douze pieds, tu rames
En vers ... et contre tout — Hommes, auvergnats, femmes. —
Tu n'as pas vu l'endroit et tu cherches l'envers.
Jeune renard en chasse ... Ils sont trop verts — tes vers.

C'est le *vers solitaire.* — On le purge. — *Ces Dames*
Sont le remède. Après tu feras de tes nerfs
Des cordes-à-boyau; quand, guitares sans âmes,
Les vers te reviendront déchantés et soufferts.

Hystérique à rebours, ta Muse est trop superbe,
Petit cochon de lait, qui n'as goûté qu'en herbe
L'âcre saveur du fruit encore défendu.

Plus tard, tu colleras sur papier tes pensées,
Fleurs d'herboriste, mais, autrefois ramassées ...
Quand il faisait beau temps au paradis perdu.

To a Sucking Juvenal

Incipe, parve puer, risu cognoscere ...

With deep strokes of your twelve foot oars, you are rowing
In lines ... against the current — Men, auvergnats, women. —
You haven't seen the good side, yet you seek reverses.
Fox-cub out hunting ... They are too sour — your verses.

You're an anchorite with lost-thread-worm. — To purge. —
Try thole-pins or pin-ups in order to be cured.
Making nerves catgut — guitars with no pluck — you'll emerge
With worm-eaten lines, disenchanted and endured.

Your Muse: stuck-up, hysterical if made to squirm;
You: young sucking-pig, who have sampled but in germ
The tart flavour of the fruit that's still forbidden.

Then later, you'll commit to paper your heart's ease,
Flowers of the botanist, but picked in olden days
When the sun was radiant over a vanished Eden.

À une Demoiselle

Pour Piano et Chant

La dent de ton Érard, râtelier osanore,
Et scie et broie à cru, sous son tic-tac nerveux,
La gamme de tes dents, autre clavier sonore ...
Touches qui ne vont pas aux cordes des cheveux!

— Cauchemar de meunier, ta: *Rêverie agile!*
— Grattage, ton: *Premier amour à quatre mains!*
Ô femme transposée en *Morceau difficile,*
Tes croches sans douleur n'ont pas d'accents humains!

Déchiffre au clavecin cet accord de ma lyre;
Télégraphe à musique, il pourra le traduire:
Cri d'os, dur, sec, qui plaque et casse — Plangorer ...

Jamais! — La *clef-de-Sol* n'est pas la clef de l'âme,
La *clef-de-Fa* n'est pas la syllabe de *Femme,*
Et deux *demi-soupirs* ... ce n'est pas soupirer.

To a Young Lady

for piano and voice

The bite of your Erard, that ivory denture,
Sets on edge and grinds down, with its highly-strung clicks,
The scale of your teeth, whose keys do not venture
To your hair-strings, though its keyboard plays tricks!

— It's a miller's nightmare, your: *Nimble reverie!*
— Butterfinger fumble, your: *First love for four hands!*
O woman transposed into *Difficult piece*,
Your painless crotchets don't make human demands!

Pick out on the harpsichord these notes of my lyre
— Musical morse-code — to signal that my desire
Is bone-screak — hard, dry bone that strikes and breaks — Plangent cries ...

Never! — The *treble clef*'s not the key to the heart,
The *clef of F* doesn't make a *Female* start,
And two *semi-quavers* ... don't quaver in lovers' sighs.

Décourageux

Ce fut un vrai poète: Il n'avait pas de chant.
Mort, il aimait le jour et dédaigna de geindre.
Peintre: il aimait son art — Il oublia de peindre ...
Il voyait trop — Et voir est un aveuglement.

— Songe-creux: bien profond il resta dans son rêve;
Sans lui donner la forme en baudruche qui crève,
Sans *ouvrir le bonhomme*, et se chercher dedans.

— Pur héros de roman: il adorait la brune,
Sans voir s'elle était blonde ... Il adorait la lune;
Mais il n'aima jamais — Il n'avait pas le temps. —

— Chercheur infatigable: Ici-bas où l'on rame,
Il regardait ramer, du haut de sa grande âme,
Fatigué de pitié pour ceux qui ramaient bien ...

Mineur de la pensée: il touchait son front blême,
Pour gratter un bouton ou gratter le problème
      Qui travaillait là — Faire rien. —

— Il parlait: "Oui, la Muse est stérile! elle est fille
D'amour, d'oisiveté, de prostitution;
Ne la déformez pas en ventre de famille
Que couvre un étalon pour la production!

"Ô vous tous qui gâchez, maçons de la pensée!
Vous tous que son caprice a touchés en amants,
— Vanité, vanité — La folle nuit passée,
Vous l'affichez *en charge* aux yeux ronds des manants!

"Elle vous effleurait, vous, comme chats qu'on noie,
Vous avez accroché son aile ou son réseau,
Fiers d'avoir dans vos mains un bout de plume d'oie,
Ou des poils à gratter, en façon de pinceau!"

Out of Pluck

He was a true poet: He didn't *lisp in numbers.*
Being dead, he loved daylight and disdained complaint.
A painter: he loved his art — He forgot to paint ...
He could see too much — And seeing is a blindness.

— Pipedreamer: so hooked he stayed in his make-believe;
Not shaping it like a bladder that's losing wind,
Not opening up the man — to seek himself within.

— Pure hero of romance: he adored dusky eve,
Without seeing if she was blond ... He adored the moon;
But he never loved — The time always passed too soon. —

— Indefatigable prospector: Here below,
From the heights of his great soul, he watched them row,
Fatigued with pity for the oarsmen who knew how ...

Miner for thought: he'd put a hand to his pale brow,
To scratch a pimple or his head, working
          Away at his problem — Doing nothing. —

— He would say: "Yes, the Muse is sterile! she's a child
Of love, of bone idleness and prostitution;
Don't deform her in the family way, defiled
By a stallion for the purposes of production!

"O all you gash structuralists, free masons of thought!
All you her passing fancies, turned paramours.
— Vanity, vanity — The mad night spent, you flaunt
And guy her for the pop-eyes of bucolic boors!

"She'd brush against you, like cats you're about to drown,
And you have caught her by her whiskers or her wing,
Proud to hold a goose quill — from the Muse's eiderdown? —
Or bristles, paint-brush shaped — a teaseler caught napping!"

179

— Il disait: "Ô naïf Océan! Ô fleurettes,
Ne sommes-nous pas là, sans peintres, ni poètes! ...
Quel vitrier a peint! quel aveugle a chanté! ...
Et quel vitrier chante en raclant sa palette,

"Ou quel aveugle a peint avec sa clarinette!
— Est-ce l'art? ..."
                              — Lui resta dans le Sublime Bête
Noyer son orgueil vide et sa virginité.

Méditerranée.

— He would say: "O naïve Ocean! O painted-tongue,
Don't we exist, without your painter or your poet! ...
What glazier has painted! what blind man has sung! ...
And what glazier sings as he scrapes his palette,

"Or what blind man has painted with his clarinet!
— Is it art? ..."
                       — He stayed in Sublime Asininity*?
To drown his empty pride and his virginity.

The Mediterranean.

*Or: Foolish Sublimity

181

Rapsodie du Sourd

À Madame D ***.

L'homme de l'art lui dit: — Fort bien, restons-en là.
Le traitement est fait: vous êtes sourd. Voilà
Comme quoi vous avez l'organe bien perdu. —
Et lui comprit trop bien, n'ayant pas entendu.

— Eh bien, merci Monsieur, vous qui daignez me rendre
      La tête comme un bon cercueil.
Désormais, à crédit, je pourrai tout entendre
      Avec un légitime orgueil ...

À l'œil — Mais gare à l'œil jaloux, gardant la place
De l'oreille au clou! ... — Non — À quoi sert de braver?
... Si j'ai sifflé trop haut le ridicule en face,
En face, et bassement, il pourra me baver! ...

Moi, mannequin muet, à fil banal! — Demain,
Dans la rue, un ami peut me prendre la main,
En me disant: vieux pot ..., ou rien, en radouci;
Et je lui répondrai — Pas mal et vous, merci! —

Si l'un me corne un mot, j'enrage de l'entendre;
Si quelqu'autre se tait: serait-ce par pitié? ...
Toujours, comme un *rebus*, je travaille à surprendre
Un mot de travers ... — Non — On m'a donc oublié!

— Ou bien — autre guitare — un officieux être
Dont la lippe me fait le mouvement de paître,
Croit me parler ... Et moi je tire, en me rongeant,
Un sourire idiot — d'un air intelligent!

— Bonnet de laine grise enfoncé sur mon âme!
Et — coup de pied de l'âne ... Hue! — Une bonne-femme
Vieille Limonadière, aussi, de la Passion!
Peut venir saliver sa sainte compassion

The Deaf Man's Rhapsody

To Madame D ***.

The *artist* says to him: — We've done what we can, near
Enough. The treatment's over: you're deaf. What's occurred
Is proof incontrovertible you've lost your ear. —
He grasped that all too well, not having caught a word.

— Well, thanks a lot, you who deign to make my head it
          Feels like a coffin inside.
From now on, I'll be hearing everything on credit
          With a legitimate sense of pride ...

On tick and optically — But watch for the jealous eye
Clapped where the ear should be! ... — No — Why the do-or-die?
... If I've hissed too loud in the face of ridicule,
It may spit in my face, make me look a soft fool! ...

I'm a dumb dummy, a puppet on a string, a *Guy*!
— Tomorrow, in the street, a friend may shake my hand
And say: You old crock ..., or nothing, no whited lie;
And I shall answer — Not bad thanks, and you? That's grand! —

I itch to hear what's blared at me — but must they shout? —
If someone's silent: is it for pity's sake? ...
I try to intercept a word, puzzle it out
As it sails by ... — I can't and I'm forgotten in its wake!

— Or else — some officious so-and-so — know the style? —
Whose blubber lips go through the motions of grazing,
Thinks he's addressing me ... Eating my heart out, I smile
An idiotic smile — with intelligent phasing!

— Grey balaclava pulled over my head, the ass!
And — unkindest kick of all ... Gee up! — A canny lass,
Mature Purveyor of Soft Drinks for the Passion!
Can come and salivate her holy compassion

Dans ma *trompe-d'Eustache*, à pleins cris, à plein cor,
Sans que je puisse au moins lui marcher sur un cor!

— Bête comme une vierge et fier comme un lépreux,
Je suis là, mais absent ... On dit: Est-ce un gâteux,
Poète muselé, hérisson à rebours? ... —
Un haussement d'épaule, et ça veut dire: un sourd.

— Hystérique tourment d'un Tantale acoustique!
Je vois voler des mots que je ne puis happer;
Gobe-mouche impuissant, mangé par un moustique,
Tête-de-turc gratis où chacun peut taper.

Ô musique céleste: entendre, sur du plâtre,
Gratter un coquillage! un rasoir, un couteau
Grinçant dans un bouchon! ... un couplet de théâtre!
Un os vivant qu'on scie! un monsieur! un rondeau! ...

— Rien — Je parle sous moi ... Des mots qu'à l'air je jette
De chic, et sans savoir si je parle en indou ...
Ou peut-être en canard, comme la clarinette
D'un aveugle bouché qui se trompe de trou.

— Va donc, balancier soûl affolé dans ma tête!
Bats en branle ce bon tam-tam, chaudron fêlé
Qui rend la voix de femme ainsi qu'une sonnette,
Qu'un coucou! ... quelquefois: un moucheron ailé ...

— Va te coucher, mon cœur! et ne bats plus de l'aile.
Dans la lanterne sourde étouffons la chandelle,
Et tout ce qui vibrait là — je ne sais plus où —
Oubliette où l'on vient de tirer le verrou.

— Soyez muette pour moi, contemplative Idole,
Tous les deux, l'un par l'autre, oubliant la parole,
Vous ne me direz mot: je ne répondrai rien ...
Et rien ne pourra dédorer l'entretien.

Le silence est d'or (Saint Jean Chrysostome).

In my *Eustachian tube*, with loud blasts of her horn,
— And not even a chance of treading on her corns!

— Silly as a virgin and proud as a leper,
I am here, but absent ... They say: Is he a crone
Dribbling, a muzzled poet, an out-of-stepper
Kicking himself? ... — Then shrug, meaning: deaf as a stone.

— The anguish an acoustic Tantalus undergoes!
I see words fly away and cannot snap them up;
Impotent fly-catcher, bitten by mosquitoes,
Free test-your-strength machine that anyone can whop.

Just to hear on plaster — celestial music ho! —
A shell scraping; a cut-throat razor, a knife blade
Squinge in a bung; a weather saw or a barbed tirade;
Living bone sawn through! a gentleman! a rondeau! ...

— Not for me, though — I speak undertones ... I bowl
Words to the winds, haphazardly: are they all in Greek?
Or perhaps, like a blind man's clarinet, in squeak!
Being hermetically sealed one mistakes the hole.

— Drunk and demented pendulum in my head, swing,
Set this tom-tom throbbing, this cracked pot, this honky-tonk
That makes the voice of a woman sound like a honk
Or a cuckoo! ... and sometimes: a midge on the wing ...

— Off to bed, my heart! don't beat your wings any more.
In this deaf dark-lantern let's snuff the candle-light
And everything vibrating there — now I've lost the site —
Where your *artist* has just bolted my dungeon door.

— Be dumb for me, contemplative Idol; let's try,
Shall we, abandoning speech, the strains of discourse;
You won't say a word to me, I shall not reply ...
And nothing will take the gilt off our intercourse.

Silence is golden (Saint John Chrysostom).

185

Frère et Sœur Jumeaux

Ils étaient tous deux seuls, oubliés là par l'âge ...
Ils promenaient toujours tous les deux, à longs pas,
Obliquant de travers, l'air piteux et sauvage ...
Et deux pauvres regards qui ne regardaient pas.

Ils allaient devant eux essuyant les risées,
— Leur parapluie aussi, vert, avec un grand bec —
Serrés l'un contre l'autre et roides, sans pensées ...
Eh bien, je les aimais — leur parapluie avec! —

Ils avaient tous les deux servi dans les gendarmes:
La Sœur à la *popote*, et l'Autre sous les armes;
Ils gardaient l'uniforme encor — veuf de galon:
Elle avait la barbiche, et lui le pantalon.

Un Dimanche de Mai que tout avait une âme,
Depuis le champignon jusqu'au paradis bleu,
Je flânais aux bois, seul — à deux aussi: la femme
Que j'aimais comme l'air ... m'en doutant assez peu.

— Soudain, au coin d'un champ, sous l'ombre verdoyante
Du parapluie éclos, nichés dans un fossé,
Mes Vieux Jumeaux, tous deux, à l'aube souriante,
Souriaient rayonnants ... quand nous avons passé.

Contre un arbre, le vieux jouait de la musette,
Comme un sourd aveugle, et sa sœur dans un sillon,
Grelottant au soleil, écoutait un grillon
Et remerciait Dieu de son beau jour de fête.

— Avez-vous remarqué l'humaine créature
Qui végète loin du vulgaire intelligent,
Et dont l'âme d'instinct, au trait de la figure,
Se lit ... — N'avez-vous pas aimé de chien couchant? ...

Twin Brother and Sister

They were both there alone, forgotten by the years ...
And both of them still cut, out striding as a pair,
Wild and sorry figures; leaning sideways, they steered
A tottery course, crestfallen, with unseeing stare.

Following their noses, they weathered squalls and jeers,
— Their umbrella did too, it was green and nasute —
Huddled up together, and stiff, with no ideas ...
I was fond of them, though — their umbrella to boot! —

Both of them had served in the mounted gendarmes:
The Sister in the mess, the Brother under arms;
They still wore the uniform — bereft of galloons:
She sporting the goatee, he the red pantaloons.

One Sunday in May when all creatures had a soul,
From the humble mushroom to the blue of the skies,
I was strolling through the woods, alone — but also
With the woman I loved like the air ... To my surprise:

There, in the corner of a field, in the verdant shade
Of the splayed umbrella and ensconced in a ditch,
My Old Twins, both of them, at radiant break of day,
Were smiling radiantly ... when we passed by their niche.

Propped against a tree, the old man played his musette,
Like someone blind and deaf, while in a dip his sister,
Shivering in the sunlight, listened to a cricket
And gave thanks to God for her fine birthday weather.

— Have you ever noticed there are human creatures
Vegetating far from your crass intelligentsia,
And whose soul can be read in their facial features,
Intuitively ... — Have you never loved a cur? ...

Ils avaient de cela — De retour dans l'enfance,
Tenant chaud l'un à l'autre, ils attendaient le jour
Ensemble pour la mort comme pour la naissance ...
— Et je les regardais en pensant à l'amour ...

Mais l'Amour que j'avais près de moi voulut rire;
Et moi, pauvre honteux de mon émotion,
J'eus le cœur de crier au vieux duo: Tityre! —
. . . .
Et j'ai fait ces vieux vers en expiation.

They had that cringing look — In second infancy,
Keeping each other warm, they awaited the day
Of their death together as they had been for birth ...
— And as I watched them I considered love on earth ...

But Eros standing by wanted to titter as
I, poor specimen, ashamed of my emotion,
Had the nerve to mock the ancient pair: Tityrus! —
. . . .
And I've made up these old lines in expiation.

Litanie du Sommeil

J'ai scié le sommeil!
— MACBETH.

Vous qui ronflez au coin d'une épouse endormie,
RUMINANT! savez-vous ce soupir: L'INSOMNIE?
— Avez-vous vu la Nuit, et le Sommeil ailé,
Papillon de minuit dans la nuit envolé,
Sans un coup d'aile ami, vous laissant sur le seuil,
Seul, dans le pot-au-noir au couvercle sans œil?
— Avez-vous navigué? ... La pensée est la houle
Ressassant le galet: ma tête ... votre boule.
— Vous êtes-vous laissé voyager en ballon?
— Non? — bien, c'est l'insomnie. — Un grand coup de talon
Là! — Vous voyez cligner des chandelles étranges:
Une femme, une Gloire en soleil, des archanges ...
Et, la nuit s'éteignant dans le jour à demi,
Vous vous réveillez coi, sans vous être endormi.

*

SOMMEIL! écoute-moi: je parlerai bien bas:
Sommeil — Ciel-de-lit de ceux qui n'en ont pas!

TOI qui planes avec l'Albatros des tempêtes,
Et qui t'assieds sur les casques-à-mèche honnêtes!
SOMMEIL! — Oreiller blanc des vierges assez bêtes!
Et Soupape à secret des vierges assez faites!
— Moelleux Matelas de l'échine en arête!
Sac noir où les chassés s'en vont cacher leur tête!
Rôdeur de boulevard extérieur! Proxénète!
Pays où le muet se réveille prophète!
Césure du vers long, et Rime du poète!

Litany of Sleep

I've sawn sleep apart!
— MACBETH

YOU who snore with your sleeping wife so near,
RUMINANT! do you know this sigh: INSOMNIA?
— Have you seen Night and winged Sleep who's flown
Into the night, leaving you at the threshold, alone
— Not a friendly wing-beat from that midnight butterfly —
Alone in the pitch-pot whose lid has no eye?
— Have you been out in a boat? ... Thought is the swell
Resifting the shingle: my head ... your creel.
— Have you let a balloon take you up? — No? — well,
That's insomnia. — A big jolt from a heel,
Like that! — You see the flickering of strange candles:
A woman, a Halo of sunshine, archangels ...
And, night having brought day to the brink,
You wake up doggo, not having slept a wink.

*

SLEEP! listen to me: I shall speak very softly:
Sleep. — Four-poster for those with no canopy!

YOU who soar with the Albatross when storms blow!
And perch on honest night-caps of calico!
SLEEP! — For quite silly virgins, a white Pillow
And for well-developed ones, a secret Overflow!
— Downy Mattress for those who suffer polio!
Black Bag where, to hide their heads, the hounded go!
Prowler of the outer boulevards! Gigolo!
Country where the dumb wake to let their people know!
Caesura of the long line, and Rhyme for Sappho!

SOMMEIL! — Loup-Garou gris! Sommeil Noir de fumée!
SOMMEIL! — Loup de velours, de dentelle embaumée!
Baiser de l'Inconnue, et Baiser de l'Aimée!
— SOMMEIL! Voleur de nuit! Folle-brise pâmée!
Parfum qui monte au ciel des tombes parfumées!
Carrosse à Cendrillon ramassant *les Traînées!*
Obscène Confesseur des dévotes mort-nées!

TOI qui viens, comme un chien, lécher la vieille plaie
Du martyr que la mort tiraille sur sa claie!
Ô sourire forcé de la crise tuée!
SOMMEIL! Brise alizée! Aurorale buée!

TROP-PLEIN de l'existence, et Torchon neuf qu'on passe
Au CAFÉ DE LA VIE, à chaque assiette grasse!
Grain d'ennui qui nous pleut de l'ennui des espaces!
Chose qui court encor, sans sillage et sans traces!
Pont-levis des fossés! Passage des impasses!

SOMMEIL! — Caméléon tout pailleté d'étoiles!
Vaisseau-fantôme errant tout seul à pleines voiles!
Femme du rendez-vous, s'enveloppant d'un voile!
SOMMEIL! — Triste Araignée, étends sur moi ta toile!

SOMMEIL auréolé! féerique Apothéose,
Exaltant le grabat du déclassé qui pose!
Patient Auditeur de l'incompris qui cause!
Refuge du pêcheur, de l'innocent qui n'ose!
Domino! Diables-bleus! Ange-gardien rose!

VOIX mortelle qui vibre aux immortelles ondes!
Réveil des échos morts et des choses profondes,
— Journal du soir: TEMPS, SIÈCLE et REVUE DES DEUX MONDES!

FONTAINE de Jouvence et Borne de l'envie!
— Toi qui viens assouvir la faim inassouvie!
Toi qui viens délier la pauvre âme ravie,
Pour la noyer d'air pur au large de la vie!

SLEEP — Grizzly Werewolf! Black Sleep in a smokescreen!
SLEEP! — Fragrant lace round a Wolf of velveteen!
Kiss from the Faire Unknowne, and Kiss from your heart's Queen!
— SLEEP! Thief of night! Frisking cat's-paw become serene!
Redolence from graves rising to heaven unseen!
Cinderella's Coach picking up each *Magdalene!*
Confessor Obscene to each pious still-born *cailín!*

YOU who come, like a dog, to lick the stigmata
Of the one racked by death on his hurdle, the martyr!
O forced smile of the crisis that's lost its aura!
SLEEP! Constant north-east Breeze! Vapours of Aurora!

SURFEIT of existence, and clean Dishcloth in the CAFÉ
OF LIFE, wiping every plate that is greasy!
Squall of tedium that rains on us from space's ennui!
Thing that tacks on, with no tracks on land or sea!
Drawbridge of moats! Way-through the blind alley!

SLEEP! — Chameleon with its star-spangled mail!
Flying Dutchman adrift alone and in full sail!
Blind Date wrapped in nothing but a filmy veil!
Doleful Spider, stretch over me your silky trail!

SLEEP with a halo! Fairy-tale Apotheosis,
Exalting the doss of the ostracized who poses!
Patient Listener to what the poor fish discloses!
Refuge of fly fishers and innocents with clean noses!
Domino! Blue-devils! Pink Guardian-angel Moses!

MORTAL Voice vibrating to immortal waves!
Waker of profundities and dead echoes from caves,
— Evening paper: OUR TIME, THE CALENDAR, THE MYTHS OF GRAVES!

FOUNT of Eternal Youth and Confine of envy!
— You who come to appease the pangs of the hungry!
Who come to the soul bewitched and set it free
To drown it in the pure air of life's open sea!

TOI qui, le rideau bas, viens lâcher la ficelle
Du Chat, du Commissaire, et de Polichinelle,
Du violoncelliste et de son violoncelle,
Et la lyre de ceux dont la Muse est pucelle!

GRAND Dieu, Maître de tout! Maître de ma Maîtresse
Qui me trompe avec toi — l'amoureuse Paresse —
Ô Bain de voluptés! Éventail de caresse!

SOMMEIL! Honnêteté des voleurs! Clair de lune
Des yeux crevés! — SOMMEIL! Roulette de fortune
De tout infortuné! Balayeur de rancune!

Ô corde-de-pendu de la Planète lourde!
Accord éolien hantant l'oreille sourde!
— Beau Conteur à dormir debout: conte ta bourde? ...
SOMMEIL! — Foyer de ceux dont morte est la falourde!

SOMMEIL — Foyer de ceux dont la falourde est morte!
Passe-partout de ceux qui sont mis à la porte!
Face-de-bois pour les créanciers et leur sorte!
Paravent du mari contre la femme-forte!

SURFACE des profonds! Profondeur des jocrisses!
Nourrice du soldat et Soldat des nourrices!
Paix des juges-de-paix! Police des polices!
SOMMEIL! — Belle-de-nuit entr'ouvrant son calice!
Larve, Ver-luisant et nocturne Cilice!
Puits de vérité de monsieur La Palisse!

SOUPIRAIL d'en haut! Rais de poussière impalpable!
Qui viens rayer du jour la lanterne implacable!

*

SOMMEIL — Écoute-moi, je parlerai bien bas:
Crépuscule flottant de l'*Être ou n'Être pas!* ...

194

YOU who, once the curtain's down, let the strings go
— Of the Cat, the Commissionaire and Punchinello,
Of the violincellist and her violincello,
And the lyre of everyone whose Muse is Virgo!

GREAT Lord, Master of all! Master of my Mistress
Who deceives me with you — loving Idleness —
O Fan of caresses! Bath of voluptuousness!

SLEEP! Honesty of thieves! Light of the moon
For put-out eyes! — SLEEP! Wheel of fortune
For all unfortunates! Quasher of the lampoon!

O Luck of the devil for this heavy Sphere:
Noose for this Planet with no hangman to fear!
Aeolian harmonies haunting the deaf ear!
— Handsome Romancer, tall story teller, liar? ...
SLEEP! — Warmth for those with no kindling for their fire!

SLEEP — Kindling for the poor folk who have none!
Pass-key for the turned-out-of-doors: a skeleton!
For creditors and their ilk: wooden jaws or lantern!
Breastwork for the husband against his Amazon!

DEPTHS of the simpleton! Surface of the deeps!
Wet-nurse for the soldier and Soldier for the nurse! Peace
For all JPs! Policy of the police!
SLEEP! — Belladonna Lily opening her fleur-de-lys!
Larva, Glow-worm and nocturnal Hair-cilice!
Well-spring of truth for Monsieur La Palisse!

AIR-SHAFT on high! Impalpable dust-laden Beam,
Coming to expunge day's implacable gleam!

*

SLEEP — Listen to me, I shall speak very softly:
Floating twilight of the *to Be or not to Be!* ...

SOMBRE lucidité! Clair-obscur! Souvenir
De l'Inouï! Marée! Horizon! Avenir!
Conte des *Mille-et-une-nuits* doux à ouïr!
Lampiste d'*Aladin* qui sais nous éblouir!
Eunuque noir! muet blanc! Derviche! Djinn! Fakir!
Conte de Fée où *le Roi* se laisse assoupir!
Forêt-vierge où *Peau-d'Âne* en pleurs va s'accroupir!
Garde-manger où l'*Ogre* encor va s'assouvir!
Tourelle où *ma sœur Anne* allait voir rien venir!
Tour où *dame Malbrouck* voyait page courir!
Où *Femme Barbe-Bleue* oyait l'heure mourir! ...
Où *Belle-au-Bois-Dormant* dormait dans un soupir!

CUIRASSE du petit! Camisole du fort!
Lampion des éteints! Éteignoir du remord!
Conscience du juste, et du pochard qui dort!
Contre-poids des poids faux de l'épicier de Sort!
Portrait enluminé de la livide Mort!

GRAND fleuve où Cupidon va retremper ses dards:
SOMMEIL! — Corne de Diane, et corne du cornard!
Couveur de magistrats et Couveur de lézards!
Marmite d'*Arlequin!* — bout de cuir, lard, homard —
SOMMEIL! — Noce de ceux qui sont dans les beaux arts.

BOULET des forcenés, Liberté des captifs!
Sabbat du somnambule et Relais des poussifs! —
SOMME! Actif du passif et Passif de l'actif!
Pavillon de *la Folle* et *Folle* du poncif! ...
— Ô viens changer de patte au cormoran pensif!

Ô brun Amant de l'Ombre! Amant honteux du jour!
Bal de nuit où Psyché veut démasquer l'Amour!
Grosse Nudité du chanoine en jupon court!
Panier-à-salade idéal! Banal four!
Omnibus où, dans l'Orbe, on fait pour rien un tour!

DARK lucidity! *Chiaroscuro!* Recollection
Of the Unheard-of! Future! High tide! Horizon!
Euphonious Tale of *Nights* — from the *Arabian!*
Genie of *Aladdin*'s lamp, out to be dazzling!
Black eunuch! white mute! Dervish! Fakir! Djinn!
Fairy tale where he who drops asleep is *King!*
Virgin forest where *Mother Goose* squats weeping!
Pantry where *the Ogre* is still replenishing!
Turret where *my sister Anne* saw nothing coming!
Tower where *Dame Malbrouck* saw a page-boy running ...
Where *Bluebeard's Wife* could hear the hour a-dying! ...
Where *Sleeping Beauty* could fall asleep, sighing!

BREASTPLATE for the weakling! Straitjacket for the tougher!
Fairy lights for those who've snuffed it! Remorse's Snuffer!
Conscience of the just man, and the dozing boozer!
Counterbalance for the short weight of the grocer,
Fate! Illuminated Portrait of livid *Rigor!*

ONCE more Cupid will dip his darts in your broad river,
SLEEP! — Horns of the cuckold and Horn of Diana!
Hatcher of magistrates and lizards' Incubator!
Hitchhiker's Nap-sack! Beach basker! Master-baker!
Harlequin's Cauldron! — hunk of fleed, leather, lobster —
SLEEP! — Dry sherry party for the fine art master!
Piss-artists' Turner prize! Hobble-de-Goya fiesta!

MILLSTONE for the raving, Freedom for the captive!
Sleepwalker's Sabbath and Relay for the restive!
Active for the passive and Passive for the active!
Meg o' Bedlam's Tent! Figment for the uncreative! ...
— Oh come and change the cormorant's stance, he's too pensive!

Brown-skinned Lover of the Shade! Ashamed in the sun!
Masked Ball with Psyche wanting Eros undone!
Gross Nudity of the petticoated canon!
Ideal Black Maria! — Salad Basket spin! Bun
In a communal oven beautifully done!
Flop, footlights' fiasco, banal and pedestrian!
Victoria in orbit on a scot-free run!

197

SOMMEIL! Drame hagard! Sommeil, molle Langueur!
Bouche d'or du silence et Bâillon du blagueur!
Berceuse des vaincus! Perchoir des coqs vainqueurs!
Alinéa du livre où dorment les longueurs!

DU jeune homme rêveur Singulier Féminin!
De la femme rêvant pluriel masculin!

SOMMEIL! — Râtelier du Pégase fringant!
SOMMEIL! — Petite pluie abattant l'ouragan!
SOMMEIL! — Dédale vague où vient le revenant!
SOMMEIL! — Long corridor où plangore le vent!

NÉANT du fainéant! Lazzarone infini!
Aurore boréale au sein du jour terni!

SOMMEIL! — Autant de pris sur notre éternité!
Tour du cadran à *blanc!* Clou du Mont-de-Piété!
Héritage en Espagne à tout déshérité!
Coup de rapière dans l'eau du fleuve Léthé!
Génie au nimbe d'or des grands hallucinés!
Nid des petits hiboux! Aile des déplumés!

IMMENSE Vache à lait dont nous sommes les veaux!
Arche où le hère et le boa changent de peaux!
Arc-en-ciel miroitant! Faux du vrai! Vrai du faux!
Ivresse que la brute appelle le repos!
Sorcière de Bohême à sayon d'oripeaux!
Tityre sous l'ombrage essayant des pipeaux!
Temps qui porte un chibouck à la place de faux!
Parque qui met un peu d'huile à ses ciseaux!
Parque qui met un peu de chanvre à ses fuseaux!
Chat qui joue avec le peloton d'Atropos!

SOMMEIL! — Manne de grâce au cœur disgracié!
. . . .

LE SOMMEIL S'ÉVEILLANT ME DIT: TU M'AS SCIÉ.
. . . .

... Hollow-eyed Drama! Sleep, loose-limbed Languor!
lden Mouth of silence and Gag of the joker!
Cradle-song for the conquered! Perch for cock conquerors!
Indenture in a volume of nodding longueurs!

FEMININE Singular for the dreamy youth (intramural)!
For the pipe-dreaming woman Masculine plural!

SLEEP! — Rack where frisky Pegasus is quickened!
SLEEP! — Light Rain laying low the hurricane!
SLEEP! — Ghostly Labyrinth for the revenant!
SLEEP! — Long Corridor down which the wind is plangent!

NOTHINGNESS for good-for-nothings! Everlasting Laze
For *lazzaroni!* Northern Lights for tarnished days!

SLEEP! So much purchase on our eternity!
The clock's Round at white heat! Three Balls for security!
Inheritance in Spain for every non-feoffee!
Rapier-thrust into the waters of the Lethe!
For the great moonstruck a golden haloed Genie!
Nesting-hole for owlets! Wing for the plucked grandee!

HUGE Milch-Cow whose moon-calves we appear!
Ark where boa changes skin with hobo or deer!
Glistening rainbow! Real for false! False for real!
Stupor the drunken boor calls a breather!
Witch in tawdry woollen tunic from Bohemia!
Tityrus trying reed-pipes in the shade of an alder!
Time bearing a chibouk in place of a reaper!
Atropos putting a drop of oil on her shear!
Clotho putting a hank of flax on her spindle!
Cat playing with Lachesis's clew of wool!

SLEEP! — Manna of grace to the disgraced heart!
. . . .

SLEEP, ON WAKING, SAYS TO ME: YOU'VE SAWN ME APART.
. . . .

199

TOI qui souffles dessus une épouse enrayée,
RUMINANT! dilatant ta pupille éraillée;
Sais-tu? ... Ne sais-tu pas ce soupir — LE RÉVEIL! —
Qui bâille au ciel, parmi les crins d'or du soleil
Et les crins fous de ta Déesse ardente et blonde? ...
— Non? ... — Sais-tu le réveil du philosophe immonde
— Le Porc — rognonnant sa prière du matin;
Ou le réveil, extrait-d'âge de la catin? ...
As-tu jamais sonné le réveil de la meute;
As-tu jamais senti l'éveil sourd de l'émeute,
Ou le réveil de plomb du malade fini? ...
As-tu vu s'étirer l'œil des Lazzaroni? ...
Sais-tu? ... ne sais-tu pas le chant de l'alouette?
— Non — Gluants sont tes cils, pâteuse est ta luette,
Ruminant! Tu n'as pas L'INSOMNIE, éveillé;
Tu n'as pas LE SOMMEIL, ô Sac ensommeillé!

(Lits divers — Une nuit de jour.)

⌐wed wife who's sedated,
rimmed, pupils dilated,
? ... Don't you know this sigh — WAKING! —
en, amid the gold flaking
e wild ones of your blond and fiery
Goddess? — NO¡ ...   you know the waking of the filthy
Philosopher — The Pig — gruntling his morning gloria;
Or the whore's, telling her she's getting hoarier! ...
Have you ever sounded reveille for pack and hunters;
Or sensed a mob subconsciously aroused by *juntas*,
Or the leaden waking of the patient near his end? ...
Have you ever seen the Lazzaroni's eyes distend? ...
Do you know? ... don't you know the skylark's early note?
— No — Sticky are your lashes, coated is your throat,
Ruminant! You don't have INSOMNIA when *you*'re awake;
You don't have SLEEP, you sleepy Bag, for sleeping's sake!

(Divers beds — One night's day)

Idylle Coupée

Avril.

C'est très parisien dans les rues
Quand l'Aurore fait le trottoir,
De voir sortir toutes les Grues
Du violon, ou de leur boudoir ...

Chanson pitoyable et gaillarde:
Chiffons fanés papillotants,
Fausse note rauque et criarde
Et petits traits crus, turlutants:

Velours ratissant la chaussée;
Grande-duchesse mal chaussée,
Cocotte qui court becqueter
Et qui dit bonjour pour chanter ...

J'aime les voir, tout plein légères,
Et, comme en façon de prières,
Entrer dire — Bonjour, gros chien —
Au *merlan*, puis au pharmacien.

J'aime les voir, chauves, déteintes,
Vierges de seize à soixante ans,
Rossignoler pas mal d'absinthes,
Perruches de tout leur printemps;

Et puis *payer le mannezingue*,
Au *Polyte* qui sert d'Arthur,
Bon jeune homme né *brandezingue*,
Dos-bleu sous la blouse d'azur.

— C'est au boulevard excentrique,
Au — *BON RETOUR DU CHAMP DU NORD* —
Là: toujours vert le jus de trique,
Rose le nez des Croque-mort ...

_, ribald sing-song:
Frippery, faded but glittery,
Raucous screeching, each note wrong,
With little coarse flashes of wittery:

Velvet scuffing pavement and gutters;
Grand duchess down at heel,
Dolly bird who clucks and flutters
To give you a peck as her *spiel* ...

I like to see them, oh so flighty,
And, as if to give your arm a twist,
Come in with — Hiya, matey —
To the barber's, or the chemist.

I like to see them, balding, jaded,
Virgins of sixteen to sixty,
Parakeets in their heyday,
Knock back absinth (green ginger whisky?),

Before the bartender gets paid,
The swine who serves as Casanova,
Such a nice young man betrayed
By drink, pimp with an apron over.

— On the way-out boulevard,
At the — *SAFE RETURN FROM NORTHERN PARTS* —
It's: six of one and put in boots,
Red-raw the noses of Death-mutes ...

Moitié panaches, moitié cire,
Nez croqués vifs au demeurant,
Et gais comme un enterrement ...
— Toujours le petit *mort* pour rire! —

Le voyou siffle — vilain merle —
Et le poète de charnier
Dans ce fumier cherche la perle,
Avec le peintre chiffonnier.

Tous les deux fouillant la pâture
De leur art ... à coups de grouins;
Sûrs toujours de trouver l'ordure.
— C'est le fonds qui manque le moins.

C'est toujours un fond chaud qui fume,
Et, par le soleil, lardé d'or ...
Le rapin nomme ça: bitume;
Et le marchand de lyre: accord.

— Ajoutez une pipe en terre
Dont la spirale fait les cieux ...
Allez: je plains votre misère,
Vous qui trouvez qu'on trouve mieux!

C'est le *Persil* des gueux sans poses,
Et des riches sans un radis ...
— Mais ce n'est pas pour vous, ces choses,
Ô provinciaux de Paris! ...

Ni pour vous, essayeurs de sauces,
Pour qui l'azur est un ragoût!
Grands empâteurs d'emplâtres fausses,
Ne fesant rien, fesant partout!

— Rembranesque! Raphaélique!
— Manet et Courbet au milieu —
... Ils donnent des noms de fabrique
À la pochade du bon Dieu!

Half puffed-up, half malleable,
Kissers chalked from life at a stroke,
As full of fun as a funeral ...
— Death's always good for a croak! —

The guttersnipe wets his whistle — churl —
And the poet of the catacombs
Searches this midden for a pearl,
With the artist in *rag 'n bones*.

Both snuffling about in the ruck
Of their art ... with their snouts, of course;
Always sure of unearthing muck.
— There's no lack of natural resource.

There's always some dungheap steaming,
And larded with gold by the sun ...
The daubster dubs it: bitumen;
And the lyric merchant: a run.

— Now add to this a clay pipe whose
Spiralling creates a heaven ...
Hell: I pity you your blues,
Smoke that only makes cloud seven!

There's the soliciting of tramps
— Naturals all — and the hard-up rich ...
— But such things are just for vamps,
Not you yokels on your Paris pitch! ...

Nor you, connoisseurs of sauces,
For whom the blue sky's a ragout
Stirred by *artistic* forces:
No work's involved, splashes will do!

— Rembrandtesque! Raphaelic!
— With Manet and Courbet aboard —
... They're cooking brand-names up to stick
On the rough sketches of the Lord!

Ces *Galimard cherchant la ligne*,
Et ces *Ducornet-né-sans-bras*,
Dont la blague, de chic, vous signe
N'importe quoi ... qu'on ne peint pas.

Dieu garde encor l'homme qui glane
Sur le soleil du promenoir,
De flairer jamais la soutane
De la vieille dame au bas noir!

... On dégèle, animal nocturne,
Et l'on se détache en vigueur;
On veut, aveugle taciturne,
À soi tout seul être blagueur.

Savates et chapeau grotesque
Deviennent de l'antique pur;
On se colle comme une fresque
Enrayonnée au pied d'un mur.

Il coule une divine flamme
Sous la peau; l'on se sent avoir
Je ne sais quoi qui fleure l'âme ...
Je ne sais — mais ne veux savoir.

La Muse malade s'étire ...
Il semble que l'huissier sursoit ...
Soi-même on cherche à se sourire,
Soi-même on a pitié de soi.

Volez, mouches et demoiselles! ...
Le gouapeur aussi vole un peu
D'idéal ... Tout n'a pas des ailes ...
Et chacun vole comme il peut.

— Un grand pendard, cocasse, triste,
Jouissait de tout ça, comme moi,
Point ne lui demandais pourquoi ...
Du reste — une gueule d'artiste —

These Galimards after a line,
And Ducornets born-with-no-arms,
As a one-off, are willing to sign
Any old thing ... without any qualms.

God still keeps the chap who's gleaning
On the sunlit patch of the arcade,
From sniffing cassock: meaning —
The old black-stockinged maid!

... You thaw out, nocturnal creature,
And breaking loose with vigour,
Want, though blind, with dead-pan features,
To be the only comic figure.

Slippers: tatty, and hat: grotesque,
Are going beyond recall;
You apply yourself like a fresco
Irradiant with your back to the wall.

Beneath your skin there really glows
A flame divine — which goes to show
You've something smacking of a soul ...
Something — but *I* don't want to know.

The Muse, off-colour, stretches ...
The bailiff appears to reprieve ...
You try to smile at your own twitches,
Self-pity is your do-believe.

Fly, ladybirds and damselflies! ...
The drifter also flies a span
In fancy ... Not everything can rise ...
And everyone *flies* as he can.

— A huge gallows-bird, gloomy, rum,
Was aroused — Mine not to wonder why —
And, like me, starting to come ...
Besides, having an artist's eye,

Il reluquait surtout la tête
Et moi je reluquais le pié.
— Jaloux ... pourquoi? c'eût été bête,
Ayant chacun notre moitié. —

Ma béatitude nagée
Jamais, jamais n'avait bravé
Sa silhouette ravagée
Plantée au milieu du pavé ...

— Mais il fut un Dieu pour ce drille:
Au soleil loupant comme ça,
Dessinant des yeux une fille ...
— Un omnibus vert l'écrasa.

He ogled above all her head,
Whereas I, I ogled her foot.
— Jealous ... what's the point? When all's said,
His foot was in the other boot. —

My perfect bliss, in a sweat,
Never had it had the nerve
To beard her ravaged silhouette
Stuck in the middle of her reserve ...

— But there was a God for this guy:
Sauntering in moonlight like that,
Outlining a *bird* with his eye ...
— A green omnibus squashed him flat.

Le Convoi du Pauvre

Paris, le 30 avril 1873,
Rue Notre-Dame-de-Lorette.

Ça monte et c'est lourd — Allons, Hue!
— Frères de renfort, votre main? ...
C'est trop! ... et je fais le gamin;
C'est mon Calvaire cette rue!

Depuis Notre-Dame-Lorette ...
— Allons! *la Cayenne* est au bout,
Frère! du cœur! encor un coup! ...
— Mais mon âme est dans la charrette:

Corbillard dur à fendre l'âme.
Vers en bas l'attire un aimant;
Et du piteux enterrement
Rit la Lorette notre dame ...

C'est bien ça — Splendeur et misère! —
Sous le voile en trous a brillé
Un bout du tréteau funéraire;
Cadre d'or riche ... et pas payé.

La pente est âpre, tout de même,
Et les stations sont des *fours*,
Au tableau remontant le cours
De l'Élysée à la Bohème ...

— Oui, camarade, il faut qu'on sue
Après son harnais et son art! ...
Après les ailes: le brancard!
Vivre notre métier — ça tue ...

The Pauper's Funeral Procession

Paris, 30th April 1873,
Rue Notre-Dame-de-Lorette.

It's uphill and this is heavy — Gee up!
— Won't somebody lend me a hand? ...
That's too many! ... I'm a cheeky pup;
This street is my Calvary! And

Notre-Dame-Lorette was just the start ...
— The Potter's Field is up above,
Show some spirit, pal! one more shove! ...
— *My* spirit, though, is in the cart:

A hearse so hard it breaks my heart.
A lodestone draws it down below;
She laughs at the piteous burial show,
Does Lady la Lorette, the tart! ...

That's right — Misery and splendour! —
Beneath the holey veil's appeared
A glint of the funerary bier;
A rich gilt frame ... and not paid for.

At any rate, the slope's quite sheer,
And each station is a let-down
As the painting nears the crown ...
The route: Elysium to Bohemia ...

— Yes, you'll have to sweat, no doubt,
In your harness and for your art! ...
For wings: before you're carried out!
To live one's calling is the killing part ...

211

Tués l'idéal et le râble!
Hue! ... Et le cœur dans le talon!

· · · · · · · · · · · · · · · · · ·
— Salut au convoi misérable
Du peintre écrémé du Salon!

— Parmi les martyrs ça te range;
C'est prononcé comme l'arrêt
De Rafaël, peintre au nom d'ange,
Par le Peintre au nom de ... courbet!

...als shaken, gone!
...o need to be relayed!
. . . .
...ree cheers for the wretched cavalcade
Of the painter creamed from *the Salon*!

— Cut, you're ranked as martyr: a claim
Pronounced according to the book
Of Raphaël, with the angel's name,
By Courbet, alias ... bill hook!

Dejéuner de Soleil

Bois de Boulogne, 1er mai.

Au Bois, les lauriers sont coupés,
Mais le *Persil* verdit encore;
Au *Serpolet*, petits coupés
Vertueux vont lever l'Aurore ...

L'Aurore brossant sa palette:
Kh'ol, carmin et poudre de riz;
Pour faire dire — la coquette —
Qu'on fait bien les ciels à Paris.

Par ce petit-lever de Mai,
Le Bois se croit à la campagne:
Et, fraîchement trait, le champagne
Semble de la mousse de lait.

Là, j'ai vu les *Chère Madame*
S'encanailler avec le frais ...
Malgré tout prendre un vrai bain d'âme!
— Vous vous engommerez après. —

... La voix à la note expansive:
— Vous comprenez; voici mon truc:
Je vends mes Memphis, et j'arrive ...
— Cent louis! ... — Eh, Eh! Bibi ... — Mon duc? ...

On presse de petites mains:
— Tiens ... assez pur cet attelage. —
Même les cochers, au dressage,
Redeviennent simples humains.

— Encor toi! vieille *Belle-Impure!*
Toujours, les pieds au plat, tu sors,
Dans ce déjeuner de nature,
Fondre un souper à huit ressorts ... —

214

fast Quickie

Bois de Boulogne, May 1st.

In the *Bois*, the laurels are trim,
But *Lady's Smock* bestrews the lawn;
In the *Wild Thyme* one-horse prim
Broughams are out to arouse Dawn ...

Dawn brushing in her palette:
Rouge, talc, kohl of the houris;
To let it be known — the coquette —
That they paint skies well in Paris.

With this petty-levee of May
The *Bois* thinks it's in the country:
And, freshly milked, the champagne
Seems to be milk-froth, all foamy.

There I've seen the *genteel fauna*
Slumming it with the *cool* of the day ...
Yet having a real soul-sauna!
— Wear your war-paint *after* the fray. —

... The voice in an effusive burst:
— You understand, as I've no king's
Ransom, I'll sell my Memphis first ...
— A hundred louis! ... — You're joking! ...

— My hansom? ... Tiny hands are squeezed:
— Hey ... this pairing-up's quite pure. — Even
Coachmen, at the breaking-in, are eased
Into simple human beings again.

Voici l'école buissonnière:
Quelques maris jaunes de teint,
Et qui *rentrent dans la carrière*
D'assez bonne heure ... le matin.

Le lapin inquiet s'arrête,
Un sergent-de-ville s'assied,
Le sportsman promène sa bête,
Et le rêveur la sienne — à pied. —

Arthur même a presque une tête,
Son faux-col s'ouvre matinal ...
Peut-être se sent-il poète,
Tout comme *Byron* — son cheval.

Diane au petit galop de chasse
Fait galoper les papillons
Et caracoler sur sa trace,
Son Tigre et les vieux beaux Lions.

Naseaux fumants, grand œil en flamme,
Crins d'étalon: cheval et femme
Saillent de l'avant! ...
                        — Peu poli.
— Pardon: *maritime* ... et joli.

*

YOU who puff above a furrowed wife who's sedated,
RUMINANT! with eyes red-rimmed, pupils dilated,
Can whistle! Do you know? ... Don't you know this sigh — WAKING! —
Which yawns to high heaven, amid the gold flaking
Of the sun's manes and the wild ones of your blond and fiery
Goddess? — No? ... — Do you know the waking of the filthy
Philosopher — The Pig — gruntling his morning gloria;
Or the whore's, telling her she's getting hoarier! ...
Have you ever sounded reveille for pack and hunters;
Or sensed a mob subconsciously aroused by *juntas*,
Or the leaden waking of the patient near his end? ...
Have you ever seen the Lazzaroni's eyes distend? ...
Do you know? ... don't you know the skylark's early note?
— No — Sticky are your lashes, coated is your throat,
Ruminant! You don't have INSOMNIA when *you*'re awake;
You don't have SLEEP, you sleepy Bag, for sleeping's sake!

(Divers beds — One night's day)

Idylle Coupée

Avril.

C'est très parisien dans les rues
Quand l'Aurore fait le trottoir,
De voir sortir toutes les Grues
Du violon, ou de leur boudoir ...

Chanson pitoyable et gaillarde:
Chiffons fanés papillotants,
Fausse note rauque et criarde
Et petits traits crus, turlutants:

Velours ratissant la chaussée;
Grande-duchesse mal chaussée,
Cocotte qui court becqueter
Et qui dit bonjour pour chanter ...

J'aime les voir, tout plein légères,
Et, comme en façon de prières,
Entrer dire — Bonjour, gros chien —
Au *merlan*, puis au pharmacien.

J'aime les voir, chauves, déteintes,
Vierges de seize à soixante ans,
Rossignoler pas mal d'absinthes,
Perruches de tout leur printemps;

Et puis *payer le mannezingue*,
Au *Polyte* qui sert d'Arthur,
Bon jeune homme né *brandezingue*,
Dos-bleu sous la blouse d'azur.

— C'est au boulevard excentrique,
Au — *BON RETOUR DU CHAMP DU NORD* —
Là: toujours vert le jus de trique,
Rose le nez des Croque-mort ...

Idyll Nipped in the Bud

April.

It's very parisian in the streets
When Aurora walks her beat,
To see all the Strumpets tootle
From the cooler or their hotel ...

Pitiable, ribald sing-song:
Frippery, faded but glittery,
Raucous screeching, each note wrong,
With little coarse flashes of wittery:

Velvet scuffing pavement and gutters;
Grand duchess down at heel,
Dolly bird who clucks and flutters
To give you a peck as her *spiel* ...

I like to see them, oh so flighty,
And, as if to give your arm a twist,
Come in with — Hiya, matey —
To the barber's, or the chemist.

I like to see them, balding, jaded,
Virgins of sixteen to sixty,
Parakeets in their heyday,
Knock back absinth (green ginger whisky?),

Before the bartender gets paid,
The swine who serves as Casanova,
Such a nice young man betrayed
By drink, pimp with an apron over.

— On the way-out boulevard,
At the — *SAFE RETURN FROM NORTHERN PARTS* —
It's: six of one and put in boots,
Red-raw the noses of Death-mutes ...

203

Moitié panaches, moitié cire,
Nez croqués vifs au demeurant,
Et gais comme un enterrement ...
— Toujours le petit *mort* pour rire! —

Le voyou siffle — vilain merle —
Et le poète de charnier
Dans ce fumier cherche la perle,
Avec le peintre chiffonnier.

Tous les deux fouillant la pâture
De leur art ... à coups de grouins;
Sûrs toujours de trouver l'ordure.
— C'est le fonds qui manque le moins.

C'est toujours un fond chaud qui fume,
Et, par le soleil, lardé d'or ...
Le rapin nomme ça: bitume;
Et le marchand de lyre: accord.

— Ajoutez une pipe en terre
Dont la spirale fait les cieux ...
Allez: je plains votre misère,
Vous qui trouvez qu'on trouve mieux!

C'est le *Persil* des gueux sans poses,
Et des riches sans un radis ...
— Mais ce n'est pas pour vous, ces choses,
Ô provinciaux de Paris! ...

Ni pour vous, essayeurs de sauces,
Pour qui l'azur est un ragoût!
Grands empâteurs d'emplâtres fausses,
Ne fesant rien, fesant partout!

— Rembranesque! Raphaélique!
— Manet et Courbet au milieu —
... Ils donnent des noms de fabrique
À la pochade du bon Dieu!

These Galimards after a line,
And Ducornets born-with-no-arms,
As a one-off, are willing to sign
Any old thing ... without any qualms.

God still keeps the chap who's gleaning
On the sunlit patch of the arcade,
From sniffing cassock: meaning —
The old black-stockinged maid!

... You thaw out, nocturnal creature,
And breaking loose with vigour,
Want, though blind, with dead-pan features,
To be the only comic figure.

Slippers: tatty, and hat: grotesque,
Are going beyond recall;
You apply yourself like a fresco
Irradiant with your back to the wall.

Beneath your skin there really glows
A flame divine — which goes to show
You've something smacking of a soul ...
Something — but *I* don't want to know.

The Muse, off-colour, stretches ...
The bailiff appears to reprieve ...
You try to smile at your own twitches,
Self-pity is your do-believe.

Fly, ladybirds and damselflies! ...
The drifter also flies a span
In fancy ... Not everything can rise ...
And everyone *flies* as he can.

— A huge gallows-bird, gloomy, rum,
Was aroused — Mine not to wonder why —
And, like me, starting to come ...
Besides, having an artist's eye,

Il reluquait surtout la tête
Et moi je reluquais le pié.
— Jaloux ... pourquoi? c'eût été bête,
Ayant chacun notre moitié. —

Ma béatitude nagée
Jamais, jamais n'avait bravé
Sa silhouette ravagée
Plantée au milieu du pavé ...

— Mais il fut un Dieu pour ce drille:
Au soleil loupant comme ça,
Dessinant des yeux une fille ...
— Un omnibus vert l'écrasa.

He ogled above all her head,
Whereas I, I ogled her foot.
— Jealous ... what's the point? When all's said,
His foot was in the other boot. —

My perfect bliss, in a sweat,
Never had it had the nerve
To beard her ravaged silhouette
Stuck in the middle of her reserve ...

— But there was a God for this guy:
Sauntering in moonlight like that,
Outlining a *bird* with his eye ...
— A green omnibus squashed him flat.

Le Convoi du Pauvre

Paris, le 30 avril 1873,
Rue Notre-Dame-de-Lorette.

Ça monte et c'est lourd — Allons, Hue!
— Frères de renfort, votre main? ...
C'est trop! ... et je fais le gamin;
C'est mon Calvaire cette rue!

Depuis Notre-Dame-Lorette ...
— Allons! *la Cayenne* est au bout,
Frère! du cœur! encor un coup! ...
— Mais mon âme est dans la charrette:

Corbillard dur à fendre l'âme.
Vers en bas l'attire un aimant;
Et du piteux enterrement
Rit la Lorette notre dame ...

C'est bien ça — Splendeur et misère! —
Sous le voile en trous a brillé
Un bout du tréteau funéraire;
Cadre d'or riche ... et pas payé.

La pente est âpre, tout de même,
Et les stations sont des *fours*,
Au tableau remontant le cours
De l'Élysée à la Bohème ...

— Oui, camarade, il faut qu'on sue
Après son harnais et son art! ...
Après les ailes: le brancard!
Vivre notre métier — ça tue ...

The Pauper's Funeral Procession

Paris, 30th April 1873,
Rue Notre-Dame-de-Lorette.

It's uphill and this is heavy — Gee up!
— Won't somebody lend me a hand? ...
That's too many! ... I'm a cheeky pup;
This street is my Calvary! And

Notre-Dame-Lorette was just the start ...
— The Potter's Field is up above,
Show some spirit, pal! one more shove! ...
— *My* spirit, though, is in the cart:

A hearse so hard it breaks my heart.
A lodestone draws it down below;
She laughs at the piteous burial show,
Does Lady la Lorette, the tart! ...

That's right — Misery and splendour! —
Beneath the holey veil's appeared
A glint of the funerary bier;
A rich gilt frame ... and not paid for.

At any rate, the slope's quite sheer,
And each station is a let-down
As the painting nears the crown ...
The route: Elysium to Bohemia ...

— Yes, you'll have to sweat, no doubt,
In your harness and for your art! ...
For wings: before you're carried out!
To live one's calling is the killing part ...

Tués l'idéal et le râble!
Hue! ... Et le cœur dans le talon!

. . . .

— Salut au convoi misérable
Du peintre écrémé du Salon!

— Parmi les martyrs ça te range;
C'est prononcé comme l'arrêt
De Rafaël, peintre au nom d'ange,
Par le Peintre au nom de ... courbet!

...als shaken, gone!
...o need to be relayed!
. . . .
...ree cheers for the wretched cavalcade
Of the painter creamed from *the Salon*!

— Cut, you're ranked as martyr: a claim
Pronounced according to the book
Of Raphaël, with the angel's name,
By Courbet, alias ... bill hook!

Dejéuner de Soleil

Bois de Boulogne, 1er mai.

Au Bois, les lauriers sont coupés,
Mais le *Persil* verdit encore;
Au *Serpolet*, petits coupés
Vertueux vont lever l'Aurore ...

L'Aurore brossant sa palette:
Kh'ol, carmin et poudre de riz;
Pour faire dire — la coquette —
Qu'on fait bien les ciels à Paris.

Par ce petit-lever de Mai,
Le Bois se croit à la campagne:
Et, fraîchement trait, le champagne
Semble de la mousse de lait.

Là, j'ai vu les *Chère Madame*
S'encanailler avec le frais ...
Malgré tout prendre un vrai bain d'âme!
— Vous vous engommerez après. —

... La voix à la note expansive:
— Vous comprenez; voici mon truc:
Je vends mes Memphis, et j'arrive ...
— Cent louis! ... — Eh, Eh! Bibi ... — Mon duc? ...

On presse de petites mains:
— Tiens ... assez pur cet attelage. —
Même les cochers, au dressage,
Redeviennent simples humains.

— Encor toi! vieille *Belle-Impure!*
Toujours, les pieds au plat, tu sors,
Dans ce déjeuner de nature,
Fondre un souper à huit ressorts ... —

214

A Flash of Pan
OR
The Breakfast Quickie

Bois de Boulogne, May 1st.

In the *Bois*, the laurels are trim,
But *Lady's Smock* bestrews the lawn;
In the *Wild Thyme* one-horse prim
Broughams are out to arouse Dawn ...

Dawn brushing in her palette:
Rouge, talc, kohl of the houris;
To let it be known — the coquette —
That they paint skies well in Paris.

With this petty-levee of May
The *Bois* thinks it's in the country:
And, freshly milked, the champagne
Seems to be milk-froth, all foamy.

There I've seen the *genteel fauna*
Slumming it with the *cool* of the day ...
Yet having a real soul-sauna!
— Wear your war-paint *after* the fray. —

... The voice in an effusive burst:
— You understand, as I've no king's
Ransom, I'll sell my Memphis first ...
— A hundred louis! ... — You're joking! ...

— My hansom? ... Tiny hands are squeezed:
— Hey ... this pairing-up's quite pure. — Even
Coachmen, at the breaking-in, are eased
Into simple human beings again.

Voici l'école buissonnière:
Quelques maris jaunes de teint,
Et qui *rentrent dans la carrière*
D'assez bonne heure ... le matin.

Le lapin inquiet s'arrête,
Un sergent-de-ville s'assied,
Le sportsman promène sa bête,
Et le rêveur la sienne — à pied. —

Arthur même a presque une tête,
Son faux-col s'ouvre matinal ...
Peut-être se sent-il poète,
Tout comme *Byron* — son cheval.

Diane au petit galop de chasse
Fait galoper les papillons
Et caracoler sur sa trace,
Son Tigre et les vieux beaux Lions.

Naseaux fumants, grand œil en flamme,
Crins d'étalon: cheval et femme
Saillent de l'avant! ...
                              — Peu poli.
— Pardon: *maritime* ... et joli.

Veder Napoli Poi Mori

See Naples and ... — Very nice, thanks, I'm just back.
                                              — Home
Of true-blue Englishmen, slapped on a blue-rinse ground!
Artists of any style forget in indigo
That ultra-marine *Forget-me-not*: the customs hound.

— O Corinne! ... there they are with my trunk, inveighing ...
Lasciate speranza, my cheroots are inside!
— O Mignon! ... they've brought my dirty linen from its hide
To rinse it in the blue of everlasting Spring!

They ask if I've *a hand* ... so I go and shake theirs!
The picture of my Sweetheart, with *morbidezza*,
Passes from hand to hand: the sanitary inspector
Sounds it, and smiles at me ... seeing it hasn't grown hairs!

I come here to extol their illustrious duds,
And they extort: I feel a rag of the first water!
Plucking out my collars, one offers me his daughter ...
Plucking out my fond illusion's collar and studs!

Naples! Squanderer of Lords Dough and Lolly-bones,
            Rich with soft bellies in the sun!
Punchinello-Gods, flea-bitten Kings on their thrones,
Clyster-piping the sky that yawns their sleep well-done! ...

Fleshpots! Soles of feet in rows! Great ... string of onions!
You whose sole adornment is a sack, or bunions!
Are still worthy — old Phœbus warms up every son! —
Of the songs of Musset, or the scorn of Byron! ...

— Boat-song mutineers, with Torsos like mandolines!
You whose métier's to be seen, not as wastrels
But gilded by sunbeams and love ... to flare your nostrils,
Poets of the open air! Beloved kith and kin!

219

Dolce Farniente! ... — Non! c'est mon sac! ... il nage
Parmi ces asticots, comme un chien crevé;
Et ma malle est hantée aussi ... comme un fromage!
Inerte, ô Galilée! et ... *è pur si muove* ...

— Ne ruolze plus ça, toi, grand Astre stupide!
Tas de pâles voyous grouillant à se nourrir;
Ce n'est plus le lézard, c'est la sangsue à vide ...
— Dernier *lazzarone* à moi la bon Dormir!

Napoli. —Dogana del porto.

Dolce Farniente! ... — No, that's my bag! ... floating
Among those maggots, like a dead dog, dead *and* rotting;
And my trunk's crawling too ... like cheese that's on its way!
Inert, O Galileo! and ... *è pur si muove* ...

— You great clot of a star! stop ruolzing those creeps,
That pile of pale yobbos wriggling to stuff their guts;
They're not the basking lizard, they're the leech that sucks ...
— As last *lazzarone* I want my Beauty sleeps!

Napoli. — Dogana del porto.

Vésuves et Cie

Pompeïa-station — Vésuve, est-ce encor toi?
Toi qui fis mon bonheur, tout petit, en Bretagne,
— Du bon temps où la foi transportait la montagne —
Sur un bel abat-jour, chez une tante à moi:

Tu te détachais noir, sur un fond transparent,
Et la lampe grillait les feux de ton cratère.
C'était le confesseur, dit-on, de ma grand'mère
Qui t'avait rapporté de Rome tout flambant ...

Plus grand, je te revis à l'Opéra-Comique.
— Rôle jadis créé par toi: *Le Dernier Jour*
De Pompeï. — Ton feu s'en allait en musique,
On te soufflait ton rôle, et ... tu ne fis qu'un four.

— Nous nous sommes revus: devant-de-cheminée,
À Marseille, en congé, sans musique, et sans feu:
Bleu sur fond rose, avec ta Méditerranée
Te renvoyant pendu, rose sur un champ bleu.

— Souvent tu vins à moi la première, ô Montagne!
Je te rends ta visite, exprès, à la campagne.
Le Vrai vésuve est toi, puisqu'on m'a *fait* cent francs!
. . . .

Mais les autres petits étaient plus ressemblants.

Pompeï, aprile.

Vesuvius & Co.

Pompeïa-halt — Vesuvius ... what, you again?
You who were my childhood joy, back in Brittany,
— In the good old days when faith could move the mountain —
On a lovely lampshade belonging to my auntie:

You stood out black on a background I could see through,
And the lamp would ignite the fires of your crater.
It was, as I've heard tell, my grandma's confessor
Who, all aglow, brought you home from Rome, *brand*-new ...

Older, at the *Opéra Comique*: — I saw you there
In the part you had once created: *The Last Day
Of Pompeï*. — In music your ardour died away,
You were prompted — primed — and ... fizzled out in hot air.

Then, on holiday in Marseilles: you were revealed
To me once more, without music or flames: a fire-screen,
Blue on a pink ground, with your Mediterranean
Reflecting you upended, pink on a blue field.

— Often, Mountain, you've been the first to visit me!
Now I'm paying you a call, on a country hike.
You're the Real vesuvius — I've been stung for 50p.!
. . . .
But the other little ones looked much more alike.

Pompeï, April.

Soneto a Napoli

ALL'SOLE, ALL'LUNA
ALL'SABATO, ALL'CANONICO
E TUTTI QUANTI

— CON PULCINELLA —

Il n'est pas de Samedi
Qui n'ait soleil à midi;
Femme ou fille soleillant,
Qui n'ait midi sans amant! ...

Lune, Bouc, Curé cafard
Qui n'ait tricorne cornard!
— Corne au front et corne au seuil
Préserve du mauvais œil. —

... *L'Ombilic du jour* filant
Son macaroni brûlant,
Avec la tarentela:

Lucia, Maz'Aniello,
Santa-Pia, Diavolo,
— CON PULCINELLA. —

Mergelina — Venerdi, aprile 15.

224

Soneto a Napoli

ALL'SOLE, ALL'LUNA
ALL'SABATO, ALL'CANONICO
E TUTTI QUANTI

— CON PULCINELLA —

There's not a single Saturday
That hasn't sun at midday;
Signorina sunning who hasn't
Noon without a gallant ..

Moon, Goat, humbug *Curé*
That isn't horned or horny!
— Horn on the forehead, horn in the doorway
Keeps the evil eye at bay. —

... *Day's Umbilicus* spinning
Out its macaroni ... burning ...
With the tarentela:

Lucia, Maz'Aniello,
Santa Pia, Diavolo,
— CON PULCINELLA. —

Mergelina —Venerdi, aprile 15.

225

À l'Etna

Sicelides Musæ, paulo majora canamus.
— VIRGILE.

Etna — j'ai monté le Vésuve ...
Le Vésuve a beaucoup baissé:
J'étais plus chaud que son effluve,
Plus que sa crête hérissé ...

— Toi que l'on compare à la femme ...
— Pourquoi? — Pour ton âge? ou ton âme
De caillou cuit? ... — Ça fait rêver ...
— Et tu t'en fais rire à crever! —

— Tu ris jaune et tousses: sans doute,
Crachant un vieil amour malsain;
La lave coule sous la croûte
De ton vieux cancer au sein.

— Couchons ensemble, Camarade!
Là — mon flanc sur ton flanc malade:
Nous sommes frères, par Vénus,
Volcan! ...
                    Un peu moins ... un peu plus ...

Palerme. — Août.

226

To Mount Etna

Sicelides Musæ, paulo majora canamus.
— VIRGIL.

Etna — I've been up Vesuvius ...
Vesuvius has gone down a lot:
I was hotter than its effluvium,
Pricklier than its arête..

You've been compared to woman ... — Why?
— Is it your age? or your hard heart
Baked to stone? ... — Makes you think ... — And die
Laughing, splitting your sides apart! —

— Your laugh is sickly and you cough:
You'll be spitting out a jaundiced love;
Lava's flowing under the crust
Of your old cancer of the breast.

— Let's lie together, Vulcan, us
Two! Like this — my side against your
Feverish side: I swear, by Venus,
We're brothers! ...
     A little less ... or more ...

Palermo. — August.

227

Le Fils de Lamartine et de Graziella

C'est ainsi que j'expiai par ces larmes écrites la dureté et l'ingratitude de mon cœur de dix-huit ans. Je ne puis jamais relire ces vers sans adorer cette fraîche image que rouleront éternellement pour moi les vagues transparentes et plaintives du golfe de Naples ... et sans me haïr moi-même; mais les âmes pardonnent là-haut. La sienne m'a pardonné. Pardonnez-moi aussi, vous!!! J'ai pleuré.

LAMARTINE, *Graziella.*
(1fr. 25c. le vol.)

À l'île de Procide, où la mer de Sorrente
Scande un flot hexamètre à la fleur d'oranger,
Un Naturel se fait une petite rente
      En *Graziellant* l'Étranger ...

L'Étrangère surtout, confite en Lamartine,
Qui paye pour fluer, vers à vers, sur les lieux ...
— Du *Cygne-de-Saint-Point* l'Homme a si bien la mine,
Qu'on croirait qu'il va rendre un vers ... harmonieux.

C'est un peintre inspiré qui lui trouva sa balle,
Sa balle de profil: — Oh mais! dit-il, voilà!
Je te baptise, au nom de la couleur locale:
— LE FILS DE LAMARTINE ET DE GRAZIELLA! —

Vrai portrait du portrait du Rafaël fort triste*, ...
Fort triste, pressentant qu'il serait décollé
De sa toile, pour vivre en la peau du *Harpiste*
Ainsi que de son fils, rafaël raffalé.

---

*Lamartine avoue quelque part qu'un seul portrait lui ressemblait alors: celui de Raphaël peint par lui-même.

Son of Lamartine and Graziella

> *This is how I atoned with these written tears for the harshness and ingratitude of my heart at the age of eighteen. I can never re-read these lines without adoring the fresh image which the transparent and plaintive waves of the gulf of Naples will unroll eternally before me ... and without despising myself; but souls in heaven forgive. Hers has forgiven me. You must forgive me too!!! I have wept.*
>
> LAMARTINE, Graziella.
> (12fr. 50c. a copy)

On Procida Island, where the Sorrento Sea
Scans hexameter waves scented orange blossom,
A Child of Nature rakes in a little income
    By *Grazielling* the Sightseer ...

Especially the Female, quite steeped in Lamartine,
Who'll pay to gush, line by line, over every scene ...
— Our Man looks so like *The-Swan-of-Saint-Point* (hem),
That they think he'll come out with some harmonious gem.

The artist was inspired who gave him a head-start,
His head in profile: Oh! said he, you do look the part!
I baptise you, in the name of local colour:
— SON OF LAMARTINE AND GRAZIELLA! —

The image of Rafaël's self-portrait, the saddest*, ...
Choked at the foreboding that he might come unstuck
From his canvas to live in the skin of *The Harpist*
And his son's, rafaël on the rocks, down on his luck.

---

* Lamartine owns somewhere that there was just one painting that looked like him at the time: Raphaël's self-portrait.

229

— Raphaël-Lamartine et fils! — Ô Fornarine-
Graziella! Vos noms font de petits profits;
L'écho dit pour deux sous: *Le Fils de Lamartine!*
Si Lamartine eût pu jamais avoir un fils!

— Et toi, Graziella ... Toi, Lesbienne Vierge!
Nom d'amour, que, sopran' il a tant déchanté! ...
Nom de joie! ... et qu'il a pleuré — Jaune cierge —
Tu n'étais vierge que de sa virginité!

— Dis: moins éoliens étaient, ô Grazielle,
Tes Mâles d'Ischia? ... que ce pieux Jocelyn
Qui tenait, à côté, la lyre et la chandelle! ...
Et, de loin, t'enterrait en chants de sacristain ...

Ces souvenirs sont loin ... — Dors, va! Dors sous les pierres
        Que voit, n'importe où, l'étranger,
Où fait paître ton Fils des familles entières
— Citron prématuré de ta Fleur d'Oranger —

Dors — l'Oranger fleurit encor ... encor se fane;
Et la rosée et le soleil ont eu ses fleurs ...
Le Poète-apothicaire en a fait sa tisane:
        Remède à vers! remède à pleurs!

— Dors — L'Oranger fleurit encor ... et la mémoire
Des jeunes d'autrefois dont l'ombre est encor là,
Qui ne t'ont pas pêchée au fond d'une écritoire ...
Et n'en pêchaient que mieux! — dis, ô *picciola!*

— Mère de l'Antechrist de Lamartine-Père,
Aurore qui mourus sous un coup d'éteignoir,
Ton Orphelin, posthume et de père et de mère,
Allait — quand tu naquis — déjà comme un vieux Soir.

Graziella! — Conception trois fois immaculée ...
D'un platonique amour, Messie et Souvenir,
Ce Fils avait vingt ans quand, Mère inoculée,
Tu mourus à seize ans! ... C'est bien tôt pour nourrir!

— *Raphaël-Lamartine & Son!* — O Fornarine-
Graziella! Your names make a little on the side;
The echo says, for a fee: *Son of Lamartine!*
Thinking he could sire one, you're taken for a ride!

— As for you, Graziella ... Thou Lesbian Vestal!
He pitched you so high ... and, with the voice of castrati,
Would sing your pet-name low ... and weep — Yellow candle —
You were only virgin with his virginity!

— Well, were they less æolian, your Males from Ischia,
Graziella? ... than that sanctimonious Jocelyn
Who kept, at the ready, his candle and his lyre! ...
And buried you, from afar, to the strains of compline ...

These memories are distant ... — Sleep now, beneath the maze
Of stones the tourist sees in any direction,
And this is where your Son has whole families graze
— Your Orange Blossom bears a premature Lemon —

Sleep — the Orange Tree blooms return in profusion ...
And then fade; dew and sunlight have had its flowers ...
The Apothecary-Poet has made an infusion
Out of them, as a cure for worms! or verse! or tears!

— Sleep on — The Orange flowers again ... and memories stir
In those who were young once and whose shadows still are,
Who haven't fished you out from an old escritoire ...
And yet, o *picciola!* have fished all the better!

— Mother of the Antechrist of Lamartine Senior,
Aurora who died when a snuffer doused your light,
Your Orphan, posthumous to father and to mother,
Was turning — when you were born — into a hoary Night.

— Thrice immaculate Conception — Graziella!
Messiah and Memorial of platonic love,
This Son was twenty when, inoculated Mother,
You died at sixteen! ... That's rather young to give suck!

231

— Pour toi: c'est ta seule œuvre mâle, ô Lamartine,
Saint-Joseph de la Muse, avec elle couché,
Et l'aidant à vêler ... par la grâce divine:
Ton fils avant la lettre est conçu sans péché! ...

— LUI se souvient très peu de ces scènes passées ...
Mais il *laisse le vent et le flot murmurer,*
Et l'Étranger, plongeant dans ses tristes pensées ...
  En tirer un franc — pour pleurer!

Et, tout bas, il vous dit, de murmure en murmures:
Que sa fille ressemble à L'AUTRE ... et qu'elle est là,
Qu'on peut pleurer, à l'heure, avec des rimes pures,
Et ... — *pour cent sous, Signor* — nommer Graziella!

Isola di Capri. — Gennaio.

— O Lamartine, he's your only male creation;
You're Saint-Joseph of the Muse, sleeping at her inn,
And helping her to calve ... by divine mediation:
Your son *avant la lettre* is conceived without sin! ...

— Of such past scenes HE has little recollection ...
And yet he *lets the wind and the waves murmur by*,
And the Sightseer, who'll be plunged in sad reflection ...
      Shell out ten francs — so he can cry!

And, in a whisper, says, to lapping from the shore,
That his daughter looks like THE GIRL ... and she is here,
So folk can weep, *right now*, in flawless rhymes, *Signor*,
And ... — *for just ten francs more* — call her Graziella!

Isola di Capri. — Gennaio.

233

Libertà*

À LA CELLULE IV BIS
(PRISON ROYALE DE GÊNES)

Lasciate ogni ...
— DANTE.

Ô belle hospitalière
Qui ne me connais pas,
Vierge publique et fière
Qui m'as ouvert les bras! ...
Rompant ma longue chaîne,
L'eunuque m'a jeté
Sur ton sein royal, Reine! ...
— Vanité, vanité! —

Comme la Vénus nue,
D'un bain de lait de chaux
Tu sors, blanche Inconnue,
Fille des noirs cachots
Où l'on pleure, d'usage ...
— Moi: jamais n'ai chanté
Que pour toi, dans ta cage,
Cage de la gaîté!

La misère parée
Est dans le grand égout;
Dépouillons la livrée
Et la chemise et tout!
Que tout mon baiser couvre
Ta franche nudité ...
Vraie ou fausse, se rouvre
Une virginité!

— Plus ce ciel louche et rose
Ni ce soleil d'enfer! ...

*Libertà. Ce mot se lit au fronton de la prison de Gênes (?)

234

Libertà*

IN CELL 4A
(OF THE ROYAL PRISON OF GENOA)

Lasciate ogni ...
— DANTE.

Sweet sister of mercy, to you
I am just one of the crowd;
O Virgin — public and proud —
You've opened your arms to me too! ...
Snapping my long chain clean
Off, your eunuch has pretty
Well tossed me onto your bosom, Queen! ...
— Vanity, vanity! —

You step like naked Venus
Out of a quicklime bath,
White Stranger in my path,
Girl from the black dungeons
Where weeping is the rule ...
— I've never sung a ditty
For anyone but you
In your cage of levity!

Bedizened misery
Is in the filthy gutter;
Let's strip her of her livery,
Her shift and other clutter!
Let my open kiss reclothe
Your candid nudity ...
Reopen what was closed:
True or false virginity!

— No more this pink shifty sky,
No more this hell-fire sun! ...

* Libertà. This word can be read on the pediment of the prison in Genoa (?)

235

— Ta paupière mi-close,
Tes cils, barreaux de fer!
Ta ceinture-dorée,
De fer! — Fidélité —
Et ta couche encastrée
Tombeau de volupté!

À nos cœurs plus d'alarmes:
Libres et bien à nous! ...
Sens planer les gendarmes,
Pigeons du rendez-vous;
Et Cupidon-Cerbère
À qui la sûreté
De nos amours est chère ...
Quatre murs! — Liberté!

Ho! l'Espérance folle
— Ce crampon — est au clou.
L'existence qui colle
Est collée à l'écrou.
Le souvenir qui hante
À l'huys est resté;
L'huys n'a pas de fente ...
— Oh le carcan ôté! —

Laissons venir la Muse,
Elle osera chanter;
Et, si le jeu t'amuse,
Je veux te la prêter ...
Ton petit lit de sangle,
Pour nous a rajouté
Les *trois bouts du triangle:*
Triple amour! — Trinité!

Plus d'huissiers aux mains sales!
Ni mains de chers amis!
Ni menottes banales! ...
— Mon nom est *Quatre-Bis.*—
Hors la terrestre croûte,
Désert mal habité,

— With eyelids ajar, each eye-
Lash is a bar of iron!
Your golden girdle is iron
Too! — Fidelity —
And the fitted bed you'll die on
The tomb of sensuality!

No more will our hearts pound:
We're free and on our own! ...
Sense *pigs* hang-gliding round
— Town pigeons — as chaperones;
And Cupid-Cerberus is here,
To whom the surety
Of our love affair is dear ...
Four walls! — Liberty!

Look! demented Hope, this
Clinging vine, can't have bail.
Strait-jacketed existence is
Confined, on tenter-hooks, in gaol.
Haunting memory links
Are still captivity;
The sally-post has no chinks ...
— No more close custody! —

Let's let the Muse bestir
Herself, and she'll dare to sing;
I'd like to lend you her
If you'll chance disporting ...
Your little trestle bed
Has made three company,
The triangle x y z:
Three-sided love! — Trinity!

No more bailiff's dirty hands!
No hands of shipmates o' mine!
No banal handcuffs! — They're banned!
— My name is Four A: a sign! —
Off earth's crust, a haven,
A desert far from the city,

Loin des mortels je goûte
Un peu d'éternité.

— Prison, sûre conquête
Où le poète est roi!
Et boudoir plus qu'honnête
Où le sage est chez soi;
Cruche, au moins ingénue,
Puits de la vérité!
Vide, quand on l'a bue ...
— Vase de pureté! —

— Seule est ta solitude,
Et béats tes ennuis
Sans pose et sans étude ...
Plus de jours, plus de nuits!
C'est tout le temps dimanche,
Et le far-niente
Dort pour moi sur la planche
De l'idéalité ...

... Jusqu'au jour de misère
Où, condamné, je sors
Seul, ramer ma galère ...
Là, n'importe où, ... dehors,
Laissant emprisonnée
À perpétuité
Cette fleur cloisonnée,
Qui fut ma liberté ...

— Va: reprends, froide et dure,
Pour le captif oison,
Ton masque, ta figure
De porte de prison ...
Que d'autres, basse race
Dont le dos est voûté,
Pour eux te trouvent basse,
Altière déité!

Cellule *4 bis*. — Genova-la-Superba.

Far from mortals I savour
A bit of eternity.

— Prison, that sound conquest
Where the poet is king!
And boudoir where the wise man's breast
Is bared — an honest fling;
Pitcher, artless, say, or *nunc*
Est ... A well of verity!
Empty, when it's been drunk ...
— A ewer of purity! —

— Alone in your solitude,
And blissful in your plights,
No adopting of attitudes ...
No more days, no more nights!
Each day's the day of the Lord,
And for me otiosity
Dozes off on a sail-board
Of ideality ...

... Until the unhappy day
When, sentenced, I emerge
Alone, to row my galley away ...
Somewhere, ... to any verge,
Leaving in the prison tower
In perpetuity
That septated flower,
Which was my liberty ...

— Now: resume, hard, cold, raw,
For the silly captive goose,
Your mask, the face you wore
To fit the hangman's noose ...
So others, the hard-done-to crew,
Backs bent and rickety,
May find you low-down too,
You high and mighty deity!

Cell 4A. — Genova-la-Superba.

Hidalgo!

Ils sont fiers ceux-là! ... comme poux sur la gale!
C'est à la don-juan qu'ils vous *font* votre malle.
Ils ne sentent pas bon, mais ils fleurent le preux:
Valeureux vauriens, crétins chevalereux!
Prenant sans demander — toujours suant la race, —
Et demandant un sol, — mais toujours pleins de grâce ...

Là, j'ai fait le croquis d'un mendiant à cheval:
— Le Cid ... un cid par un *été* de carnaval:

— Je cheminais — à pied — traînant une compagne;
Le soleil craquelait la route en blanc-d'Espagne;
Et *le cid* fut sur nous en un temps de galop ...
Là, me pressant entre le mur et le garrot:
— Ah! seigneur *Cavalier*, d'honneur! sur ma parole!
Je mendie à genoux: un oignon ... une obole? ... —
(Et son cheval paissait mon col.) — Pauvre animal,
Il vous aime déjà! Ne prenez pas à mal ...
— Au large! — Oh! mais: au moins votre bout de cigare? ...
La Vierge vous le rende. — Allons: au large! ou: gare! ...
(Son pied nu prenait ma poche en étrier.)
— Pitié pour un infirme, ô seigneur-cavalier ...
— Tiens donc un sou ... — Señor, que jamais je n'oublie
Votre Grâce! Pardon, je vous ai retardé ...
Señora: Merci, toi! pour être si jolie ...
Ma Jolie, et: Merci pour m'avoir regardé!

(Cosas de España.)

240

Hidalgo!

They're as proud as they come! ... like *sucking lice* on mange!
They take you in, don-juan style, then itch for change.
They don't smell good, but they've an odour of gallantry:
Valorous numskulls, chivalrous ignorami!
Taking without a by-your-leave — they ooze breeding
And beg for a sou, — so silver-tongued your heart's bleeding ...

That's my beggar-on-horseback sketch — to the life, I swear:
— The Cid ... a fair-weather cid, fiesta in the air:

— I was travelling — on foot — a lady-friend in tow;
In cracks of Spanish chalk the sun criss-crossed the road;
And *el cid* was upon us at a galloping pace ...
When between wall and withers my body was braced:
— Ah! my lord *Caballero*, glory be, 'pon my soul!
I'm begging on my knees: an onion ... an obol ... —
(Now his steed was cropping my collar.) — Poor Neddy!
Don't be offended, he's fond of you already!
— Keep off! — Just your cigar butt, every little helps ...
The Virgin will repay you. — Look: clear off! or else! ...
(His bare foot was taking my pocket for a stirrup.)
— Pity a poor cripple, sir Knight, I'm so hard up ...
— Here's a sou then ... — Señor, may I never forget
Your Grace! Forgive me, I've detained you, I'm in your debt ...
Señora: Thanks to you for being so pretty ...
My Beauty, and: Thanks too for having looked at me!

(Cosas de España.)

Paria

Qu'ils se payent des républiques,
Hommes libres! — carcan au cou —
Qu'ils peuplent leurs nids domestiques! ...
— Moi je suis le maigre coucou.

— Moi, — cœur eunuque, dératé
De ce qui mouille et ce qui vibre ...
Que me chante leur Liberté,
À moi? toujours seul. Toujours libre.

— Ma Patrie ... elle est par le monde;
Et, puisque la planète est ronde,
Je ne crains pas d'en voir le bout ...
Ma patrie est où je la plante:
Terre ou mer, elle est sous la plante
De mes pieds — quand je suis debout.

— Quand je suis couché: ma patrie
C'est la couche seule et meurtrie
Où je vais forcer dans mes bras
Ma moitié, comme moi sans âme;
Et ma moitié: c'est une femme ...
Une femme que je n'ai pas.

— L'idéal à moi: c'est un songe
Creux; mon horizon — l'imprévu —
Et le mal du pays me ronge ...
Du pays que je n'ai pas vu.

Que les moutons suivent leur route,
De Carcassonne à Tombouctou ...
— Moi, ma route me suit. Sans doute
Elle me suivra n'importe où.

Pariah

Let them stand themselves republics,
Your free men! — their necks in a lasso —
Let them feather their domestic
Nests! ... — I am the starved cuckoo.

— I'm a eunuch soul, lacerate
From what wets dreams and would vibrate ...
What does their Freedom mean to me?
Who am always alone. Always free.

— My Country ... is where I'm bound;
And, because the planet is round,
I'm not afraid to see its ending ...
My country's wherever I'm at:
On land or sea, it's under the flat
Of my feet — when I am standing.

— When I am lying: my country
Is the lonely and bruised divan
Where into my arms I shall force
My better half, soulless like me;
And my better half is a woman ...
A woman I don't have, of course.

— My ideal is merely daydream;
My horizon — the unforeseen —
And homesickness gnaws at me ...
For the land I have yet to see.

Let the sheep follow their sheep-track
From Carcassonne to Timbucktoo ...
— My track follows me; it has the knack
Of always keeping me in view.

Mon pavillon sur moi frissonne,
Il a le ciel pour couronne:
C'est la brise dans mes cheveux ...
Et, dans n'importe quelle langue
Je puis subir une harangue;
Je puis me taire si je veux.

Ma pensée est un souffle aride:
C'est l'air. L'air est à moi partout.
Et ma parole est l'écho vide
Qui ne dit rien — et c'est tout.

Mon passé: c'est ce que j'oublie.
La seule chose qui me lie
C'est ma main dans mon autre main.
Mon souvenir — Rien — C'est ma trace.
Mon présent, c'est tout ce qui passe ...
Mon avenir — Demain ... demain ...

Je ne connais pas mon semblable;
Moi, je suis ce que je me fais.
— *Le Moi humain est haïssable* ...
— Je ne m'aime ni ne me hais.

— Allons! la vie est une fille
Qui m'a pris à son bon plaisir ...
Le mien, c'est: la mettre en guenille,
La prostituer sans désir.

— Des dieux? ... — Par hasard j'ai pu naître;
Peut-être en est-il — par hasard ...
Ceux-là, s'ils veulent me connaître,
Me trouveront bien quelque part.

— Où que je meure: ma patrie
S'ouvrira bien, sans qu'on l'en prie,
Assez grande pour mon linceul ...
Un linceul encor: pour que faire? ...
Puisque ma patrie est en terre
Mon os ira bien là tout seul ...

244

My Blue Peter's quivering still,
With the welkin for its crown:
That's the breeze through my hair ...
And, in any language anywhere,
A homily won't get me down;
I can shut myself up at will.

My thinking is a sirocco:
All wind. Dry as dust air is mine.
My word's the empty echo
That says nothing — which is fine.

Now, what I forget's my past.
The sole thing that forges a band
Is my hand in my other hand.
My memory — gone — is my wake.
My present's what doesn't last
Tomorrow ... that's still at stake.

I don't know my fellow creatures;
I am what I make myself.
— *The human Self is odious* ...
— I neither love nor hate myself.

— Ah well! life's nothing but a flirt
Who's having her way till she tire ...
I dress her in a ragged skirt,
Prostitute her without desire.

— The gods? ... — By a fluke I was spawned;
It could be there's gods — by pure chance ...
If they want to know me, they're warned:
I'll be leading them quite a dance.

— Wherever I die: my native heath
Will open up, no need to implore,
Wide enough for my winding sheet ...
A shroud indeed: what on earth for? ...
Since my country is in the ground
My bones will get there safe and sound ...

ARMOR

ARMOR

Paysage Mauvais

Sables de vieux os — Le flot râle
Des glas: crevant bruit sur bruit ...
— Palud pâle, où la lune avale
De gros vers, pour passer la nuit.

Calme de peste, où la fièvre
Cuit ... Le follet damné languit.
— Herbe puante où le lièvre
Est un sorcier poltron qui fuit ...

— La Lavandière blanche étale
Des trépassés le linge sale,
Au *soleil des loups* ... — Les crapauds,

Petits chantres mélancoliques
Empoisonnent de leurs coliques,
Les champignons, leurs escabeaux.

Marais de Guérande. — Avril.

Malevolent Landscape

Sands of old bones — The sea draws
Last gasps: its swell bursting, sound on sound ...
— To see the night through, the moon trawls
Pallid swamp, gulping fat worms down.

— Calm of the plague, kiln of fever ...
The damned will o' the wisp is languishing.
— Through fetid grass the lily-livered
Warlock of a hare is vanishing ...

— The white Washerwoman spreads
The dirty linen of the dead
Under *the wolves' sun* ... — Schools

Of toads, small, melancholy
Succentors, with their bags of colic,
Poison the mushrooms, their stools.

Guérande Marsh. — April.

Nature Morte

Des coucous l'*Angelus* funèbre
A fait sursauter, à ténèbre,
Le coucou, pendule du vieux,

Et le chat-huant, sentinelle,
Dans sa carcasse à la chandelle
Qui flamboie à travers ses yeux.

— Écoute se taire la chouette ...
— Un cri de bois: C'est *la brouette*
De la Mort, le long du chemin ...

Et, d'un vol joyeux, la corneille
Fait le tour du toit où l'on veille
Le défunt qui s'en va demain.

Bretagne. — Avril.

Still Life

The cuckoos' funereal *Angelus*
Has made the cuckoo in grandfather's
Clock dart out at tenebrae,

And the sentinel tawny owl
Jump out of its skin, with a candle
Blazing through each eye.

— Hear the screech owl forbear
To hoot ... A creak of wood somewhere
Along the road is *Death's wheelbarrow* ...

— See the crow, joy in flight, rake
The roof that harbours a wake
For the dead man who leaves tomorrow.

Brittany. — April.

Un Riche en Bretagne

O fortunatos nimium, sua si ...
— VIRGILE.

C'est le bon riche, c'est un vieux pauvre en Bretagne,
Oui, pouilleux de pavé sans eau pure et sans ciel!
— Lui, c'est un philosophe-errant dans la campagne;
Il aime son pain noir sec — pas beurré de fiel ...
S'il n'en a pas: bonsoir. — Il connaît une crèche
Où la vache lui prête un peu de paille fraîche,
Il s'endort, rêvassant planche-à-pain au milieu,
Et s'éveille au matin en bayant au Bon-Dieu.
— *Panem nostrum* ... — Sa faim a le goût d'espérance ...
Un *Benedicite* s'exhale de sa panse;
Il sait bien que pour lui l'œil d'en haut est ouvert
Dans ce coin d'où tomba la manne du désert
Et le pain de son sac ...
                Il va de ferme en ferme.
Et jamais à son pas la porte ne se ferme,
— Car sa venue est bien. — Il entre à la maison
Pour allumer sa pipe en soufflant un tison ...
Et s'assied. — Quand on a quelque chose, on lui donne;
Alors, il se secoue et rit, tousse et rognonne
Un *Pater* en hébreu. Puis, son bâton en main,
Il reprend sa tournée en disant: à demain.
Le gros chien de la cour en passant le caresse ...
— Avec ça, peut-on pas se passer de maîtresse? ...
Et, — qui sait, — dans les champs, un beau jour, la beauté
Peut s'amuser à faire aussi la charité ...

A Rich Man in Brittany

O fortunatos nimium, sua si ...
— VIRGIL.

He's rich, this Breton hobo, who is poor and old,
Yes, and homeless, unwashed, lousy, with not far to fall!
— He's a philosopher-errant of the open road,
Partial to dry black bread — not buttered with gall ...
If there is none: good-night. — He knows of a manger
Where the cow loans a little fresh straw to the stranger;
There he'll fall asleep, dream of feasting at the bread-board,
And wake up in the morning, agape at the Good Lord
— *Panem nostrum* ... — His hunger has the savour of hope ...
A belly *Benedicite* is given full scope;
Well he knows that the eye above is never shut,
In its twinkling there fell manna in the desert
And the bread in his pouch ...
                                    From farm to farm he goes.
At the sound of his step there are no doors that close,
— For his coming's propitious. — In he comes and,
Having lighted his pipe by blowing on a firebrand,
Sits down. — When there's food to spare folk are generous;
So he bestirs himself and laughs, coughs and chunners
A *pater* in Hebrew. Then, taking up his cane
With an: I'll be back — he's off on his rounds again.
The huge dog in the yard rubs up against his leg ...
— With nuzzling like that, do you really need your Meg? ...
And, — who knows, — in the fields, one fine day, an empress
May let her hair down too and distribute largesse ...

— Lui, n'est pas pauvre: il est *Un Pauvre*, — et s'en contente.
C'est un petit rentier, moins l'ennui de la rente.
Seul, il se chante vêpre en berçant son ennui ...
— Travailler — Pour que faire? — ... On travaille pour lui.
Point ne doit déroger, il perdrait la pratique;
Il doit garder intact son vieux blason mystique.
— Noblesse oblige. — Il est saint: à chaque foyer
Sa niche est là, tout près du grillon familier.
Bon messager boiteux, il a plus d'une histoire
À faire froid au dos, quand la nuit est bien noire ...
N'a-t-il pas vu, rôdeur, durant les clairs minuits
Dans la lande danser les *cornandons* maudits ...

— Il est simple ... peut-être. — Heureux ceux qui sont simples! ...
À la lune, n'a-t-il jamais cueilli des simples? ...
— Il est sorcier peut-être ... et, sur le mauvais seuil,
Pourrait, en s'en allant, jeter le mauvais œil ...
— Mais non: mieux vaut porter bonheur; dans les familles,
Proposer ou chercher des maris pour les filles.
Il est de noce alors, très humble desservant
De *la part du bon-dieu.* — Dieu doit être content:
Plein comme feu Noé, son Pauvre est ramassé
Le lendemain matin au revers d'un fossé.

Ah, s'il avait été senti du doux Virgile ...
Il eût été traduit par monsieur Delille,
Comme un *"trop fortuné s'il connût son bonheur ..."*

— Merci: ça le connaît, ce marmiteux seigneur!

Saint-Thégonnec.

254

— He isn't poor: he's *A Pauper*, — and is content;
He's of independent means but dependent.
Alone, to lull his tedium, he intones a hymn ...
— Work — Name one good reason why! ... People work for him.
He must not stoop to that, he would lose his knack;
His ancient mystic blazon must be kept intact.
— *Noblesse oblige*. — He's blessed: a household messenger
Of the gods, who limps to where homely crickets chirr —
To his own special niche. He's a fund of yarns
To send shivers down your spine, when the night is very dark ...
Prowling the moors, has he not spied on clear midnights
The tripping of accursèd *cornandon* sprites ...

— He is simple ... may be. — Blessèd are the simple! ...
And by moonlight has he never picked a simple? ...
— Perhaps he's a warlock, if not welcomed, who
Could cast the evil eye as he's bidding you adieu ...
— No: it's better to bring good luck; be exhorter
Of likely husbands for the marriageable daughter.
Then he's in on the rite, this very humble *priest*
Of God and *the poor man's portion*. — God must be pleased:
Half-seas over like old Noah, his Pauper is hitched
The following morning from the bottom of a ditch.

Now, if he had been conveyed by gentle Virgil ...
He might have been translated by Mister Delille,
As one "*too fortunate if he should know his hire ..*"

— Thanks: he knows what's what, this poverty-stricken squire!

Saint-Thégonnec.

Saint Tupetu de Tu-Pe-Tu

C'est au pays de Léon. — Est une petite chapelle à saint Tupetu. (En breton: *D'un côté ou de l'autre.*)

Une fois l'an, les croyants — fatalistes chrétiens — s'y rendent en pèlerinage, afin d'obtenir, par l'entremise du Saint, le dénoûment fatal de toute affaire nouée: la délivrance d'un malade tenace ou d'une vache pleine; ou, tout au moins, quelque signe de l'avenir: tel que c'est écrit là-haut. — *Puisque cela doit être, autant que cela soit de suite ... d'un côté ou de l'autre.* — *Tu-pe-tu.*

L'oracle fonctionne pendant la grand'messe: l'officiant fait faire, pour chacun, un tour à la *Roulette-de-chance*, grand cercle en bois fixé à la voûte et manœuvré par une longue corde que Tupetu tient lui-même dans sa main de granit. La roue, garnie de clochettes, tourne en carillonnant; son point d'arrêt présage l'arrêt du destin: — *D'un côté ou de l'autre.*

Et chacun s'en va comme il est venu, quitte à revenir l'an prochain ... *Tu-pe-tu* finit fatalement par avoir son effet.

Il est, dans la vieille Armorique,
Un saint — des saints le plus pointu —
Pointu comme un clocher gothique
Et comme son nom: TUPETU.

Son petit clocheton de pierre
Semble prêt à changer de bout ...
Il lui faut, pour tenir debout,
Beaucoup de foi ... beaucoup de lierre ...

Et, dans sa chapelle ouverte, entre
— Tête ou pieds — tout franc Breton
Pour lui tâter l'œuf dans le ventre,
L'œuf du destin: C'est oui? — c'est non?

— Plus fort que sainte Cunégonde
Ou Cucugnan de Quilbignon ...
Petit prophète au pauvre monde,
Saint de la veine ou du guignon,

Il tient sa *Roulette-de-chance*
Qu'il vous fait aller pour cinq sous;
Ça dit bien, mieux qu'une balance,
Si l'on est dessus ou dessous.

Saint One or T'other of One-Ort-Other

In Léon country: Is a small chapel dedicated to Saint Tupetu. (In Breton: *On the one hand or the other, whichever way the wind blows.*)

Once a year, believers — Christian fatalists — make a pilgrimage there to obtain, through the mediation of the Saint, the inevitable unravelling of every knotty circumstance: delivery from a tenacious illness or of a cow with calf; or, at the very least, some forecast of what the future has in store: as it is written on high. — *Since it must be to the extent that it will be ... one way or the other.* — *Tu-pe-tu.*

The oracle functions during high mass: the officiant sees to it that everyone has a turn of *the Roulette Wheel,* a large wooden ring fixed to the vault and worked by a long rope held by Tupetu in his granite hand. The wheel, trimmed with little bells, chimes as it turns; its point of rest presages the halting of destiny: — *On one side or the other.*

And everyone goes away as he has come, even if it means returning the following year ... *One-Ort-Other* ends, inevitably, by having an effect.

There is, in old Armorica,
A saint — the sharpest brother —
Pointed as a Gothic bell-tower
And as his name: ONE OR T'OTHER.

Though in stone his little belfry
'S about to swivel upside down ...
It needs, just to hold its own,
A lot of faith ... a lot of ivy ...

And, into his open chapel
— Head or feet first — true Bretons go
To palp the egg near her navel,
The egg of fate: Is it yes? — or no?

— Robuster than Saint Cunégonde
Or Cucugnan of Quilbignon ...
The poor man's prophet, the bond-
Saint of good luck or ill omen,

He holds onto his *Roulette Wheel*
He has you spin for a franc or two;
Better than scales, it can reveal
Whether things will turn out for you.

C'est la roulette sans pareille,
Et les grelots qui sont parmi
Vont, là-haut, chatouiller l'oreille
Du coquin de Sort endormi.

Sonnette de la Providence,
Et serinette du Destin;
Carillon faux, mais argentin;
Grelottière de l'Espérance ...

Tu-pe-tu — D'un bord ou de l'autre!
Tu-pe-tu — Banco — Quitte-ou-tout!
Juge-de-paix sans patenôtre ...
TUPETU, saint valet d'atout!

Tu-pe-tu — Pas de milieu! ...
TUPETU, sorcier à musique,
Croupier du tourniquet mystique
Pour les macarons du Bon-Dieu! ...

Médecin héroïque, il pousse
Le mourant à sauter le pas:
Soit dans la vie à la rescousse ...
Soit, à pieds joints, en plein trépas:

— *Tu-pe-tu!* cheval couronné!
— *Tu-pe-tu!* qu'on saute ou qu'on butte!
— *Tu-pe-tu!* vieillard obstiné! ...
Au bout du fossé la culbute!

TUPETU, saint tout juste honnête,
Petit Janus chair et poisson!
Saint confesseur à double tête,
Saint confesseur à double fond! ...

— Pile-ou-face de la vertu,
Ambigu patron des pucelles
Qui viennent t'offrir des chandelles ...
Jésuite! tu dis: — *Tu-pe-tu!* ...

It's a roulette wheel without a peer,
With tintinnabula that leap
Up to the vault and tickle the ear
Of that rascal Fate who's fast asleep.

Luck's bird-organ that twitters;
Tinkler of Providence; carillon
— Out of tune but silver-toned;
Jingler of Hope, with the jitters ...

One-ort-other! — on or off the roster!
One-ort-other — Banco — Peaks or slumps!
Magistrate without a paternoster ...
ONE OR T'OTHER, holy knave of trumps!

One-ort-other — No in-between wiles! ...
ONE OR T'OTHER, musical wizard,
Croupier of the mystic turnstile
For the stewards of the Lord! ...

Heroic doctor for the dying man
Who takes the plunge at his dictates,
Either to cross the Rubicon ...
Or, feet bound, into death's straits:

— *One-ort-other!* broken-kneed *hoss*!
— *One-ort-other!* covered or shored-up!
— *One-ort-other!* stiff-necked old chap! ...
Finally certain to take a toss!

Saint ONE OR T'OTHER, thorough-paced,
Little Janus fish and fowl!
Holy confessor who's double-faced,
Holy confessor who's double-bowelled ! ...

— Heads or tails of that coin, virtue,
Patron of virgins — two-way split —
Who come to offer candles to you...
You say: — You can choose! ... — Jesuit!

La Rapsode Foraine
ET
Le Pardon de Sainte-Anne

La Palud, 27 Août, jour du Pardon.

Bénite est l'infertile plage
Où, comme la mer, tout est nud.
Sainte est la chapelle sauvage
De Sainte-Anne-de-la-Palud …

De la Bonne Femme Sainte Anne
Grand'tante du petit Jésus,
En bois pourri dans sa soutane
Riche … plus riche que Crésus!

Contre elle la petite Vierge,
Fuseau frêle, attend l'*Angelus*;
Au coin, Joseph tenant son cierge,
Niche, en saint qu'on ne fête plus …

. . . .

C'est le *Pardon*. — Liesse et mystères —
Déjà l'herbe rase a des poux …
— *Sainte Anne, Onguent des belles-mères!*
Consolation des époux! …

Des paroisses environnantes:
De Plougastel et Loc-Tudy,
Ils viennent tous planter leurs tentes,
Trois nuits, trois jours — jusqu'au lundi.

Trois jours, trois nuits, la palud grogne,
Selon l'antique rituel,
— Chœur séraphique et chant d'ivrogne —
Le CANTIQUE SPIRITUEL.

* * *

260

The Strolling Balladeer
The Pardon of Saint-Anne

La Palud, 27th August, day of the *Pardon*.

Blessed is the barren strand
Where, like the sea, all is bare.
Holy the chapel of Saint-Anne-
Of-the-Marsh with its wild air ...

Of Saint Anne whose heart's so good,
Grandmama to little Jesus;
Around her frame of rotted wood
A rich cope ... richer than Croesus!

By her the Virgin, distaff frail
And small, awaits the *Angelus*;
In a niche, holding his candle,
Joseph's ensconced, superfluous ...

. . . .

It's the *Pardon*. — Mysteries and gala —
Bald grass already crawls with lice ...
— *Saint Anne, Balm of mothers-in-law!*
And of husbands, Solace! ...

From the parishes round about:
From Plougastel and Loc-Tudy,
They come, all set on camping out,
Three nights, three days — till Monday.

Three days, three nights, the marshland grunts,
In a ritual custom prolongs,
— Seraphic choir and roaring drunks —
The *SPIRITUAL SONG OF SONGS*.

* * *

261

Mère taillée à coups de hache,
Tout cœur de chêne duret bon;
Sous l'or de ta robe se cache
L'âme en pièce d'un franc-Breton!

*

— Vieille verte à face usée
Comme la pierre du torrent,
Par des larmes d'amour creusée,
Séchée avec des pleurs de sang ...

*

— Toi dont la mamelle tarie
S'est refait, pour avoir porté
La Virginité de Marie,
Une mâle virginité!

*

— Servante-maîtresse altière,
Très-haute devant le Très-Haut;
Au pauvre monde, pas fière,
Dame pleine de comme-il-faut!

*

— Bâton des aveugles! Béquille
Des vieilles! Bras des nouveau-nés!
Mère de Madame ta fille!
Parente des abandonnés!

*

— Ô Fleur de la pucelle neuve!
Fruit de l'épouse au sein grossi!
Reposoir de la femme veuve ...
Et du veuf Dame-de-merci!

*

Mother hewn by an axe's blows,
Good and strong, true heart of oak;
There hides beneath your golden robe
A bona fide *Breton soul.*

*

— Hale old dame whose face is worn
Like a stone by the river's flood,
By tears of love it's lined and drawn,
Then dried with tears of blood ...

*

— You whose shrivelled breasts ran dry,
Gave suck once more because you bore
Mary's Virginity,
A virile virginity!

*

— Both servant and proud mistress,
Most high before the Most High;
Not proud to the poor and distressed,
Lady of utmost courtesy!

*

— White stick of the blind! Crutch for
The old! Arms for the newly born!
Mother of Our Lady your daughter!
Kinswoman of the forlorn!

*

— Of the burgeoning girl, the Flower!
Fruit of the wife with swelling breast!
Lady of comfort for the widower ...
For the widow, Haven of rest!

*

— Arche de Joachim! Aïeule!
Médaille de cuivre effacé!
Gui sacré! Trèfle-quatre-feuille!
Mont d'Horeb! Souche de Jessé!

*

— Ô toi qui recouvrais la cendre,
Qui filais comme on fait chez nous,
Quand le soir venait à descendre,
Tenant l'ENFANT sur tes genoux;

*

Toi qui fus là, seule, pour faire
Son maillot neuf à Bethléem,
Et là, pour coudre son suaire
Douloureux, à Jérusalem! ...

*

Des croix profondes sont tes rides,
Tes cheveux sont blancs comme fils ...
— Préserve des regards arides
Le berceau de nos petits-fils!

*

Fais venir et conserve en joie
Ceux à naître et ceux qui sont nés.
Et verse, sans que Dieu te voie,
L'eau de tes yeux sur les damnés!

*

Reprends dans leur chemise blanche
Les petits qui sont en langueur ...
Rappelle à l'éternel Dimanche
Les vieux qui traînent en longueur.

*

Ark of Joachim! Ancestress!
Medallion of well-worn copper!
Sacred mistletoe! Four-leaved clover!
Mount Horeb! Stem of Jesse!

*

— O you have banked up the gleeds,
You've spun as we still do today,
And held the BOYCHILD *on your knees*
When the dark of evening came;

*

You were there, alone, to make
His swaddling clothes in Bethlehem,
And there to sew for his dear sake
His dolorous shroud in Jerusalem! ...

*

Deep-scored crosses are your wrinkles,
Your hair is as white as thread ...
— Preserve our grandsons' cradles
From the arid stares we dread!

*

Grant life and joy to all men bred
And those about to be.
And, without God seeing, shed
Tears on those in purgatory!

*

Take to your breast in his white shift
The ill or sickly little one ...
To an eternal Sabbath lift
The old whose lives are dragging on.

*

265

— Dragon-gardien de la Vierge,
Garde la crèche sous ton œil.
Que, près de toi, Joseph-concierge
Garde la propreté du seuil!

*

Prends pitié de la fille-mère,
Du petit au bord du chemin ...
Si quelqu'un leur jette la pierre,
Que la pierre se change en pain!

*

— Dame bonne en mer et sur terre,
Montre-nous le ciel et le port,
Dans la tempête ou dans la guerre ...
Ô Fanal de la bonne mort!

*

Humble: à tes pieds n'as point d'étoile,
Humble ... et brave pour protéger!
Dans la nue apparaît ton voile,
Pâle auréole du danger.

*

— Aux perdus dont la vie est grise,
(— Sauf respect — perdus de boisson)
Montre le clocher de l'église
Et le chemin de la maison.

*

Prête ta douce et chaste flamme
Aux chrétiens qui sont ici ...
Ton remède de bonne femme
Pour les bêtes-à-corne aussi!

*

— *Dragon-guardian of the Virgin,*
Keep the crib under your watchful eye.
Near you, let Joseph-the-concierge
Keep the doorstep clean and tidy!

*

Take pity on the child in tatters,
And on his mother who's unwed ...
If someone throws a stone at them
Let the stone be changed to bread!

*

— *O Lady, kind on sea and shore,*
Show us the harbour and clear sky
In time of storm or time of war ...
Beacon for all those called to die!

*

Humble: you've no star at your feet,
Humble ... and a guardian angel!
In the clouds your veil appears,
Pale aureole of the danger.

*

— *For all lost souls, maudlin people,*
(— Saving you — they're often stoned)
Set their sights upon your steeple
Then point them down the road to home.

*

To all Christians gathered here
Lend your pure and gentle flame ...
Your old wives' panacea
To horned creatures that go lame!

*

267

Montre à nos femmes et servantes
L'ouvrage et la fécondité ...
— Le bonjour aux âmes parentes
Qui sont bien dans l'éternité!

     *

Nous mettrons un cordon de cire,
De cire-vierge jaune, autour
De ta chapelle; et ferons dire
Ta messe basse au point du jour.

     *

— Préserve notre cheminée
Des sorts et du monde-malin ...
À Pâques te sera donnée
Une quenouille avec du lin.

     *

Si nos corps sont puants sur terre,
Ta grâce est un bain de santé;
Répands sur nous, au cimetière,
Ta bonne odeur-de-sainteté.

     *

— À l'an prochain! — Voici ton cierge:
(C'est deux livres qu'il a coûté)
... Respects à Madame la Vierge,
Sans oublier la Trinité.

    * * *

... Et les fidèles, en chemise,
— Sainte Anne, ayez pitié de nous! —
Font trois fois le tour de l'église
En se traînant sur leurs genoux;

Teach our servant-girls and wives
Needlework and fecundity ...
— Kind regards to our relatives
Already in eternity!

*

At Easter you shall have a gift:
A distaff with a skein of flax.
We'll surround your chapel with
A braid of yellow virgin wax;

*

And we we shall say your low mass
— Or have it said — at break of day.
— Keep our homes from hocus-pocus,
From evil spells and sorcery ...

*

If our bodies stink on earth,
Your grace is a bath of purity;
Then in the graveyard please asperge
Us with your odour: sanctity.

*

— Here's to next year! — And in your honour
A candle: (two whole francs it cost me)
... Our respects to the Madonna,
Not forgetting the Trinity.

* * *

... And the faithful, in chemises,
— Saint Anne, have mercy on us! —
Drag themselves on bended knees
Three times round the church, no less:

Et boivent l'eau miraculeuse
Où les Job teigneux ont lavé
Leur nudité contagieuse ...
— *Allez: la Foi vous a sauvé!* —

C'est là que tiennent leurs cénacles
Les pauvres, frères de Jésus.
— Ce n'est pas la cour des miracles,
Les trous sont vrais: *Vide latus!*

Sont-ils pas divins sur leurs claies,
Qu'auréole un nimbe vermeil,
Ces propriétaires de plaies,
Rubis vivants sous le soleil! ...

En aboyant, un rachitique
Secoue un moignon désossé,
Coudoyant un épileptique
Qui travaille dans un fossé.

Là, ce tronc d'homme où croît l'ulcère,
Contre un tronc d'arbre où croît le gui;
Ici, c'est la fille et la mère
Dansant la danse de Saint-Guy.

Cet autre pare le cautère
De son petit enfant malsain:
— L'enfant se doit à son vieux père ...
— Et le chancre est un gagne-pain!

Là, c'est l'idiot de naissance,
Un *visité par Gabriel,*
Dans l'extase de l'innocence ...
— L'innocent est près du ciel! —

— Tiens, passant, regarde: tout passe ...
L'œil de l'idiot est resté,
Car il est en état-de-grâce ...
— Et la Grâce est l'Éternité! —

Drinking from miraculous springs
Where scabby Jobs have dipped their bowls
And washed their contagious skins ...
— *Go: your Faith has made you whole!* —

This is where the poor hold council,
Brothers in the order of Jesus.
— It's not the court of miracles,
The holes are real: *Vide latus!*

Are they not divine, in glory
On their hurdles, their haloes bright,
These proud possessors of running sores,
Rubies glinting in the sunlight! ...

Barking, a rachitic
With a boneless stump to twitch
Rubs shoulders with an epileptic
Having convulsions in a ditch.

There, a man's trunk — with an ulcer —
Against a tree's trunk — with mistletoe;
Here, a daughter and her mother
Dancing with St Vitus's woe.

This one titivates the pustules
His small ailing son's been given:
— The child plays to his father's rules ...
— He festers for a living!

That one's a natural, the dunce,
A genuine Tom o' Bedlam,
In the bliss of innocence ...
— The innocent is close to heaven! —

— Look, passer-by, the idiot's eye
Stays put — all else passes. For he
Is in a state of grace, that's why ...
— And Grace is for eternity! —

Parmi les autres, après vêpre,
Qui sont d'eau bénite arrosés,
Un cadavre, vivant de lèpre,
Fleurit — souvenir des croisés ...

Puis tous ceux que les Rois de France
Guérissaient d'un toucher de doigts ...
— Mais la France n'a plus de rois,
Et leur dieu suspend sa clémence.

— Charité dans leurs écuelles! ...
Nos aïeux ensemble ont porté
Ces fleurs de lis en écrouelles
Dont ces *choisis* ont hérité.

— *Miserere* pour les ripailles
Des *Ankokrignets* et *Kakous!* ...
Ces moignons-là sont des tenailles,
Ces béquilles donnent des coups.

Risquez-vous donc là, gens ingambes,
Mais gare pour votre toison:
Gare aux bras crochus! gare aux jambes
En *kyriè-éleison!*

... Et détourne-toi, jeune fille,
Qui viens là voir, et prendre l'air ...
Peut-être, sous l'autre guenille,
Percerait la guenille en chair ...

C'est qu'ils chassent là sur leurs terres!
Leurs peaux sont leurs blasons béants:
— Le droit-du-seigneur à leurs serres! ...
Le droit du Seigneur de céans! —

Tas d'*ex-voto* de carne impure,
Charnier d'élus pour les cieux,
Chez le Seigneur ils sont chez eux!
— Ne sont-ils pas sa créature ...

Among the rest, after vespers,
Who are by holy water sprayed,
A corpse, alive with leprosy,
Flowers — souvenir of the crusades ...

And all those healed by the Kings of France
With a touch of their little finger ...
— With no more kings there's little chance
That the divine touch will linger.

— Alms in their begging bowls, sir! ...
Those fleur-de-lis that our forebears
Wore as a brand are scrofula
To which these *elect* are heirs.

— *Miserere* for the capers
Of the *Ankokrignets* and *Kakous!*
Those stumps of limbs are pincers,
Those crutches land smart blows.

Venture there, but on nimble pegs;
Watch out for your fleece, — like Jason —
Watch for hooked arms! watch out for legs
Laid in *kyriè-éleison!*

... But turn away, you young lass,
Who've only come to see the view ...
It may be from their other rags
Their rag of flesh will poke through ...

Their skins gaping escutcheons,
They're hunting on their preserves:
— *Droit-du-seigneur* to their clutches! ...
The rights that the Lord reserves! —

Heap of *ex-votos* of tainted meat,
Charnel house of heaven's elect,
Under the Lord's table they've got their feet!
Are they not each his subject ...

Ils grouillent dans le cimetière
On dirait les morts déroutés
N'ayant tiré de sous la pierre
Que des membres mal reboutés.

— Nous, taisons-nous! ... Ils sont sacrés.
C'est la faute d'Adam punie,
Le doigt d'En-haut les a marqués:
— La Droite d'En-haut soit bénie!

Du grand troupeau, boucs émissaires
Chargés des forfaits d'ici-bas,
Sur eux Dieu purge ses colères! ...
— Le pasteur de Sainte-Anne est gras. —
. . . .

Mais une note pantelante,
Écho grelottant dans le vent
Vient battre la rumeur bêlante
De ce purgatoire ambulant.

Une forme humaine qui beugle
Contre le *calvaire* se tient;
C'est comme une moitié d'aveugle:
Elle est borgne, et n'a pas de chien ...

C'est une rapsode foraine
Qui donne aux gens pour un liard
L'*Istoyre de la Magdalayne*,
Du Juif-Errant ou d'*Abaylar*.

Elle hâle comme une plainte,
Comme une plainte de la faim,
Et, longue comme un jour sans pain,
Lamentablement, sa complainte ...

— Ça chante comme ça respire,
Triste oiseau sans plume et sans nid
Vaguant où son instinct l'attire:
Autour des Bon-Dieu de granit ...

274

They're swarming in the cemetery:
You'd think they'd come from under the stones
And found themselves all at sea
With ill-knit limbs and ill-set bones.

— Let's say no more! ... They're holy men.
Adam's fault is thus chastised —
The finger of the Lord has branded them:
The Right Hand of the Lord be praised!

Scape-goats from the ample flock,
They must atone for the world's misdeeds,
On them God is purging his wrath! ...
— The pastor of Saint-Anne's well-heeled.—

. . . .

But a panting note, whose tremors
Quiver in the wind and echo,
Rises above the bleating clamours
Of this itinerant limbo.

It's bellowing like a calf,
This human shape by the calvary;
Like a blind man's better half:
No dog, but one eye that can see ...

It's a strolling balladeer who'd fain
Recount to anyone for a sou
The Storye of Magdalayne,
Or *Abaylar* or *the Wandering Jew*.

It wails — a sound like keening,
Drawn out as someone who's faint
With hunger might be, whining
Lamentably, its plaint ...

— It sings as easily as breathes,
Sad bird with no feathers or nest
Roaming where its instinct leads:
Near granite statues of the Blest ...

275

Ça peut parler aussi, sans doute.
Ça peut penser comme ça voit:
Toujours devant soi la grand'route ...
— Et, quand ç'a deux sous ... ça les boit.

— Femme: on dirait hélas — sa nippe
Lui pend, ficelée en jupon;
Sa dent noire serre une pipe
Éteinte ... — Oh, la vie a du bon! —

Son nom ... ça se nomme Misère.
Ça s'est trouvé né par hasard.
Ça sera trouvé mort par terre ...
La même chose — quelque part.

— Si tu la rencontres, Poète,
Avec son vieux sac de soldat:
C'est notre sœur ... donne — c'est fête —
Pour sa pipe, un peu de tabac! ...

Tu verras dans sa face creuse
Se creuser, comme dans du bois,
Un sourire; et sa main galeuse
Te faire un vrai signe de croix.

It can talk as well, I suppose.
As clearly as it sees, it thinks:
Ahead of it lie the open roads ...
— And, with a copper or two ... it drinks.

Its clothes hang off it, tied up like
A smock. — It's a woman: alas!
Her blackened teeth grip a pipe
That's out ... — Life is a pretty pass! —

Her name ... is Want or Misery.
She found herself born by mischance.
She will be found dead in the street ...
Somewhere, but who'll so much as glance?

— If you should meet her, Poet,
With her old campaigner's pack:
Give her for her pipe — this is a *fête*
And she's our sister — an ounce of shag.

You'll see in her furrowed face,
Gouged, like wood, right across,
A smile; and her scabby hand trace
For you a true sign of the cross.

Cris d'Aveugle

(Sur l'air bas-breton *Ann hini goz.*)

  L'œil tué n'est pas mort
  Un coin le fend encor
Encloué je suis sans cercueil
On m'a planté le clou dans l'œil
  L'œil cloué n'est pas mort
  Et le coin entre encor

  Deus misericors
  Deus misericors
Le marteau bat ma tête en bois
Le marteau qui ferra la croix
  Deus misericors
  Deus misericors

  Les oiseaux croque-morts
  Ont donc peur à mon corps
Mon Golgotha n'est pas fini
Lamma lamma sabacthani
  Colombes de la Mort
  Soiffez après mon corps

  Rouge comme un sabord
  La plaie est sur le bord
Comme la gencive bavant
D'une vieille qui rit sans dent
  La plaie est sur le bord
  Rouge comme un sabord

  Je vois des cercles d'or
  Le soleil blanc me mord
J'ai deux trous percés par un fer
Rougi dans la forge d'enfer
  Je vois un cercle d'or
  Le feu d'en haut me mord

Blind Man's Cries

(To the Low-Breton tune: *Ann hini goz.*)

It's not dead the eye once killed
A splinter splits it still
Nailed down coffinless I lie
The nail's been driven through my eye
The split eye's not dead though killed
And the splinter splits it still

Deus misericors
Deus misericors
The hammer strikes my wooden head
The hammer that saw the cross rough-shod
Deus misericors
Deus misericors

Graveyard birds that peck red raw
Does my body fill them with awe
From my Golgotha I'm not yet free
Lamma lamma sabacthani
You Doves of Death grow hoarse
Going thirsty for my corse

Red as any porthole's jaw
Is the side that bears the sore
Very like the slavering gum
Of some cackling toothless bum
The side that bears the sore
Is red as any porthole's maw

Circlets of gold are what I see
The white hot sun bites into me
A red hot spear twice pierced my skull
Struck it was in the forge of hell
A circle of gold is what I see
Fire from heaven bites into me

279

Dans la moelle se tord
Une larme qui sort
Je vois dedans le paradis
Miserere, De profundis
Dans mon crâne se tord
Du soufre en pleur qui sort

Bienheureux le bon mort
Le mort sauvé qui dort
Heureux les martyrs, les élus
Avec la Vierge et son Jésus
Ô bienheureux le mort
Le mort jugé qui dort

Un Chevalier dehors
Repose sans remords
Dans le cimetière bénit
Dans sa sieste de granit
L'homme en pierre dehors
A deux yeux sans remords

Ho je vous sens encor
Landes jaunes d'Armor
Je sens mon rosaire à mes doigts
Et le Christ en os sur le bois
À toi je baye encor
Ô ciel défunt d'Armor

Pardon de prier fort
Seigneur si c'est le sort
Mes yeux, deux bénitiers ardents
Le diable a mis ses doigts dedans
Pardon de crier fort
Seigneur contre le sort

Wrung from my very marrow
Is a tear now watch it flow
Within it I see paradise
Miserere, De profundis
From my skull right through the bone
Are wrung out tears of brimstone

Blessed is he who's earned release
Who being saved can sleep in peace
Happy the martyrs, the chosen
Also the Virgin and her Son
O blessed is he who's found release
He's been judged and sleeps in peace

A certain Knight upon his horse
Rests outside without remorse
In God's consecrated acre
In his granite-like siesta
This man of stone upon his horse
Has two eyes and no remorse

Oh still I feel you at my core
You yellow heathland of Armor
I'm feeling when I tell my beads
Christ in his bones up on the tree
I gape at you as I did of yore
You long-lost skies of Armor

For praying hard forgive me Lord
If such a fate is my reward
My eyes' two stoups are burning since
The devil's dipped his fingers in
For crying out loud forgive me Lord
If such a fate is my reward

J'entends le vent du nord
Qui bugle comme un cor
C'est l'hallali des trépassés
J'aboie après mon tour assez
J'entends le vent du nord
J'entends le glas du cor

Menez-Arrez.

I can hear the north wind mourn
Like the winding of a horn
It is the mort for the deceased
I bay for my turn I've hardly ceased
I can hear the north wind mourn
And the last post of the horn

Menez-Arrez.

La Pastorale de Conlie

PAR UN MOBILISÉ DU MORBIHAN

Moral jeunes troupes excellent.
OFF.

Qui nous avait levés dans le *Mois-noir* — Novembre —
    Et parqués comme des troupeaux
Pour laisser dans la boue, au *Mois-plus-noir* — Décembre —
    Des peaux de mouton et nos peaux!

Qui nous a lâchés là: vides, sans espérance,
    Sans un levain de désespoir!
Nous entre-regardant, comme cherchant la France ...
    Comiques, fesant peur à voir!

— Soldats tant qu'on voudra! ... soldat est donc un être
    Fait pour perdre le goût du pain? ...
Nous allions mendier; on nous envoyait paître:
    Et ... nous paissions à la fin!

— S'il vous plaît: Quelque chose à mettre dans nos bouches? ...
    — Héros et bêtes à moitié! —
... Ou quelque chose là: du cœur ou des cartouches:
    — On nous a laissé la pitié!

L'aumône: on nous la fit — Qu'elle leur soit rendue
    À ces bienheureux uhlans soûls!
Qui venaient nous jeter une balle perdue ...
    Et pour rire! ... comme des sous.

On eût dit un radeau de naufragés. — Misère —
    Nous crevions devant l'horizon.
Nos yeux troubles restaient tendus vers une terre ...
    Un cri nous montait: Trahison!

The Pastoral of Conlie

BY A CONSCRIPT FROM MORBIHAN

Young troops' morale excellent.
OFF.

Who had levied us in the *Black-Month* — November —
    And like flocks had penned us in
Only to leave, in the *Blacker-Month* — December —
    And the mud, sheepskins and our skin!

Who just dumped us there: with no hope and empty hands,
    Without a leaven of despair!
Eyeing one another, as if in search of France ...
    So comical-fearsome our air!

— Soldiers to our bootstraps! ... if soldier means an ass
    Born for losing the taste for bread! ...
We were about to beg some; they put us out to grass:
    And ... we were grazing to be fed!

— Please, we must have a bite to eat, say sausages ...
    — We're half-animal, half-hero! —
... Or something else in here: courage or cartridges:
    — All that we've been left with's woe!

Alms: we were given them — But let's give back the lot
    To those blissful, drunken Uhlans!
Who kept coming to take pot-shots at us — crackpots —
    ... Pfennigs from heaven: spent for fun!

Picture a raft of shipwrecked sailors — Blood and sand —
    Dying for the sight of a sail.
Our blear eyes were straining for the sight of dry land ...
    A cry rose from us: Betrayal!

285

— Trahison! ... c'est la guerre! On trouve à qui l'on crie! ...
      — Nous: pas besoin ... — Pourquoi trahis? ...
J'en ai vu parmi nous, sur la Terre-Patrie,
      Se mourir du mal-du-pays.

— Oh, qu'elle s'en allait morne, la douce vie! ...
      Soupir qui sentait le remord
De ne pouvoir serrer sur sa lèvre une hostie,
      Entre ses dents la mâle-mort! ...

— Un grand enfant nous vint, aidé par deux gendarmes,
      — Celui-là ne comprenait pas —
Tout barbouillé de vin, de sueur et de larmes,
      Avec un *biniou* sous son bras.

Il s'assit dans la neige en disant: Ça m'amuse
      De jouer mes airs; laissez-moi. —
Et, le surlendemain, avec sa cornemuse,
      Nous l'avons enterré — Pourquoi! ...

Pourquoi? dites-leur donc! Vous du Quatre-Septembre!
      À ces vingt mille croupissants! ...
Citoyens-décréteurs de victoires en chambre,
      Tyrans forains impuissants!

— La parole est à vous — la parole est légère! ...
      La Honte est fille ... elle passa —
Ceux dont les pieds verdis sortent à fleur-de-terre
      Se taisent ... — Trop vert pour vous, ça!

— Ha! Bordeaux, n'est-ce pas, c'est une riche ville ...
      Encore en France, n'est-ce pas? ...
Elle avait chaud partout votre garde mobile,
      Sous les balcons marquant le pas?

La résurrection de nos boutons de guêtres
      Est loin pour vous faire songer;
Et, vos noms, je les vois collés partout, ô Maîtres! ...
      — La honte ne sait plus ronger. —

286

— Betrayal! ... that's war! You learn who's in command! ...
        — For us, there's no need ... — Why betrayed? ...
I've seen some in our midst, in their own fatherland,
        So homesick they've a foot in the grave.

— Oh, how bitter sweet life was, as it gave up the ghost! ...
        With a sigh of remorse on its breath,
It laboured in vain to press its lips to a host,
        When it gripped in its teeth foul death! ...

— A stripling appeared, helped along by two gendarmes,
        — He couldn't comprehend our fears —
With a *biniou* — Breton bagpipes — under his arm,
        And all smeared with wine, sweat and tears.

He sat down in the snow and said: I do enjoy
        Playing my tunes; just leave me be. —
In a couple of days, with his bagpipes deployed,
        We buried him — Why precisely! ...

Yes, why? tell me then! You Fourth of Septemberites!
        Tell those twenty thousand wallowers! ...
You armchair-decreers of how to win dogfights,
        Alien tyrants, camp followers!

— Speak up, the floor is yours — spoken words can misfire! ...
        Shame's a virgin ... she went her way —
Those whose slimy feet are sticking in the quagmire
        Stay silent ... — Too near the bone, eh!

— Now! Bordeaux, you must agree, is a very rich town ...
        Still part of France? what's the old rhyme? ...
They kept their all warm, your militia of renown,
        Under the balconies marking time?

The resurrection of the buttons on our gaiters
        Is too far removed to give you pause;
And your names, they're pasted up, O Men-of-Status! ...
        — Shame, sans teeth, no longer gnaws. —

— Nos chefs ... ils fesaient bien de se trouver malades!
              Armés en faux-turcs-espagnols
On en vit quelques-uns essayer des parades
              Avec la troupe des Guignols.

— *Le moral: excellent* — Ces rois avaient des reines,
              Parmi leurs sacs-de-nuit de cour ...
À la botte vernie il faut robes à traînes;
              La vaillance est sœur de l'amour.

— Assez! — Plus n'en fallait de fanfare guerrière
              À nous, brutes garde-moutons,
Nous: ceux-là qui restaient simples, à leur manière,
              Soldats, catholiques, Bretons ...

À ceux-là qui tombaient bayant à la bataille,
              Ramas de vermine sans nom,
Espérant le premier qui vînt crier: Canaille!
              Au canon, la chair à canon! ...

— Allons donc: l'abattoir! — Bestiaux galeux qu'on rosse,
              On nous fournit aux Prussiens;
Et, nous voyant rouler-plat sous les coups de crosse,
              Des Français aboyaient — Bons chiens!

Hallali! ramenés! — Les perdus ... Dieu les compte, —
              Abreuvés de banals dédains;
Poussés, traînant au pied la savate et la honte,
              Cracher sur nos foyers éteints!
       . . . .

— Va: toi qui n'es pas bue, ô fosse de Conlie!
              De nos jeunes sangs appauvris,
Qu'en voyant regermer tes blés gras, on oublie
              Nos os qui végétaient pourris,

— Our chiefs ... did well to discover they were ailing!
      Armed to the teeth like *Spanish-Turks*,
Some did try out parades in full regalia
      With the Punchinello squad: the jerks.

— *Morale: excellent* — Every king had his queen
      On his palliasse Valhalla ...
With patent leather boots you need gowns of sateen;
      The sister of love is valour.

— Enough! martial fanfares weren't needed any more
      For us, brutish shepherd sons,
Us: the ones who, in their simple way, were still raw
      Privates, Catholics, Bretons.

For those who, with mouths wide open, fell in battle,
      Pack of vermin, downtrodden,
In hopes that someone would come and shout: You rabble!
      To the cannons, cannon-fodder! ...

Mangy, belaboured cattle: To the abattoir!
      We're provisions for the Prussians;
And, there were Frenchmen barking — What good dogs they are! —
      To see us felled by the butts of guns.

The mort! reined off! — Lost souls ... God counts them all the same, —
      Watered with contempt, they called us names;
Egged each other on, slipshod in worn slippers and shame,
      To spit on our extinguished flames!
      . . . .

— O grave, Conlie midden, you who are not sated
      With our every son of a gun,
Let folk forget, when your plump ears have germinated,
      Our bones, vegetating, rotten,

La chair plaquée après nos blouses en guenilles
       — Fumier tout seul rassemblé ...
— Ne mangez pas ce pain, mères et jeunes filles!
       L'*ergot* de mort est dans le blé.

1870.

The flesh that was caked on our ragged dungarees
        — Dung-heap amassed in its own sweet
Way ... — Don't eat the bread though, mothers and brides-to-be!
        The *ergot* of death is in the wheat.

1870.

GENS DE MERS

SEAFARERS

Point n'ai fait un tas d'océans
Comme les Messieurs d'Orléans,
Ulysses à vapeur en quête ...
Ni l'Archipel en capitan;
Ni le Transatlantique autant
Qu'une chanteuse d'opérette.

Mais il fut flottant, mon berceau,
Fait comme le nid de l'oiseau
Qui couve ses œufs sur la houle ...
Mon lit d'amour fut un hamac;
Et, pour tantôt, j'espère un sac
Lesté d'un bon caillou qui coule.

— Marin, je sens mon matelot
Comme le bonhomme Callot
Sentait son illustre bonhomme ...
— *Va,* bonhomme de mer *mal fait!*
Va, Muse à la voix de rogomme!
Va, Chef-d'œuvre de cabaret!

I ain't sailed a heap of oceans
Like Orleans braggadocians,
Steamboat Ulysses on some quest ...
Nor swaggered the Archipelago;
Nor the Transatlantic swell
That operetta singers breast.

But it floated, my cradle did,
Woven like the nest of the bird
That hatches its eggs on the waves ...
My bed of love was a hammock;
Here's hoping I'll end in a sack
Weighed down by a stone to my grave.

— Like that mere engraver Callot
Sensed his illustrious fellow,
So I, swabbie, sense my first mate ...
— Aweigh, ungainly Jack-afloat!
Aweigh, Muse with a drunkard's croak!
Aweigh, Masterpiece on the slate!

Matelots

Vos marins de quinquets à l'Opéra ... comique,
Sous un frac en bleu-ciel jurent "Mille sabords!"
Et, sur les boulevards, le survivant chronique
Du *Vengeur* vend l'onguent à tuer les rats morts.
Le *Jûn'homme infligé d'un bras* — même en voyage —
Infortuné, chantant par suite de naufrage;
La femme en bain de mer qui tord ses bras au flot;
Et l'amiral *** — Ce n'est pas matelot! —
— Matelots — quelle brusque et nerveuse saillie
Fait cette *Race à part* sur la race faillie!
Comme ils vous mettent tous, *terriens*, au même sac!
— *Un curé dans ton lit, un' fill' dans mon hamac!* —
. . . .

— On ne les connaît pas, ces gens à rudes nœuds.
Ils ont le mal de mer sur vos *planchers à bœufs*;
À terre — oiseaux palmés — ils sont gauches et veules.
Ils sont mal culottés comme leurs brûle-gueules.
Quand le roulis leur manque ... ils se sentent rouler:
— *À terre, on a beau boire, on ne peut désoûler!*

— On ne les connaît pas. — Eux: que leur fait la terre? ...
Une relâche, avec l'hôpital militaire,
Des filles, la prison, des horions, du vin ...
Le reste: Eh bien, après? — Est-ce que c'est marin? ...

— Eux ils sont matelots. — À travers les tortures,
Les luttes, les dangers, les larges aventures,
Leur *face-à-coups-de-hache* a pris un tic nerveux
D'insouciant dédain pour ce qui n'est pas Eux ...
C'est qu'ils se sentent bien, ces chiens! Ce sont des mâles!
— Eux: l'Océan! — et vous: les plates-bandes sales;
Vous êtes des *terriens*, en un mot, des *troupiers*:
— *De la terre de pipe et de la sueur de pieds!* —

Able Seamen

Your argand-lamp sailors at the ... comic Opera
In sky-blue tuxedos all swear "Herrings & sprats!"
And, on the boulevards, the chronic survivor
Of the *Avenger* sells ointment for killing dead rats.
The *Young Salt* who has lost an arm — on a day-trip —
Hapless wight, singing that the sea has wrecked his ship;
The girl in a bubble bath of brine crooking her arms
To the billows; and Admiral *Asterisk* ... — Such charms
Are not naval!
          — But sea-dogs have you by the throat
— This gruff and sinewy tribe that's out of the ruck!
They put you all, landlubbers, into the same boat!
— *A parson in your bed, a wench in my hammock!* —

. . . .

— They're unplumbed depths, rough 'n ready, gnarled 'n scabby,
Feeling sea-sick on your *ox-floor* terra firma;
Web-footed birds on land, they are gauche and flabby.
They're as badly seasoned as their clay throat-burner.
When their sea-legs miss the roll, they're out of their cups:
— *On land, however much we sup, we never sober up!*

— They're unplumbed depths. — What's ashore mean then to 'em? ...
A port of call, with the military hospital,
Skirt, the nick, punch-ups, booze ... The rest: a vacuum.
What else could there be? — And would it be nautical? ...

— They're able seamen. — Having faced extremity,
Withstood peril, *the devil and the deep blue sea*,
Their rough-hewn features have assumed a nervous tic
Of casual disdain for what doesn't touch their quick ...
Because their tails are up! Real sea-dogs! And real males!
— Theirs: the Ocean! — and yours: filthy flower-beds. Your tails
Between your legs, landlubbers all, and rather wet —
To coin a phrase: *Clay-pipe clay and sweaty-feet sweat!* —

Eux sont les *vieux-de-cale* et les *frères-la-côte*,
Gens au cœur sur la main, et toujours la main haute;
Des natures en barre! — Et capables de tout ...
— Faites-en donc autant! ... Ils sont *de mauvais goût* ...
— Peut-être ... Ils ont chez vous des amours tolérées
Par un *grippe-Jésus** accueillant leurs entrées ...
— Eh! faut-il pas du cœur au ventre quelque part,
Pour entrer en plein jour là — bagne-lupanar,
Qu'ils nomment le *Cap-Horn*, dans leur langue hâlée:
— Le cap Horn, noir séjour de tempête grêlée —
Et se coller en vrac, sans crampe d'estomac,
De la chair à chiquer — comme un nœud de tabac!

Jetant leur solde avec leur trop-plein de tendresse,
À tout vent; ils vont là comme ils vont à la messe ...
Ces anges mal léchés, ces durs enfants perdus!
— Leur tête a du requin et du petit-Jésus.

Ils aiment à tout crin: Ils aiment plaie et bosse,
La Bonne-Vierge, avec le gendarme qu'on rosse;
Ils font des vœux à tout ... mais leur vœu caressé
A toujours l'habit bleu d'un *Jésus-Christ*† rossé.

— Allez: ce franc cynique a sa grâce native ...
Comme il vous toise un chef, à sa façon naïve!
Comme il connaît son maître: — *Un d'un seul bloc de bois!*
— *Un mauvais chien toujours qu'un bon enfant parfois!*
· ·

— Allez: à bord, chez eux, ils ont leur poésie!
Ces brutes ont des chants ivres d'âme saisie
Improvisés aux quarts sur le gaillard-d'avant ...
— Ils ne s'en doutent pas, eux, poème vivant.

---

* *Grippe-Jésus*: petit nom marin du gendarme.
† *Jésus-Christ*: du même au même.

They're the *gaffers-o'-the-hold* and *shipmates-o'-the-coast*,
Men with their hearts on their sleeve, and who rule the roast;
Of gold ingot mettle! — So capable, they are braced
For anything ... Can you boast that? ... They're *in bad taste* ...
— Could well be ... They sow their oats ashore. And the arms
Of the law are welcoming — tolerant *gendarmes!* ...
— You don't half need some spunk to lay aboard and board
In broad daylight in that hard-labour house of bawds
They call *Cape-Horn* in their weather-beaten lingo:
— Cape-Horn: dark haunt whose hailstones pockmark and sting you —
And get stuck hugger-mugger, without cramp in the gut,
On flesh to sink their teeth in — like chews of their cut!

Flinging their pay with an overflow of tenderness
To the four winds; they go there as they'd go to mass ...
These rough-cast angels, these tough little-boys-lost
Whose cross-grained faces are a shark and a cherub crossed!

They love hell for leather: They love set-tos and throws,
The Virgin Mary, and the *bill* who'll feel their blows;
They'll have a go at anything ... and hardly stop
For breath to black the blue of a well-clobbered *cop.*

— Yet this out-and-out cynic has an inborn grace ...
He sizes up a superior, knowing his place
And who his master is: — *Hewn from a single block!*
— *Good-natured now and then, but surly round the clock!*

. . . .

— What's more: on board, their realm, they have their poetry!
These unlicked bears roar a spirited shanty
That's well-oiled when improvised on fo'c'sle watches ...
— Live poems themselves, they haven't quite fathomed this.

— Ils ont toujours, pour leur *bonne femme de mère,*
Une larme d'enfant, ces héros de misère;
Pour leur *Douce-Jolie,* une larme d'amour! ...
Au pays — loin — ils ont, espérant leur retour,
Ces gens de cuivre rouge, une pâle fiancée
Que, pour la mer jolie, un jour ils ont laissée.
Elle attend vaguement ... comme on attend là-bas.
Eux ils portent son nom tatoué sur leur bras.
Peut-être elle sera veuve avant d'être épouse ...
— Car la mer est bien grande et la mer est jalouse. —
Mais elle sera fière, à travers un sanglot,
De pouvoir dire encore: — Il était matelot! ...

— C'est plus qu'un homme aussi devant la mer géante,
Ce matelot entier! ...
           Piétinant sous la plante
De son pied marin le pont près de crouler:
Tiens bon! Ça le connaît, ça va le désoûler.
Il finit comme ça, simple en sa grande allure,
D'un bloc: — *Un trou dans l'eau, quoi! ... pas de fioriture.* —
. . . .

On en voit revenir pourtant: bris de naufrage,
Ramassis de scorbut et hachis d'abordage ...
Cassés, défigurés, dépaysés, perclus:
— Un œil en moins. — Et vous, en avez-vous en plus?
— La fièvre jaune. — Eh bien, et vous, l'avez-vous rose?
— Une balafre. — Ah, c'est signé! ... C'est quelque chose!
— Et le bras en pantenne. — Oui, c'est un biscaïen,
Le reste c'est le bel ouvrage au chirurgien.
— Et ce trou dans la joue? — Un ancien coup de pique.
— Cette bosse? — *À tribord?* ... excusez: c'est ma chique.
— Ça? — Rien: une *foutaise,* un pruneau dans la main,
Ça sert de baromètre, et vous verrez demain:
Je ne vous dis que ça, sûr! quand je sens ma crampe ...
Allez, on n'en fait plus de coques de ma trempe!
On m'a pendu deux fois ... —
              Et l'honnête forban
Creuse un bateau de bois pour un petit enfant.

— For the good mother who bore them, they'll always shed
A child's tear, these heroes who wouldn't be seen dead
Blubbing at pain; for their sweetheart they've a lover's tear! ...
Back at home, she awaits her bronzed sea-dog in fear
And trembling for his return; off he went one day
Leaving, for the bounding main, a pale fiancée.
She waits abstractedly ... as folk in Brittany do.
He wears her name upon his arm as a tattoo.
Perhaps she'll be a widow before she is a bride ...
— For the sea is jealous and the sea is very wide. —
But she'll hold her head up high, still proud that she can
Say, through sobs in her voice: — He was a sailorman! ...

— He's more than a man too, this quintessential tar;
Faced with the giant sea, he's flawless! ...
                                        Pacing the spar-
Deck about to give beneath his sea-legs: Avast!
He's used to this, it'll sober him up. His last
Moment comes: he goes, simple, majestic, man and skills
All of a piece: — *A hole in the water! ... no frills.* —
. . . .

You see some come back though: flotsam from a shipwreck,
Scurvy's remains and mincemeat from the quarter-deck ...
The broken, disfigured, *fish out of water*, lame:
— Minus an eye. — And you, have you got plus the same?
— Yellow fever. — And are you suffering from the pink?
— A gash that's left a scar. — Signed, that, with blood for ink!
— And an arm in shreds. — A Biscayen had its wish,
The rest's the smart workmanship of the surgeon-fish.
— And that hole in your cheek? — A pike once caused a snag.
— That swelling? — *To starboard?* Sorry, mate, that's my shag.
— That? — It's *nowt*, a bullet through the hand, a warning,
Works like a weather-glass, you'll see in the morning:
I'll only tell you, though, when it starts to twinge ... Somehow,
They don't seem to make craft of the first water now!
I've even been hanged twice ... —
                                        And the bluff buccaneer
Hollows out a wooden boat for a child on the pier.

— Ils durent comme ça, reniflant la tempête,
Riches de gloire et de trois cents francs de retraite,
Vieux culots de gargousse, épaves de héros! ...
— Héros? — ils riraient bien! ... — Non merci: matelots!

— Matelots! — Ce n'est pas vous, jeunes *mateluches*,
Pour qui les femmes ont toujours des coqueluches ...
Ah, les vieux avaient de plus fiers appétits!
En haussant leur épaule ils vous trouvent petits.
À treize ans ils mangeaient de l'Anglais, les corsaires!
Vous, vous n'êtes que des *pelletas* militaires ...
Allez, on n'en fait plus de ces *purs, premier brin!*
Tout s'en va ... tout! La mer ... elle n'est plus *marin!*
De leur temps, elle était plus salée et sauvage.
Mais, à présent, rien n'a plus de pucelage ...
La mer ... La mer n'est plus qu'une fille à soldats! ...

— Vous, matelots, rêvez, en faisant vos cent pas
Comme dans les grands quarts ... Paisible rêverie
De carcasse qui geint, de mât craqué qui crie ...
— Aux pompes! ...
      — Non: fini! — Les beaux jours sont passés:
— *Adieu mon beau navire aux trois mâts pavoisés!*
· · · · · · · · · · · · · · · · · · · ·

Tel qu'une vieille coque, au sec et dégréée,
Où vient encor parfois clapoter la marée:
Âme-de-mer en peine est le vieux matelot
Attendant, échoué ... — quoi: la mort?
                  — Non, le flot.

Île d'Ouessant. — Avril.

— That's how they endure, sniffing the storm's intention,
Rich with glory and three hundred francs as pension,
Old salt-petre holders, wrecks of heroes, ex-whalers! ...
— Heroes? — they'd snort at that! ... — Nay, we're *nobbut* sailors!

— Sailors! — That's not you young'uns, sailor-lad upstarts,
For whom the womenfolk have a soft spot in their hearts ...
Ah, the old'uns had more prodigious appetites!
One shrug of the shoulders says: you're small fry in their sights.
At thirteen these corsairs ate Englishmen galore!
At any age, *you*'re only fit for a small cod-war!
They don't make A1 seamen now, ready for the fray!
All things pass ... every one! The sea ... has had its day!
Then it was more salty and, being wild, could roar.
Now, *nowt* can be pure-bred, nothing's virgin any more ...
The sea ... The sea is nothing but a soldiers' whore! ...

— You sea-dogs, dream on of your sentry-go of yore
When you did the long watches ... Cosy day-dreaming
Of the groaning carcase and the cracked mast screaming ...
— Man the pumps! ...
             — No: all's gone! — the good old days are wrecked:
— *Farewell my handsome bark whose masts were flag-bedecked!*
. . . .

You're like an old two-master, high, dry, unrigged;
Sometimes still the sea comes lapping against your side:
Sea-soul in torment, you, old *matlow*, are a brig
Waiting there, stranded ... — for what: for death?
                                    — No, the tide.

Ushant. — April.

303

Le Bossu Bitor*

Un pauvre diable aussi vaillant qu'un autre,
Quatrième et dernier à bord d'un petit *cotre* ...
Fier d'être matelot et de manger pour rien,
Il remplaçait le *coq*, le mousse et le chien;
Et comptait, comme ça, quarante ans de service,
Sur *le rôle* toujours inscrit comme — *novice!* —

... Un vrai bossu: cou tors et retors, très madré,
Dans sa coque il gardait sa petite influence;
Car chacun sait qu'en mer un bossu porte chance ...
— Rien ne f ...iche malheur comme femme ou curé!

Son nom: c'était Bitor — nom de mer et de guerre —
Il disait que c'était un tremblement de terre
Qui, jeune et fait au tour, l'avait tout démoli:
Lui, son navire et des cocotiers ... au Chili.

. . . .

Le soleil est noyé. — C'est le soir— dans le port
Le navire bercé sur ses câbles, s'endort
Seul; et le clapotis bas de l'eau morte et lourde,
Chuchote un gros baiser sous sa carène sourde.
Parmi les yeux du brai flottant qui luit en plaque,
Le ciel miroité semble une immense flaque.

Le long des quais déserts où grouillait un chaos
S'étend le calme plat ...
                          Quelques vagues échos ...
Quelque novice seul, resté mélancolique,
Se chante son pays avec une musique ...
De loin en loin, répond le jappement hagard,
Intermittent, d'un chien de bord qui fait le quart,

---

* Le *bitors* est un gros fil à voile tordu en double et goudronné.

The Hunchback Bitor*

A poor little devil as spirited as they come,
The fourth and last on board a little *galleon* ...
Proud of being a sailor and of *dining* scot-free,
He stood in for cook, cabin-boy and dog's-body;
And he had done just that for forty years in service,
On the muster-roll still registered as — *novice!* —

... A real hunchback: neck awry, veins varicose,
In his shell he retained his slight ascendancy;
Hunchbacks bring good luck at sea, as everyone knows ...
— Nothing breeds misfortune like a woman or a priest!

His name was Bitor — *nom de mer* and *nom de guerre* —
He'd say an earthquake, when he was young and debonair,
Had contorted his frame, bent him willy-nilly:
Him, his cutter and some coconut palms ... in Chile.

. . . .

The sun is drowned. — It is evening — in the harbour
The schooner, rocking on her cables, falls asleep
Alone; and the low lapping of the tide at its neap
Whispers a lavish kiss beneath her deaf garboard.
Among the eyes of floating tar that gleams in blobs,
The sky, like an immense puddle, glistens and throbs.

Along the deserted quays where throngs of people milled
Stretches a dead calm ...
                                    Odd echoes are not quite stilled ...
Some lone apprentice, dejected and down at heart,
Sings to himself of his homeland to a guitar ...
He's answered from time to time by the wild, fitful
Yapping of a ship's dog, forgotten on the fo'c'sle,
Keeping the dog-watch ...

* *bitors*: is stout rope yarn twisted double and tarred.

Oublié sur le pont ...
                    Tout le monde est à terre.
Les matelots farauds s'en sont allés — mystère! —
Faire, à grands coups de gueule et de botte ... l'amour.
— Doux repos tant sué dans les labeurs du jour. —
Entendez-vous là-bas, dans les culs-de-sac louches,
Roucouler leur chanson ces tourtereaux farouches! ...

— Chantez! La vie est courte et drôlement cordée!
Hâle à toi, si tu peux, une bonne bordée
À jouer de la fille, à jouer du couteau ...
Roucoulez mes Amours! Qui sait: demain! ... tantôt ...

... Tantôt, tantôt ... la ronde en écrémant la ville,
Vous soulage en douceur quelque traînard tranquille
Pour le coller en vrac, léger échantillon,
Bleu saignant et vainqueur, au clou. — Tradition. —

. . . .

Mais les soirs étaient doux aussi pour le Bitor,
Il était libre aussi, maître et gardien à bord ...
Lové tout de son long sur un rond de cordage,
Se sentant somnoler comme un chat ... comme un sage,
Se repassant l'oreille avec ses doigts poilus,
Voluptueux, pensif, et n'en pensant pas plus,
Laissant mollir son corps dénoué de paresse,
Son petit œil vairon noyé de morbidesse! ...

— Un *loustic* en passant lui caressait les os:
Il riait de son mieux et faisait le gros dos.
. . . .

Tout le monde a pourtant quelque bosse en la tête ...
Bitor aussi — c'était de se payer la fête!

Everyone else is on shore.
The spruced-up sailors have set off — Excelsior! —
To have, with loud shouts and kicks in the air, it away.
— Sweet repose so sweated for in the toils of the day. —
Can you hear them down blind alleys, duly shady,
Those rampant turtle-doves cooing to their lady! ...
Sing on! Life is short and of the strangest weave! ...
Haul away, if you can, and overstay your leave
To ply the wench, to play at knives, to call the tune ...
Coo on, Bill-and-cooers! Who knows: tomorrow! ... soon ...

... Soon, soon ... the night-watch creaming the town of blackguards
Discreetly removes some inoffensive laggard
To bung him, any old how, sample of their mission:
One bleeding conquering tyro, in clink. — Tradition. —

. . . .

But the evenings were a solace too for Bitor,
He was free to be captain and first mate on board ...
Curled up tight in a ball on the coil of a rope,
Feeling himself doze off like a cat ... like a pope,
Ironing an ear with his hairy fingers, in short:
Voluptuous, pensive, not giving it a thought,
His body going slack, unknotted by indolence,
His small wall-eye steeped in languid quiescence! ...

— Some joker passing by would stroke the bones of this *jack*:
He'd laugh as best he could and then he'd arch his back.

. . . .

Everyone has some hunch, though usually in the head ...
Bitor had one too — namely, to paint the town red!

Et cela lui prenait, comme un commandement
De Dieu: vers la Noël, et juste une fois l'an.
Ce jour-là, sur la brune, il s'ensauvait à terre
Comme un rat dont on a cacheté le derrière ...
— Tiens: Bitor disparu. — C'est son jour de sabbats:
Il en a pour deux nuits: réglé comme un compas.
— C'est un sorcier pour sûr ... —
                                        Aucun n'aurait pu dire,
Même on n'en riait plus; c'était fini de rire.

Au deuxième matin, le *bordailleur* rentrait
Sur ses jambes en pieds-de-banc-de-cabaret,
Louvoyant bord-sur-bord ...
                                        Morne, vers la cuisine
Il piquait droit, chantant ses vêpres ou matine,
Et jetait en pleurant ses savates au feu ...
— Pourquoi — nul ne savait, et lui s'en doutait peu.
... J'y sens je ne sais quoi d'assez mélancolique,
Comme un vague fumet d'holocauste à l'antique ...

C'était la fin; plus morne et plus tordu, le hère
Se reprenait hâler son bitor de misère ...

. . . .

— C'est un soir, près Noël. — Le cotre est à bon port,
L'équipage au diable, et Bitor ... toujours Bitor.
C'est le grand jour qu'il s'est donné pour prendre terre:
Il fait noir, il est gris. — L'or n'est qu'une chimère!
Il tient, dans un vieux bas de laine, un sac de sous ...
Son pantalon à mettre et: — La terre est à nous! —

... Un pantalon jadis *cuisse-de-nymphe-émue*,
Couleur tendre à mourir! ... et trop tôt devenue
Merdoie ... excepté dans les plis *rose-d'amour*,
Gardiens de la couleur, gardiens du pur contour ...

And it came over him, like a veritable *fiat*
From God: about Christmas time and just once a year.
The day'd arrive; at dusk, he'd make a dash for land
Like an excise rat whose backside's been stamped or tanned ...
— Hey: Bitor's disappeared. — It's his sabbath rumpus:
Two nights of revelling: steady as a compass.
— He's a warlock for sure ... —
                                    What might he be after?
He's a joke no longer; there is an end to laughter.

The second morning the *short-tacker* would return,
His legs like the legs of a bench in a tavern,
Rolling gunwale under ...
                          He'd head for the galley,
Despondent, chanting his vespers or reveille,
And tearful, toss his down-at-heel shoes on the fire ...
Why — no one knew, and *he* didn't think to enquire.
... I can sense something that makes me quite disheartened,
A whiff of late burnt offerings ...
                                    It was the end;
More downcast and more twisted, the poor blighter
Pulled himself together to bear his yoke, his plight ...

. . . .

— One evening, round Christmas. — The schooner's safe in port,
The crew's gone to the devil, and Bitor's ... still Bitor.
It's the great day he's appointed for his appearance:
It is dark, he's lit up. Gold's a mere chimera!
He's got a woollen sock, old maybe, but well-lined ...
He's just to put his trousers on and: — The land is mine! —

... An erstwhile flesh-pink pair of breeches — tingling flesh —
Such a delicate shade! ... which are no longer fresh
But goose-shit green ... except in the love-pink folds,
Guardians of colour, guardians of the purest moulds ...

Enfin il s'est lavé, gratté — rude toilette!
— Ah! c'est que ce n'est pas, non plus, tous les jours fête! ...
Un cache-nez lilas lui cache les genoux,
— Encore un coup-de-suif! et: La terre est à nous!
... La terre: un bouchon, quoi! ... — Mais Bitor se sent riche:
D'argent, comme un bourgeois: d'amour, comme un caniche ...
— Pourquoi pas le *Cap-Horn**! ... Le sérail — Pourquoi pas! ...
— Syrènes du *Cap-Horn*, vous lui tendez les bras! ...

. . . .

Au fond de la venelle est la lanterne rouge,
Phare du matelot, *Stella maris* du bouge ...
— Qui va là? — Ce n'est plus Bitor! c'est un héros,
Un Lauzun qui se frotte aux plus gros numéros! ...
C'est Triboulet tordu comme un ver par sa haine! ...
Ou c'est Alain Chartier, sous un baiser de reine! ...
Lagardère en manteau qui va se redresser! ...
— Non: C'est un bienheureux honteux — Laissez passer.
C'est une chair enfin que ce bout de rognure!
Un partageux qui veut son morceau de nature.
C'est une passion qui regarde en dessous
L'amour ... pour le voler! ... — L'amour à trente sous!

— Va donc Paillasse! Et le trousse-galant t'emporte!
Tiens: c'est là! ... C'est un mur — Heurte encor! ... C'est la porte:
As-tu peur! —
              Il écoute ... Enfin: un bruit de clefs,
Le judas darde un rais: — Hô, quoi que vous voulez?
— J'ai de l'argent. — Combien es-tu? Voyons ta tête ...
Bon. Gare à n'entrer qu'un; la maison est honnête;
Fais voir ton sac un peu? ... Tu feras travailler? ... —

... *Ce bagne-lupanar*
Qu'ils nomment le Cap-Horn, *dans leur langue hâlée.*
(Les Matelots, page 298.)

310

At last he's washed and scratched — abrasive ablution!
Because not every day's a day for celebration! ...
A lilac nose-band hides his knees — they're aquiline!
— Just one more dressing-down! and: The land is mine!
... The land: a bull and bush! ... — But Bitor has oodles
Of money, like a bourgeois; of love, like poodles ...
— Why not the *Cape-Horn!* ... The seraglio — Why not! ...
— Luring *Cape-Horn* sirens, *you*'ll find his ticklish spot! ...

. . . .

At the ginnel's end the red light's above the door:
Beacon for the sailor, *Stella maris* of the whore ...
— Who goes there? — He's Bitor no more! he's a hero,
A Lauzun who'd have hobnobbed even with Nero! ...
Triboulet twisted like a worm by his hatred! ...
Or Alain Chartier, whom a queen's kiss recreated! ...
Lagardère in his cloak who'll stand erect again! ...
— No: He's a blissful faint-heart, whom we'll not detain.
This scrap of rind, this paring's truly flesh and blood!
He wants fair shares for all, a nip of nature's bud.
His obsession: to look up skirts for love; thence
To steal it away! ... — Love? — Love for a handful o' pence!

On then, Pagliacci! May the sweating sickness floor
You! You're there! ... That's a wall — Stumble on! ... That's the door:
Are you scared! —
                  He listens ... At last, a sound of keys,
The spy-hole stabs a beam: — Ahoy, waddya want? Jeez! ...
— I've got money. — You alone? Let's look at your face ...
Right. Mind only one comes in; this is an honest place;
Let's have a squint at your shekels? ... You'll make 'em talk? ... —

Et la serrure grince, on vient d'entrebâiller;
Bitor pique une tête entre l'huys et l'hôtesse,
Comme un chien dépendu qui se rue à la messe.
— Eh, là-bas! l'enragé, quoi que tu veux ici?
Qu'on te f ...iche droit, quoi? pas dégoûté! Merci! ...
Quoi qui te faut, bosco? ... des nymphes, des pucelles
Hop! à qui le Mayeux? Eh là-bas, les donzelles! ... —

Bitor lui prit le bras: — Tiens, voici pour toi, gouine:
Cache-moi quelque part ... tiens: là ... — C'est la cuisine.
— Bon. Tu m'en conduiras une ... et propre! combien? ...
— Tire ton sac. — Voilà. — Parole! il a du bien! ...
Pour lors nous en avons du premier brin: *cossuses*;
Mais on ne t'en a pas fait exprès des *bossuses* ...
Bah! la nuit tous les chats sont gris. Reste là voir,
Puisque c'est ton caprice; as pas peur, c'est tout noir. —

.   .   .   .

Une porte s'ouvrit. C'est la salle allumée.
Silhouettes grouillant à travers la fumée:
Les amateurs beuglant, ronflant, trinquant, rendus;
— Des Anglais, jouissant comme de vrais pendus,
Se cuvent, pleins de tout et de béatitude;
— Des Yankees longs, et roide-soûls par habitude,
Assis en deux, et tour à tour tirant au mur
Leur jet de jus de chique, au but, et toujours sûr;
— Des Hollandais salés, lardés de couperose;
— De blonds Norwégiens hercules de chlorose;
— Des Espagnols avec leurs figures en os;
— Des baleiniers huileux comme des cachalots;
— D'honnêtes caboteurs bien carrés d'envergures,
Calfatés de goudron sur toutes les coutures;
— Des Nègres blancs, avec des mulâtres lippus;
— Des Chinois, le chignon roulé sous un *gibus*,

The door opens a chink, the bolt squeaking like chalk;
Bitor takes a header between doorpost and hostess,
Like an unhanged dog dashing off to mass post-haste.
— Hey, you with the hump, you're rabid, waddya want here?
Straightenin' out *and* a hump! not squeamish, are yer, dear!
What's yer requirements? ... nymphet, virgin or masseuse ...
Who's the Judy for this Punch? Jump to it, Delilahs! ... —

Bitor took her arm: — Here's something for you, vixen:
Now, hide me somewhere ... there will do ... — That's the kitchen.
— Good. Now, send me a nympho down ... who's clean! How much? ...
— Let's see what you're worth. — Look. — 'Strewth! he's good for a touch! ....
In that case we've some of the smartest: well-endowed;
Only we haven't a hump-backed kitten to do you proud ...
Hell though! at night all cats are grey. Wait here, your itch
Is our command; don't be afeard, it's black as pitch. —

. . . .

A door sprang open. The brightly lit tap-room's here.
Silhouettes seething in the smoky atmosphere:
Barflies buzzing, tipplers: hail-fellow or maudlin,
Bellowers clinking their glasses, snorers, all-in;
Englishmen elated with three sheeets in the wind,
Sleep off their hootch, full of owt* and beatitude,

— Elongated Yankees are, as habit warrants, slewed
And, sitting in pairs, take it in turns to let fly
Jets of tobacco juice at their targets — bull's eye;
— Well-salted Dutchmen larded with psoriasis;
— Blond Norwegian hercules, green with chlorosis;
— Spaniards with the bony features of men marooned;
— Sperm whalers oily with the whales that they've harpooned;
— Clean-cut square-rigged coasters with their sail-cloth abeam,
Caulked with melted pitch and oakum in every seam;
— Albino Negroes with blubber-lipped mulattos;
— Chignons tucked under their crush-hats, Chinese *matelots*,

* particularly stout.

313

Vêtus d'un frac flambant-neuf et d'un parapluie;
— Des chauffeurs venus là pour essuyer leur suie;
— Des Allemands chantant l'amour en orphéon,
Leur patrie et leur chope ... avec accordéon;
— Un noble Italien, jouant avec un mousse
Qui roule deux gros yeux sous sa tignasse rousse;
— Des Grecs plats; des Bretons à tête biscornue;
— L'escouade d'un vaisseau russe, en grande tenue;
— Des Gascons adorés pour leur galant bagoût ...
Et quelques renégats — écume du ragoût. —

Là, plus loin dans le fond sur les banquettes grasses,
Des novices légers s'*affalent* sur les Grâces
De corvée ... Elles sont d'un gras encourageant;
Ça se paye au tonnage, on en veut pour l'argent ...
Et, quand on *largue tout*, il faut que la viande
Tombe, comme un *hunier qui se déferle en bande!*

— On a des petits noms: *Chiourme, Jany-Gratis,*
Bout-dehors, Fond-de-Vase, Anspeck, Garcette-à-ris.
— C'est gréé comme il faut: satin rose et dentelle;
Ils ne trouvent jamais la mariée assez belle ...
— Du velours pour frotter à cru leur cuir tanné!
Et du fard, pour torcher leur baiser boucané! ...
À leurs ceintures d'or, faut ceinture dorée!
Allons! — *Ciel moutonné, comme femme fardée*
N'a pas longue durée à ces Pachas d'un jour ...
— *N'en faut du vin! n'en faut du rouge! ... et de l'amour!*
. . . .

Bitor regardait ça — comment on fait la joie —
Chauve-souris fixant les albatros en proie ...
Son rêve fut secoué par une grosse voix:
— Eh, dis donc, l'oiseau bleu, c'est-y fini ton choix?
— Oui: (Ses yeux verts vrillaient la nuit de la cuisine)
... La grosse dame en rose avec sa crinoline! ...
— Ça: c'est *Mary-Saloppe*, elle a son plein et dort. —
Lui, dégainant le bas qui tenait son trésor:
— Je te dis que je veux la belle dame rose! ...

314

Spick in brand-new frock-coats, with umbrellas to boot;
— Stokers who've come in here to mop away their soot;
— *Krauts* singing love and *das Vaterland* with one accord
And accordeon ... to each mug of beer that's poured;
— A noble Italian, with a cabin-boy in tow —
Shock of red hair, wide eyes rolling, and in the know;
— Dull Greeks; Bretons, heads in the shape of a shillelagh;
— A Russian ship's crew in full-dress regalia;
— Gallant Gascons adored for their glib how-d'ye-do ...
And a few renegades — scum of this Irish stew. —

Down at the farthest end, on the grease-stained benches,
Greenhorn apprentices get embayed by the wenches:
The Graces on fatigue ... Plump inducement to berth!
They're paid for by tonnage, you want your money's worth ...
And, when you slip your moorings, the meat must fall free
From the bone, like a tops'l shaken out fully!

— They've got pet-names: *Galley-arse, On-tap-Abigail,*
Ends-away, Bed-of-ooze, Hand's-turn, Cat-o'-nine-tail.
— All dolled up to the nines in pink satin and lace;
You'll never find your bride has so much chic and grace ...
— Velvet for rubbing down their weather-beaten hide!
And lipstick to wipe their kisses on — sun-tanned, smoke-dried! ...
The *girls* need golden girdles for their golden waists!
— *A fleecy sky, like a woman with painted face*
Is gone in a twinkling for these one-night Pashas ...
— We want wine! we want it red! ... and love like the clappers!

. . . .

And Bitor saw it all — how pleasure has its sway —
A bat sensing the albatrosses here are prey ...
His daydream was jolted by an elbowing voice:
— How about it, bluebird, now have you made your choice?
— Aye aye: (His green eyes drilled the gloom of the kitchen)
... The fat one in pink, the one in the crinoline! ...
— Her? that's Slutty-Mary, she's had her full measure
And's asleep. — He, unsheathing the sock with his treasure:
— I tell you that I want the lovely pink lady! ...

— Ç'a-t'y du vice! ... Ah-ça: t'es porté sur la chose? ...
Pour avec elle, alors, tu feras dix cocus,
Dix tout frais de ce soir! ... Vas-y pour tes écus
Et paye en double: On va t'*amatelotter*. Monte ...
— Non ici ... — Dans le noir? ... allons faut pas de honte!
Je veux ici! — Pas mèche, avec les règlements.
— Et— moi je veux! — C'est bon ... mais t'endors pas dedans ...

Ohé là-bas! debout au quart, *Mary-Saloppe!*
— Eh, c'est pas moi *de quart!* — C'est pour prendre une chope,
C'est rien *la corvée* ... accoste: il y a gras!
— De quoi donc? — Va, c'est un qu'a de l'or plein ses bas,
Un bossu dans un sac, qui veut pas qu'on l'évente ...
— Bon: qu'y prenne son soûl, j'ai le mien! j'ai ma pente.
— Va, c'est dans la cuisine ...

         — Eh! voyons-toi, Bichon ...
T'es tortu, mais j'ai pas peur d'un tire-bouchon!
Viens ... Si ça t'est égal: éclairons la chandelle?
— Non. — Je voudrais te voir, j'aime Polichinelle ...
Ah je te tiens; on sait jouer Colin-Maillard! ...
La matrulle ferma la porte ...
        — Ah tortillard! ...

. . . .

— Charivari! — Pour qui? — Quelle ronde infernale,
Quel paquet crevé roule en hurlant dans la salle? ...
— Ah, peau de cervelas! ah, tu veux du chahut!
À poil! à poil! on va te *caréner* tout cru!
Ah, tu grognes, cochon! Attends, tu veux la goutte:
Tiens son ballon! ... Allons, avale-moi ça ... toute!
Gare au grappin, il croche! Ah! le cancre qui mord!
C'est le diable bouilli! ... —

        C'était l'heureux Bitor.

— Carognes, criait-il, mollissez! ... je régale ...
— Carognes? ... Ah, roussin! mauvais comme la gale!
Tu régales, Limonadier de la Passion?

316

— He's vicious with it! ... So: you're stuck on your sadie? ...
You'll cuckold ten mates, you know, with that *cocksnooker*,
Ten fresh this evening! ... Go on, you've got the lucre,
And pay double: We'll hammock you with her. Up you go ...
— No, here ... — In the dark? ... no need to be ashamed though!
— I want it here! — No chance, there's regulations to keep.
— An' I say I must! — Alright ... but don't fall asleep ...

Ahoy there, scrubber! Up on deck, Slutty-Mary!
— Eh, it's not me on tout! — It's to down a canary,
Nothing irksome ... heave alongside: there's quite a haul!
— What of? — He's got stockings stuffed with the wherewithal,
A hunchback in the bag, who don't want to be exposed ...
— Right: let him have his fill, I've had mine, heaven knows.
— It's in the kitchen then ...

                  — Hey! let's see you, ducky ...
You're all screwed up, but reckon a corkscrew's lucky!
Come on ... Let's light the candle, that's if you don't mind?
— I do. — Let me see Mister Punch, you're quite a find ...
Got you; it's Blind-Man's-Buff then, and I'm Pursuer! ... —
The madam closed the door ...
                   — Ah my little screwer! ...

. . . .

— Pots and pan music! Infernal break-dance! — Who for?
— What punctured bundle rolls howling across the floor? ...
— Aha, salami skin! ah, you want a shindy!
Strip him, lads! we'll scour you in the raw! You windy?
Ah, you're grunting, pig! Hold on, you want a tot:
Grab his snout, you lubbers ... Now swallow this ... the lot!
Mind his grapnel, it nips! Agh! the beggar's snappy!
The devil's on the boil! ... —

         It was Bitor, happy.

— You ratbags you, he cried, ease off! ... this round's on me ...
— Ratbags? ... You clapped-out carthorse! mangy as v.d.!
You stand *us* a treat, Soft-drinks boy at Christ's Passion?

On te régalera, va! double ration!
Pou crochard qui montais nous piquer nos *punaises!*
Cancre qui viens manger nos *peaux!* ... Pas de foutaises,
Vous autres: Toi, *la mère*, apporte de là haut,
Un grand tapis de lit, en double et comme-y-faut! ...
Voilà! —
         Dix bras tendus halent la couverture
— Le *tortillou* dessus! ... On va la danser dure;
Saute, Paillasse! hop là! ... —
                C'est que le matelot,
Bon enfant, est très dur quand il est *rigolot.*
Sa colère: c'est bon. — Sa joie: ah, pas de grâce! ...
Ces dames rigolaient ...
              — Attrape: pile ou face?
Ah, le malin! quel vice! Il échoue en côté! —
... Sur sa bosse grêlaient, avec quelle gaîté!
Des bouts de corde en l'air sifflant comme couleuvres;
Les sifflets de gabier, rossignols de manœuvres,
Commandaient et rossignolaient à l'unisson ...
— Tiens bon! ... —
        Pelotonné, le pauvre hérisson
Volait, rebondissait, roulait. Enfin la plainte
Qu'il rendait comme un cri de poulie est éteinte ...
— Tiens bon! il fait exprès ... Il est dur, l'entêté! ...
C'est un lapin! ça veut le jus plus pimenté:
Attends! ... —
    Quelques couteaux pleuvent ... *Mary-Saloppe*
D'un beau mouvement, hèle: — À moi sa place! — Tope!
Amène tout en vrac! largue! ... —
              Le jouet mort
S'aplatit sur la planche et rebondit encor ...

Comme après un doux rêve, il rouvrit son œil louche
Et trouble ... Il essuya dans le coin de sa bouche,
Un peu d'écume avec sa chique en sang ... — C'est bien;
C'est fini, matelot ... Un coup de *sacré-chien!*
Ça vous remet le cœur; bois! ... —

We'll treat *you*, o.k.! and give you double ration!
You crab-louse, come to latch on to *our* blood suckers,
Our bed-buggers, knave come to pinch *our* tarts! ... Don't fuck us
About, you cunts: You, *Ma* Célestine, bring us down
A double bedspread, and double quick — for this *clown!* ...
Here we go! —
                    Ten arms outstretch: five shipmates form a star:
— Up with Quasimodo! ... We'll dance him good and hard;
Jump, Jack pudding! Up, higher! ... —
                              Sailors have this trait:
Salt of the earth, they're so callous in their horseplay.
Their anger is good. — Their joy: no mercy prevails! ...
The *ladies* were tickled to death ...
                              — Catch: heads or tails?
Ha, he's a sly one! and depraved! he's *gone to earth!* —
— There hailed down on his hump, with what a show of mirth!
Lengths of rope hissing through the air like vipers;
Nightingales of the rigging, the bosun's pipers
Were whistling commands, singing out in unison ...
— Lay on! ... —
                Curled up on himself, the poor hedgehog spun
A somersault, rebounded, rolled. At last his moan,
Like the screech of a pulley, becomes a drone ...
And dies away. — Keep on! he's bluffing ... and stubborn! ...
Plucky though! he wants it hotted up, the drubbing:
Avast ... —
            A few knives rain down ... Slutty-Mary hails
On a kindly impulse: — Let me stand in, and sail
To windward! — Done! Cast off, lads! ... —
                              The lifeless plaything
Falls flat on the *deck* and goes on rebounding ...

As from a lovely dream, he opened his eyes, squinting
And hazy ... He wiped from the corner of his mouth
A little foam with his bloodied shag ... — Right enough;
It's over, sailor ... Here's a drop of the hard stuff!
This'll buck you up; drink! ... —

       Il prit avec peine
Tout l'argent qui restait dans son bon bas de laine
Et regardant *Mary-Saloppe:* — C'est pour toi,
Pour boire ... en souvenir. — Vrai? baise-moi donc, quoi! ...
Vous autres, laissez-le, grands lâches! mateluches!
C'est mon amant de cœur ... on a ses coqueluches!
... Toi: file à l'embellie, en double, l'asticot:
L'échouage est mauvais, mon pauvre saligot! ... —

Son œil marécageux, larme de crocodile,
La regardait encore ... — Allons, mon garçon, file! —

. . . .

C'est tout. Le lendemain, et jours suivants, à bord
Il manquait. — Le navire est parti sans Bitor. —

. . . .

Plus tard, l'eau soulevait une masse vaseuse
Dans le dock. On trouva des plaques de vareuse ...
Un cadavre bossu, ballonné, démasqué
Par les crabes. Et ça fut jeté sur le quai,
Tout comme l'autre soir, sur une couverture.
Restant de crabe, encore il servit de pâture
Au rire du public, et les gamins d'enfants
Jouant au bord de l'eau noire sous le beau temps,
Sur sa bosse tapaient comme sur un tambour
Crevé ...
   — Le pauvre corps avait connu l'amour!

Marseille. — La Joliette. — Mai.

Racked with pain, he disbursed

All the money that was left in his woollen *purse*
And gazing at Slutty-Mary: — This is for you,
For drinks ... in memory. — Get on? fuck me, boy blue! ...
Leave him alone, you swine, *girt* cowards! pseudo-tars!
He's my darling lovebird ... don juan of Lascars!
... And you, clear off in the lull, at the double, quick:
Running aground's no good, my poor little jellyprick! ... —

His quagmiry eye, with its crocodile tear,
Was still fixed on her ... — Go on, my wriggler, steer clear! —

. . . .

That's all. The next day, and the following, on board
He went missing. — The ship set sail without Bitor. —

. . . .

Days later, the sea roads brought up a slimy mass
In the dock. Blobs of sou'wester were seen to pass ...
A cadaver, hunchbacked, bloated, unmasked by tide
And marauding crabs, was tossed up on the quayside,
Just like the other evening, upon a blanket.
Crabs' left-over then, it still served as fodder fit
For the public's sniggers, and, playing at the brink
Of the black water, when the weather was fine, imp
Waifs and strays would tap on its hump as on a split
Drum-skin ...
As for love, the poor body had known it!

Marseilles. — La Joliette. — May.

Le Rénegat

Ça c'est un renégat. Contumace partout:
        Pour ne rien faire, ça fait tout.
Écumé de partout et d'ailleurs; crâne et lâche,
Écumeur amphibie, à la course, à la tâche;
Esclave, flibustier, nègre, blanc, ou soldat,
Bravo: fait tout ce qui concerne tout état;
Singe, limier de femme ... ou même, au besoin, femme;
Prophète *in partibus*, à tant par kilo d'âme;
Pendu, bourreau, poison, flûtiste, médecin,
Eunuque; ou mendiant, un coutelas en main ...

La mort le connaît bien, mais n'en a plus envie ...
Recraché par la mort, recraché par la vie,
Ça mange de l'humain, de l'or, de l'excrément,
Du plomb, de l'ambroisie ... ou rien — Ce que ça sent. —

— Son nom? — Il a changé de peau, comme chemise ...
Dans toutes langues c'est: Ignace ou Cydalyse,
Todos los santos ... Mais il ne porte plus ça;
Il a bien effacé son *T.F.* de forçat! ...

— Qui l'a poussé ... l'amour? — Il a jeté sa gourme!
Il a tout violé: potence et garde-chiourme.
— La haine? — Non. — Le vol? — Il a refusé mieux.
— Coup de barre du vice? — Il n'est pas vicieux;
Non ... dans le ventre il a de la fille-de-joie,
C'est un tempérament ... un artiste de proie.

. . . .

— Au diable même il n'a pas fait miséricorde.
— Hale encore! — Il a tout pourri jusqu'à la corde,
Il a tué toute *bête*, éreinté tous les coups ...

Pur, à force d'avoir purgé tous les dégoûts.

Baléares.

322

The Renegade

This one's a turncoat. Turns tail, putting in his spoke:
    Makes great efforts not to do a stroke.
Skimmed off from everywhere or elsc; has spunk and funk,
Freebooter in harness, privateer on the run,
Slave, buccaneer, nigger, whitey, soldier, punk,
Pest, poison, third degree, G.P., amphibian
Scum; cut-throat: does the dirty deeds for any state,
Ape, woman's bloodhound ... or, if need be, woman;
At a loss plays false, prophet in a heathen land,
To each according to his pound of soul; hangman,
Hanged, hanger-on, tosser-off, piper, bosun's mate,
Eunuch; or beggar with a cutlass in his hand.

Death knows him well, but does not want him any more ...
Spat out then by death, spat out now by life — too raw! ...
He eats anything human, gold, excrement,
Lead, ambrosia ... or nothing at all — What a stench. —

— What's his name? — He's changed his skin, as one changes fleas ...
In every tongue it's: Ignatius or Cydalise,
Todos los santos ... too many for him to stand;
He's thoroughly scrubbed out his *Hard Labour* brand! ...

— Who pushed him ... love? — He's let off steam, run at the nose!
He's profaned everything: prison screw and gallows.
— Hatred then? — No. — Or theft? — He's turned down better gifts.
— Has he swung vice's tiller? — He's no vicious trait;
In him there's something of the wanton wanting lifts,
He's a randy disposition ... an artist of prey.
. . . .
— He has shown no mercy, given the devil his due.
— Heave ho once more! — He's rotted everything right through,
He's killed off every quarry, taken all the blows ...

Pure, by dint of having purged everything he loathes.

The Balearics.

Aurora

APPAREILLAGE D'UN BRICK CORSAIRE

Quand l'on fut toujours vertueux
L'on aime à voir lever l'aurore ...

Cent vingt *corsairiens*, gens de corde et de sac,
À bord de la *Mary-Gratis*, ont mis leur sac.
— Il est temps, les enfants! on a roulé sa bosse ...
Hisse! — C'est le grand-foc qui va payer la noce.
Étarque! — Leur argent les fasse tous cocus! ...
La drisse du grand-foc leur rendra leurs écus ...
— Hisse hoé! ... *C'est pas tant le gendarm' qué jé r'grette!*
— Hisse hoà! ... *C'est pas ça! Naviguons, ma brunette!*

Va donc *Mary-Gratis*, brick écumeur d'Anglais!
Vire à pic et dérape! ... — Un coquin de vent frais
Largue, en vrai matelot, les voiles de l'aurore;
L'écho des cabarets de terre beugle encore ...
Eux répondent en chœur, perchés dans les huniers,
Comme des colibris au haut des cocotiers:
　　　"Jusqu'au revoir, la belle,
　　　Bientôt nous reviendrons ..."

Ils ont bien passé là quatre nuits de liesse,
Moitié sous le comptoir et moitié sur l'hôtesse ...
　　　" ...Tâchez d'être fidèle,
　　　Nous serons bons garçons ..."

— Évente les huniers! ... *C'est pas ça qué jé r'grette ...*
— Brasse et borde partout! ... *Naviguons ma brunette!*
— *Adieu, séjour de guigne!* ... Et roule, et cours bon bord ...
Va, la *Mary-Gratis!* — au nord-est quart de nord. —

Aurora

THE WEIGHING OF A CORSAIR BRIG

When one has stayed virtuous
One loves to see the dawn rise ...

A hundred and twenty pirateers, ripe for the gallows all,
Have dumped on board the *Mary-Gratis* kitbag and caul.
— It's high time, my lads! our stones have rolled fast and free ...
Sway up! — It's the main jib that will pay for our spree.
Hoist home! — Let their cash wittol them out of their senses! ...
The main jib's halyard will return their expenses ...
Heave ho! ... *It's not the gendarme I can't get over!*
Heave ho! ... *It's not that! Let's sail, my brown-haired rover!*

Come on, *Mary-Gratis*, and every Englishman quail!
Heave short and cast off! ... — A rapscallion fresh gale
Shakes out, like a true sailor, the sails of daybreak;
The echo from *The Sailors Arms* lows in your wake ...
They respond in chorus, perched above the yardarm,
Like humming birds at the top of a coconut palm:
          "*We'll be back soon,*
          My love, till then adieu ..."

They've spent four nights ashore in such joyous excess,
Half under the table and half on mine hostess ...
          "*... Try to be true*
          To us, we'll be true to you ..."

— Fill the topsails! ... *It's not that I can't get over ...*
— Brace in and haul taut! ... *Let's sail, my brown-haired rover!*
— *Farewell, ill-starred resort!* ... And roll, and stand well off ...
Tack, miss *Mary-Gratis!* — and steer nor'east by north.—

... Et la *Mary-Gratis*, en flibustant l'écume,
Bordant le lit du vent se gîte dans la brume.
Et le grand flot du large en sursaut réveillé
À terre va bâiller, s'étirant sur le roc:
     Roul' ta bosse, tout est payé
     Hiss' le grand foc !

. . . .

Ils cinglent déjà loin. Et, couvrant leur sillage,
La houle qui roulait leur chanson sur la plage
Murmure sourdement, revenant sur ses pas:
— Tout est payé, la belle! ... ils ne reviendront pas.

... And miss *Mary-Gratis*, freebooting with a list,
Catching the eye of the wind, puts up in the mist.
The waves of the open sea, woken with a start,
Will flow to yawn on land and stretch on a rocky rib:
     Roll on, all's paid, sweetheart,
      Hoist home the jib!

. . . .

They scud before the wind now. And, covering their track,
The swell that rolled their boat-song right over the beach
Sounds muted and muffled as it ebbs out of reach:
— All's paid for, my lovely! ... no, they won't be back.

Le Novice en Partance
et Sentimental

À la déçente des marins ches Marijane serre à boire & à
manger couche à pieds et à cheval.
DÉBIT.

Le temps était si beau, la mer était si belle ...
   Qu'on dirait qu'y en avait pas.
Je promenais, un coup encore, ma Donzelle,
   À terre, tous deux, sous mon bras.

C'était donc, pour du coup, la dernière journée.
   Comme-ça: ça m'était égal ...
Ça n'en était pas moins la suprême tournée
   Et j'étais sensitif pas mal.

... Tous les ans, plus ou moins, je relâchais près d'elle
   — Un mois de mouillage à passer —
Et je la relâchais tout fraîchement fidèle ...
   Et toujours à recommencer.

Donc, quand la barque était à l'ancre, sans malice
   J'accostais, novice vainqueur,
Pour mouiller un pied d'ancre, Espérance propice! ...
   Un pied d'ancre dans son cœur!

Elle donnait la main à manger mon décompte
   Et mes avances à manger.
Car, pour un *mathurin** faraud, c'est une honte:
   De ne pas rembarquer léger.

J'emportais ses cheveux, pour en cas de naufrage,
   Et ses adieux au long-cours.
Et je lui rapportais des objets de sauvage,
   Que le douanier saisit toujours.

* *Mathurin: Dumanet* maritime.

328

Tyro About to Sail
and Sentimental

The Sailors Arms Mine Hostess Marijane serves eats & drinks
puts you up on horseback & on foot.
LICENSED.

The weather was so fine, the sea so beautiful ...
       So clear you'd think they were not there.
I was walking out my girl again, dutiful
       Ashore with her, to our affair.

It really was, this time for sure, the final day.
       One way: it was all one to me ...
Yet it was the crowning jaunt, a last making-of-hay,
       And I took it softheartedly.

Every year, near enough, I'd put into her port
       — One month of anchorage to spend —
And then I'd ease her off, ever faithful once more ...
       Till next we'd vow love knows no end.

So, when the barque was in the roads, I'd throw a rope
       And board her — malice played no part,
Me the conquering tyro — to drop, propitious Hope! ...
       An anchor fluke into her heart!

She'd help shell out my pay so I could travel light
       And help eat into my credit.
For, for a sprightly *jack-tar*, if there's an appetite
       It's a sin not to have fed it.

Then, for fear of shipwreck, with a lock of her hair
       And fond farewells I'm ocean-bound.
And I'll bring back for her the most exotic ware,
       Which the customs always impound.

Je me l'imaginais pendant les traversées,
　　Moi-même et naturellement.
Je m'en imaginais d'autres aussi — censées
　　Elle — dans mon tempérament.

Mon nom mâle à son nom femelle se jumelle,
　　Bout-à-bout et par à peu-près:
Moi je suis Jean-Marie et c'est Mary-Jane elle ...
　　Elle ni moi *n'ons* fait exprès.

... Notre chien de métier est chose assez jolie
　　Pour un leste et gueusard amant;
Toujours pour démarrer on trouve l'embellie:
　　— Un pleur ... Et saille de l'avant!

Et hisse le grand foc! — la loi me le commande. —
　　Largue les *garcettes**, sans gant!
Étarque à bloc! — L'homme est libre et la mer est grande —
　　La femme: un sillage! ... Et bon vent! —

On a toujours, puisque c'est dans notre nature,
　　— Coulant en douceur, comme tout —
Filé son câble par le bout, sans *fignolure* ...
　　Filé son câble par le bout!

— File! ... La passion n'est jamais défrisée.
　　— Évente tout et pique au nord!
Borde la brigantine et porte à la risée! ...
　　— On prend sa capote et s'endort ...

— Et file le parfait amour! à ma manière,
　　Ce n'est pas la bonne: tant mieux!
C'est encor la meilleure et dernière et première ...
　　As pas peur d'échouer, mon vieux!

---

* *Garcettes*. — Bouts de corde qui servent à serrer les voiles.

I'd conjure up her picture while each voyage lasted,
  For I was naturally inclined.
I imagined others too, but they were mere impasto
  In my amorous frame of mind.

Our names, roughly speaking, are round about the same,
  Put hers back to front with mine:
We're twins — I'm Jean-Marie and she is Mary-Jane ...
  We haven't done it by design.

... Our job's pretty gruelling but it works like a charm
  For a no-hold-barred young devil;
When you want to cast off, you find that you're becalmed:
  — One tear ... And you can feel the swell!

— We're off! Trice the main jib! — It's sea-laws that decide. —
  Loose the beckets*, with both hands bare!
Hoist chock-a-block! — Man is free and the sea is wide —
  Woman: a wake! ... May the wind blow fair! —

We've always, because it's in our very nature,
  — Unwinding handsomely, once started —
Slipped our cable, run it out, with no *finicure* ...
  Slipped our cable and departed!

— Let go! ... Passion's never far from the wind. — Hurry!
  Head due north exposing all sheets!
Haul the spanker taut and stand in to the flurry! ...
  — Whoever dons his watch-coat sleeps ...

— And lives love's young dream! like I do or burst!
  — If mine's not the proper one, I rate
It all the more! It's still the best and last and first ...
  Now don't go fearing failure, mate!

* Beckets. — Loops of rope used for holding the sails tight.

331

Ah! la mer et l'amour! — On sait — c'est variable ...
        Aujourd'hui: zéphyrs et houris!
Et demain ... c'est un grain: Vente la peau du diable!
        Debout au quart! croche des ris! ...

— Nous fesons le bonheur d'un tas de malheureuses,
        Gabiers-volants de Cupidon! ...
Et la lame de l'ouest nous rince les pleureuses ...
        — Encore une! et lave le pont!

. . . .

Comme ça moi je suis. Elle, c'était la rose
        D'amour, et du débit d'ici ...
Nous cherchions tous deux à nous dire quelque chose
        De triste. — C'est plus propre aussi. —

... Elle ne disait rien — Moi: pas plus. — Et sans doute,
        La chose aurait duré longtemps ...
Quand elle dit, d'un coup, au milieu de la route:
        — Ah Jésus! comme il fait beau temps. —

J'y pensais justement, et peut-être avant elle ...
        Comme avec un même cœur, quoi!
Donc, je dis à mon tour: — Oh! oui, mademoiselle,
        Oui ... Les vents halent le *noroî* ...

— Ah! pour où partez-vous? — Ah! pour notre voyage ...
        — Des pays mauvais? — Pas meilleurs ...
— Pourquoi? — Pour faire un tour, démoisir l'équipage ...
        Pour quelque part, et pas ailleurs:

New-York ... Saint-Malo ... — Que partout Dieu vous garde!
        — Oh! ... Le saint homme y peut s'asseoir;
Ça c'est notre métier à nous, ça nous regarde:
        Éveillatifs, l'œil au bossoir!

— Oh! ne blasphémez pas! Que la Vierge vous veille!
        — Oui: que je vous rapporte encor

Aha! the sea and love! — They're changeable — we know ...
     Today: it's zephyrs and houris!
And tomorrow ... a squall: Blow, you bitch of a wind, blow!
     Stand in the nest! hand in the reefs! ...

— We're answers to maidens' prayers, our sisters' keepers,
     Flying topmen at Cupid's beck! ...
And the waves from the west rinse away the weepers ...
     — Here's another! and swill the deck!

.   .   .   .

That's how I am. And she was the compass, the rose
     Of love, and of the local bar ...
Both of us tried to say something ... sad, I suppose.
     That's only right, better by far ...

... She'd say not a word — I was tongue-tied. — And perhaps,
     Things would have carried on this way ...
But abruptly she said, as she stopped in her tracks:
     — Sweet Jesus! what a lovely day. —

That's just what I was thinking — great minds think alike ...
     I may have thought it first, if pressed!
Great hearts beat as one! — Oh yes, I said, yes, you're right ...
     The winds are veering to nor'west ...

— Ah! where are you bound for this time? — Well, we're off to ...
     — Horrid lands? — No better than a score ...
— But why? — It's just a voyage, to unrust the crew ...
     Sail somewhere we've not been before:

New-York ... Saint-Malo ... — May God preserve you then!
     Your God can get lost ... and his ghost!
It's none of his business, it's ours, a task for men:
     Wide-awake, at the look-out post!

— Oh! you mustn't blaspheme! The Virgin protect you!
     — Right, shall I bring you back, they're sold

333

Une bonne Vierge à la façon de Marseille:
    Pieds, mains, et tête et tout, en or? ...

— Votre navire est-il bon pour la mer lointaine?
    — Ah! pour ça, je ne sais pas trop,
Mademoiselle; c'est l'affaire au capitaine,
    Pas à vous, ni moi matelot.

— Mais le navire a-t-il un beau nom de baptême?
    — C'est un *brick* ... pour son petit nom;
Un espèce de nom de dieu ... toujours le même,
    Ou de sa moitié: *Junon* ...

— Je tremblerai pour vous, quand la mer se tourmente ...
    — Tiens bon, va! la coque a deux bords ...
On sait patiner ça! comme on fait d'une amante ...
    — Mais les mauvais maux? ... — Oh! des sorts!

— Je tremble aussi que vous n'oubliez mes tendresses
    Parmi vos reines de là-bas ...
— Beaux cadavres de femme: oui! mais noirs et singesses ...
    Et puis: voyez, là, sur mon bras:

C'est l'*Hôtel de l'Hymen, dont deux cœurs en gargousse*
    Tatoués à perpétuité!
Et *la petite bonne-femme en frac de mousse*:
    C'est vous, en portrait ... pas flatté.

— Pour lors, c'est donc demain que vous quittez? ... — Peut-être.
    — Déjà! ... — Peut-être après-demain.
— Regardez en appareillant, vers ma fenêtre:
    On fera bonjour de la main.

— C'est bon. Jusqu'au retour de n'importe où, m'amie ...
    Du Tropique ou Noukahiva.
Tâchez d'être fidèle, et moi: sans avarie ...
    Une autre fois mieux! ... Adieu-vat!

Brest-Recouvrance.

334

And made in Marseilles, a little Virgin Mary statue:
      Feet, hands, head an' all, made of gold? ...

— Is your vessel shipshape for the distant ocean?
      — Ah! it's the captain's job to know
Things like that, not yours or mine; I haven't a notion
      For I'm only a *matelot.*

— But was your ship baptised with a beautiful name?
      — It's a *brig* ... and was christened: Oh,
It's the goddam name of a god ... always the same,
      Or of his better half: *Juno* ...

— I'll be worried when the sea gets wild ... — Don't distress
      Yourself, love, the hull's got two sides ...
You can feel for them, as you might feel a mistress! ...
      — But what of the worst dos? ... — Rough rides!

— I'll worry too that you'll forget my caresses,
      Your girls overseas have such charms ...
— Fine bodies of women: yes! but ugly, negresses ...
      And look: here, see these on my arm:

That's Hymen Hotel, with two hearts in a cartouche;
      It's on for ever, this tattoo!
And this trim little lass in a cabin boy's ruche
      Is your spitting image, is *you.*

— So it's tomorrow that you're off then? ... — May be.
      — So soon! ... — Or the following day.
— Look up at my window as you sail out to sea:
      I'll wave you *god speed* on your way.

— Yes do. And till we return from wherever we ply,
      From the Tropic or Noukahiva,
Try to stay faithful and, bar *damage* or wreck, I
      Will too ... Now *I'll love ya an' leave ya!*

Brest-Recouvrance.

La Goutte

Sous un seul hunier — le dernier — à la cape,
Le navire était soûl; l'eau sur nous faisait nappe.
— Aux pompes, faillis chiens! — L'équipage fit — non. —

— Le hunier! le hunier! ...
                          C'est un coup de canon,
Un grand froufrou de soie à travers la tourmente.

— Le hunier emporté! — C'est la fin. Quelqu'un chante. —
— Tais-toi, Lascar! — Tantôt. — Le hunier emporté! ...
— Pare le foc, quelqu'un de bonne volonté! ...
— Moi. — Toi, lascar? — Je chantais ça, moi, capitaine.
— Va. — Non: la goutte avant? — Non, après. — Pas la peine:
La grande tasse est là pour un coup ... —
                                      Pour braver,
Quoi! mourir pour mourir et ne rien sauver ...
— Fais comme tu pourras: Coupe. Et gare à la drisse.
— Merci —
          D'un bond de singe il saute, de la lisse,
Sur le beaupré noyé, dans les agrès pendants.
— Bravo! —
           Nous regardions, la mort entre les dents.

— Garçons, tous à la drisse! à nous! pare l'écoute! ...
(Le coup de grâce enfin ...) — Hisse! barre au vent toute!
Hurrah! nous abattons! ... —
                            Et le foc déferlé
Redresse en un clin d'œil le navire acculé.
C'est le salut à nous qui bat dans cette loque
Fuyant devant le temps! Encor paré la coque!
— Hurrah pour le lascar! — Le lascar? ...
                                       — À la mer.
— Disparu? — Disparu — Bon, ce n'est pas trop cher.

. . . .

The Drink

Hove to, the ship was tipsy, with water lashing o-
Ver us, beneath a solitary topsail — the last.
— To the pumps, you mongrel sea-dogs! — The crew swore — No. —

— The topsail! the topsail! ...
                    There goes a cannon blast,
A loud swishswish of silk tearing right through the gale.

— The topsail's gone! — We've had it now. Someone's singing. —
— Stow it, Lascar! — Aye aye sir. — We've lost our topsail! ...
— One of you, trim the jib, if there's someone willing! ...
— I am. — You, lascar? — That's what I was singing, cap'n.
— Go on then. — No: tot first? — No, after. That'd be twice,
Seein' as the drink's down there as well ...
                         — Risk mishap 'n
By Christ! dying for dying's sake don't cut no ice ...
— Do what you can: Cut. And watch for the halyard's pull.
— Thanks —
          He monkey-leaps from the rail on the bowsprit
That's going under, into the hanging tackle.
— Bravo! —
          We just watched, scared to death, sensing this was it.

— All to the halyards, lads! trim the sheet or we whelm! ...
(At last the *coup de grâce* ...) — Heave! hard up with the helm!
Hurray! We're changing course! ... —
                     And the jib, unfurled,
Ups the ship in a trice that was down in the world.
There's our salvation beating in that tattered coat
Sent flying before the weather! The shell's afloat!
— Three cheers for the lascar! — The lascar? ...
                          — Overboard.
— Gone? — Gone for good — Well, it's a loss we can afford.

. . . .

— Ouf! c'est fait — Toi, Lascar! — Moi, Lascar, capitaine,
La lame m'a rincé de dessus la poulaine,
Le même coup de mer m'a ramené gratis ...
Allons, mes poux n'auront pas besoin d'onguent-gris.

— Accoste, tout le monde! Et toi, Lascar, écoute:
Nous te devons la vie ... — Après? — Pour ça? ... — La goutte!
Mais c'était pas pour ça, n'allez pas croire, au moins ...
— Viens m'embrasser! — Attrape à torcher les grouins.
J'suis pas beau, capitain', mais, soit dit en famille,
Je vous ai fait plaisir plus qu'une belle fille? ...

. . . .

Le capitaine mit, ce jour, sur son rapport:
— *Gros temps. Laissé porter. Rien de neuf à bord.* —

À bord.

— Whew! that's done — What, you, Lascar! — Right in one, it's me.
The waves washed me over the bow of the cutter
And the same rough sea, cap'n, brought me back buckshee ...
One thing, my fleas won't need treating with blue butter.

— Draw alongside, you lot! And you, Lascar, listen:
We owe you our lives ... — Which is worth? — Let's see ... — A drink!
But it wasn't for that, now you mustn't start to think ...
— Come and give us a kiss! — Wipe your chops on this 'un.
I'm not a good-looker, but, I say it as should,
I've pleasured you, cap'n, more'n any wench could? ...

. . . .

That day, the captain put in his official report:
— *Heavy weather. Gave ship her head. Nothing new aboard.* —

On board.

Bambine

Tu dors sous les panais, capitaine Bambine
Du remorqueur havrais *L'Aimable Proserpine*,
Qui, vingt-huit ans, fit voir au Parisien béant,
Pour vingt sous: *L'OCÉAN! L'OCÉAN!! L'OCÉAN!!!*

Train de plaisir au large. — On double la jetée —
En rade: *y a-z-un peu d'gomme* ... — Une mer démontée —
Et *la cargaison* râle: — Ah! commandant! assez!
Assez, pour notre argent, de tempête! cessez! —

Bambine ne dit mot. Un bon coup de mer passe
Sur les infortunés: — Ah, capitaine! grâce! ...
— C'est bon ... si ces messieurs et dam's ont leur content? ...
C'est pas pour mon plaisir, moi, v's'êtes mon chargement:
Pare à virer ... —

    Malheur! le coquin de navire
Donne en grand sur un banc ... — Stoppe! — Fini de rire ...
Et talonne à tout rompre, et roule bord sur bord
Balayé par la lame: — À la fin, c'est trop fort! ... —

Et *la cargaison* rend des cris ... rend tout! rend l'âme.
Bambine fait les cent pas.
     Un ange, une femme
Le prend: — C'est ennuyeux ça, conducteur! cessez!
Faites-moi mettre à terre, à la fin! c'est assez! —

Bambine l'élongeant d'un long regard austère:
— À terre! q'vous avez dit? ... vous avez dit: à terre ...
À terre! pas dégoûtaî! ... Moi-z'aussi, foi d'mat'lot,
J'voudrais ben! ... attendu q'si t'-ta-l'heure l'prim'flot
Ne soulag' pas la coque: vous et moi, mes princesses,
J'bêrons ben, sauf respect, la lavure éd'nos fesses! —

Il reprit ses cent pas, tout à fait mal bordé:
— À terre! ... j'crâis f ...tre ben! Les femm's! ... pas dégoûté!

Havre-de-Grâce. La Hève. — Août.

Bambine

Now you're pushing up the daisies, Captain Bambine
Of the Le Havre tugboat *L'Aimable Proserpine*,
Who, for twenty-eight years, let gawping Parisians see
THE OCEAN! THE OCEAN!! THE OCEAN!!! almost for free.

Pleasure-cruise in the offing. — Once round the jetty
In the roads: talk about the swank ... — A dirty sea —
And *the cargo*'s retching: — Enough, my man! it's choppy!
We've had our money's worth of tempest! now stop it! —

Bambine keeps his counsel. A heavy green sea breaks
Over the queasy: — Please, captain! for pity's sake! ...
— That's fine ... if you've had your fill then, ladies and gents? ...
I'm not here for my pleasure, you're my consignment:
Ready about ... —

              Disaster! the swine of a boat
Bears round on a sandbank ... — Stop! it's beyond a joke ...
And bumps, shivers her timbers and rolls gunwale under
Swept by the surge: — This is too much, a ghastly blunder! ... —

And the *cargo* gives vent to cries ... gives in to danger!
Gives up the ghost. Bambine paces the deck.
                          An angel,
A lady, grips his arm: — This is tiresome, driver!
Have me put ashore, I must be a survivor!

Bambine paying her out with a long stern stare:
— Ashore! that what you said? ... you said: ashore ... that's rare!
Ashore! she don't want much! ... Me too, I swear to God,
I'd damn well like the chance to, but if this right sod
Of a swell don't soon ease up: me 'n you, princesses
'll be supping, with respect, the swill up our arses! —

He continued to pace the deck, caught on the raw:
— Women! ... they don't want much! I'll be buggered! ashore!

Havre-de-Grâce. La Hève. — August.

Cap'taine Ledoux

À LA BONNE RELÂCHE DES CABOTEURS
VEUVE-CAP'TAINE GALMICHE
CHAUDIÈRE POUR LES MARINS — COOK-HOUSE
BRANDY — LIQŒUR
 — POULIAGE —

Tiens, c'est l'cap'tain' Ledoux! ... eh quel bon vent vous pousse?
— Un *bon frais,* m'am' Galmiche, à fair' plier mon pouce:
R'lâchés en avarie, en rade, avec mon *lougre* ...
— Auguss'! on se hiss' pas comm' ça desur les g'noux
Des cap'tain's! ... — Eh, laissez, l'chérubin! c'est à vous?
— Mon portrait craché hein? ... — Ah ...

                                        Ah! l'vilain p'tit bougre.

Saint-Malo-de-l'Isle.

342

Cap'n Ledoux

AT THE COASTERS PORT OF CALL
WIDOW OF CAP'N GALMICHE
SNUGGERY FOR SEAMEN — COOKHOUSE
BRANDY — LIQŒUR
— BLOCKS & TACKLE —

Well, it's Cap'n Ledoux! ... and what good wind blows you here?
— A fresh gale, ma'am, enough to make my wind-thumb veer:
We're laid up now, me and my broken-down *lugger* ...
— Auguss'! you don't go hoistin' y'sen on the knee
Of cap'ns! ... — Oh, let him be, is he yours, the laddie?
— The dead spit eh? ... — Ah ...

                    Ah! the ugly little bugger.

Saint-Mâlo-de-l'Isle.

343

Lettre du Mexique

La Vera-Cruz, 10 février.

"Vous m'avez confié le petit. — Il est mort.
Et plus d'un camarade avec, pauvre cher être.
L'équipage ... y en a plus. Il reviendra peut-être
    Quelques-uns de nous. — C'est le sort —

"Rien n'est beau comme ça — Matelot — pour un homme;
Tout le monde en voudrait à terre — C'est bien sûr.
Sans le désagrément. Rien que ça: Voyez comme
    Déjà l'apprentissage est dur.

"Je pleure en marquant ça, moi, vieux *Frère-la-côte.*
J'aurais donné ma peau joliment sans façon
Pour vous le renvoyer ... Moi, ce n'est pas ma faute:
    Ce mal-là n'a pas de raison.

"La fièvre est ici comme Mars en carême.
Au cimetière on va toucher sa ration.
Le zouave a nommé ça — Parisien quand-même —
    Le jardin d'acclimatation.

"Consolez-vous. Le monde y crève comme mouches.
   ... J'ai trouvé dans son sac des souvenirs de cœur:
Un portrait de fille, et deux petites babouches,
    Et: marqué — *Cadeau pour ma sœur.* —

"Il fait dire à *maman*: qu'il a fait sa prière.
Au père: qu'il serait mieux mort dans un combat.
Deux anges étaient là sur son heure dernière:
    Un matelot. Un vieux soldat."

Toulon, 24 mai.

Letter From Mexico

Vera-Cruz, 10th February.

"You entrusted your boy to me. — He is dead.
And more than one shipmate along with him, poor mite.
The crew ... there's none left. A few of us, when all's said
       And done, may be back. — That's fate —

"Nothing's so fine as being a sailor — for a man;
We're the envy of landlubbers — That's sure enough.
Barring the hardships. And there's nothing but: Even
       Being apprenticed is tough.

"I weep to tell you this, as an old fellow-salt.
I'd have readily given my skin there and then
So I could send him back to you ... It's not my fault:
       This sickness has no reason.

"The fever's upon us — as it was bound to be.
At the graveyard there's many'll draw their ration.
The Zouave — he's from Paris though — has called it *the*
       Acclimatization garden.

"Take comfort. People are dying off here like flies.
I've found in his kitbag a thing or two he prized:
A girl's picture and a pair of Turkish slippers
       Marked: *Present for my sister.*

"He wants me to tell his *mum:* he's said his prayers.
He'd rather have died in battle, tell his father.
Two angels were with him in his final hour:
       A sailor. An old soldier."

Toulon, 24th May.

Le Mousse

Mousse: il est donc marin, ton père? ...
— Pêcheur. Perdu depuis longtemps.
En découchant d'avec ma mère,
Il a couché dans les brisants ...

Maman lui garde au cimetière
Une tombe — et rien dedans. —
C'est moi son mari sur la terre,
Pour gagner du pain aux enfants:

Deux petits. — Alors, sur la plage,
Rien n'est revenu du naufrage? ...
— Son garde-pipe et son sabot ...

La mère pleure, le dimanche,
Pour repos ... Moi: j'ai ma revanche
Quand je serai grand — matelot! —

Baie des Trépassés.

The Cabin-Boy

So you've a sailor for a father?
— A fisherman. Godforsaken
Long ago. He's sleeping in Arthur's
Bosom where mother cannot waken

Him ... In the cemetery she tends
A grave — and there's nothing in it. —
I'm her husband on land, depends
On me, she does, for bread: I win it

For her'n the two kids. — Did nothing float
Back to the beach, then, from the boat? ...
— His pipe-rack and one *sabot* ... An'

On Sundays, mother's always grievin',
Wants peace of mind ... I'll get even
As a grown-up ... sea-faring man! —

Dead Men's Bay.

Au Vieux Roscoff

BERCEUSE EN NORD-OUEST MINEUR

Trou de flibustiers, vieux nid
À corsaires! — dans la tourmente,
Dors ton bon somme de granit
Sur tes caves que le flot hante ...

Ronfle à la mer, ronfle à la brise;
Ta corne dans la brume grise,
Ton pied marin dans les brisans ...
— Dors: tu peux fermer ton œil borgne
Ouvert sur le large, et qui lorgne
Les Anglais, depuis trois cents ans.

— Dors, vieille coque bien ancrée;
Les margats et les cormorans
Tes grands poètes d'ouragans
Viendront chanter à la marée ...

— Dors, vieille fille-à-matelots;
Plus ne te soûleront ces flots
Qui te faisaient une ceinture
Dorée, aux nuits rouges de vin,
De sang, de feu! — Dors ... Sur ton sein
L'or ne fondra plus en friture.

— Où sont les noms de tes amants ...
— La mer et la gloire étaient folles! —
Noms de lascars! noms de géants!
Crachés des gueules d'espingoles ...

To Old Roscoff

LULLABY IN NORTH-WEST MINOR

Filibusters' hide-out, ancient nest
Of pirates! — while the wild storm blows,
Sleep your good granite sleep, at rest
On cellars haunted by the billows ...

Boom at the sea, snore at the breeze;
Your fog-horn sounding through the fog,
Your sea-legs standing in green seas ...
— Sleep: you can close your one wall-eye
Open to the open sea to spy
For three centuries the English dog.

— Sleep, old firmly-anchored hull;
The *margets* and the cormorants
Your great poets of hurricanes
Will come and sing when the tide is full ...

— Sleep, you old sailors' concubine;
These waves won't, as in olden
Days, befuddle you or be your golden
Girdle on nights red with wine,
Blood and fire! — Sleep ... in your lap
Gold will no longer melt in boiling fat.

— Where are the names of your old flames ...
— Glory was light-headed, sea mad-capped! —
When blunderbuss muzzles spat
Names of lascars! giants' names!

349

Où battaient-ils, ces pavillons,
Écharpant ton ciel en haillons! ...
— Dors au ciel de plomb sur tes dunes ...
Dors: plus ne viendront ricocher
Les boulets morts, sur ton clocher
Criblé — comme un prunier — de prunes ...

— Dors: sous les noires cheminées,
Écoute rêver tes enfants,
Mousses de quatre-vingt-dix ans,
Épaves des belles années ...

. . . .

Il dort ton bon canon de fer,
À plat-ventre aussi dans sa souille.
Grêlé par les lunes d'hyver ...
Il dort son lourd sommeil de rouille.
— Va: ronfle au vent, vieux ronfleur,
Tiens toujours ta gueule enragée
Braquée à l'Anglais! ... et chargée
De maigre jonc-marin en fleur.

Roscoff. — Décembre.

Where did you fly your colours, those flags
Swathing your sky in slashed rags! ...
Sleep under a sky that is lead
On your dunes ... Sleep: there will be
No more cannon-balls — they're long dead —
To ricochet as they drum
A tattoo on your belfry
Riddled — like a plum tree is with plums ...

— Sleep: beneath your black chimney-stacks,
Listen to your children dreaming,
Cabin-boys of ninety deeming
The old days good now they are wrecks ...

. . . .

Your fine iron cannon's in a swoon,
Flat on its belly in the dust,
Pock-marked by each wintry moon ...
Sleeping its heavy sleep of rust.

— Roar on, old snorer, at the wind,
Always keep your rabid muzzle
Trained on the English dog! ... and primed
With thin sprigs of flowering furze.

Roscoff. — December.

351

Le Douanier

ÉLÉGIE DE CORPS-DE-GARDE
À LA MÉMOIRE DES DOUANIERS
GARDES-CÔTES MIS À LA RETRAITE
LE 30 NOVEMBRE 1869

Quoi, l'on te fend l'oreille! est-il vrai qu'on te rogne,
Douanier? ... Tu vas mourir et pourrir sans façon,
Gablou? ... — Non! car je vais t'empailler — Qui qu'en grogne! —
Mais, sans te déflorer: avec une chanson;
Et te coller ici, boucané de mes rimes,
Comme les varechs secs des herbiers maritimes.

    — Ange gardien culotté par les brises,
        Pénate des falaises grises,
        Vieux oiseau salé du bon Dieu
        Qui flânes dans la tempête,
        Sans auréole à la tête,
        Sans aile à ton habit bleu! ...

        Je t'aime, modeste amphibie
        Et ta bonne trogne d'amour,
        Anémone de mer fourbie
        Épanouie à mon *bonjour!* ...
        Et j'aime ton *bonjour*, brave homme,
        Roucoulé dans ton estomac,
        Tout gargarisé de rogomme
        Et tanné de jus de tabac!
        J'aime ton petit corps de garde
        Haut perché comme un goéland
            Qui regarde
        Dans les quatre aires-de-vent.

        Là, rat de mer solitaire,
        Bien loin du contrebandier
        Tu rumines ta chimère:
        — Les galons de brigadier! —

The Tide-Waiter

GUARD-ROOM ELEGY
TO THE MEMORY OF THE COASTGUARD
CUSTOMS OFFICERS PENSIONED OFF
ON NOVEMBER 30TH 1869

What, you, struck off! Is it true they've clipped your wings, tide-
Waiter, *salt-tax man*? ... You'll die and putrefy quite
Unceremoniously? ... — No! for I'll pack you tight
With straw — Grumble who may! — and with a song embed
You here, but without deflowering you, smoke-dried
By my rhymes, like dry kelp in a seaweed-drying shed.

    — Guardian angel seasoned by breezes,
        Daemon of the grey cliffs you haunt,
        Salty old sea-bird of the Lord Jesus
        Airing your heels in a storm,
        With no halo to daunt,
        No wings to your blue uniform! ...

        Modest amphibian, I'm fond
        Of you, your cherubic conk
        And bloated physionomy,
        That furbished sea-anemone
        In full bloom at my *how-d'ye-do!* ...
        And I love your *hello, matey,*
        Cooed from your belly or your boots,
        Gargled with hootch of potatey
        And tanned with tobacco juice!
        I like your small body, guard,
        Perched high up like a seagull
            Looking hard
        To the four points of the needle.

        There, solitary exciseman,
        With no smugglers anywhere near,
        You ruminate your fancy:
        — The gold-braid of an overseer! —

Puis un petit coup-de-blague
Doux comme un demi-sommeil ...
Et puis: bâiller à la vague,
Philosopher au soleil ...

La nuit, quand fait la rafale
La chair-de-poule au flot pâle,
Hululant dans le roc noir ...
Se promène une ombre errante;
Soudain: une pipe ardente
Rutile ... — Ah! douanier, bonsoir.

. . . .

— Tout se trouvait en toi, bonne femme cynique:
Brantôme, Anacréon, Barême et le Portique;
Homère-troubadour, vieille Muse qui chique!
Poète trop senti pour être poétique! ...
— Tout: sorcier, sage-femme et briquet phosphorique,
Rose-des-vents, sacré gui, lierre bacchique,
Thermomètre à l'alcool, coucou droit à musique,
Oracle, écho, docteur, almanach, empirique,
Curé voltairien, huître politique ...
— Sphinx d'assiette d'un sou, ton douanier souvenir
Lisait le bordereau même de l'avenir!

— Tu connaissais Phœbé, Phœbus, et les marées ...
Les amarres d'amour sur les grèves ancrées
Sous le vent des rochers; et tout amant fraudeur
Sous ta coupe passait le colis de son cœur ...
— Tu reniflais le temps, quinze jours à l'avance,
Et les noces: neuf mois ... et l'état de la France;
Tu savais tous les noms, les cancans d'alentour,
Et de terre et de mer, et de nuit et de jour! ...

Je te disais ce que je savais écrire ...
Et nous nous comprenions — tu ne savais pas lire —
Mais ta philosophie était un puits profond
Où j'aimais à cracher, rêveur ... pour faire un rond.

354

Then out with the tobacco,
Soothing as a drowse begun ...
And then: yawn at the billow,
Be philosophic in the sun ...

At night, when the growing squall
Raises goose-flesh on the pallid waves,
And ululates in black rock-caves ...
A shadowy figure walks tall;
Suddenly: a pipe is aglow,
Gleaming red ... — Aha! tidesman, hello.

. . . .

— There was everything in you, good biddy cynic:
Brantôme, Anacreon, Ready Reckoner, Stoic;
Homer the troubadour, old baccy-chewing Muse!
Poet too true to life to be truly poetic! ...
— Everything: warlock, midwife, tinder-box, time-fuse,
Compass-card, rose-of-the-winds, sacred mistletoe,
Bacchic ivy, alcohol thermometer, echo,
Musical cuckoo-clock, oracle, doctor, almanach,
Empiricist, Voltairian priest, political quack
Or oyster ... — Poor man's Sphinx, your coastguard memory
Would see the future's docket and read its summary!

— You knew Phoebe and Phoebus, each and every tide ...
Every mooring place where love let her anchor slide
To leeward of the rocks; and cheating Romeos
Smuggled their heart's moonshine under your very nose ...
— You'd sniff out the weather a fortnight in advance,
And the weddings: nine months ... and the state of France;
You knew all the names, the tittle-tattle hearsay
Of round-about, of land and sea, of night and day! ...

I'd tell you what I knew I could write ... You would heed
And we'd have an understanding — you couldn't read —
But your philosophy was a deep well I'd spit
Down, in the clouds ... to cause a ripple, to make a hit.

. . . .

Un jour — ce fut ton jour! — Je te vis redoutable:
  Sous ton bras fiévreux cahotait la table
  Où nageait, épars, du papier timbré;
  La plume crachait dans tes mains alertes
  Et sur ton front noir, tes lunettes vertes
  Sillonnaient d'éclairs ton nez cabré ...

  Contre deux rasoirs d'Albion perfide,
  Nous verbalisions! tu verbalisais!
  "Plus les deux susdits ... dont un baril vide ..."
  J'avais composé, tu repolissais ...

. . . .

— Comme un songe passés, douanier, ces jours de fête!
Fais valoir maintenant tes droits à la retraite ...
— Brigadier, brigadier, vous n'aurez plus raison! ...
— Plus de longue journée à gratter l'horizon,
Plus de sieste au soleil, plus de pipe à la lune,
Plus de nuit à l'affût des lapins sur la dune ...
Plus rien, quoi! ... que *la goutte* et le ressouvenir ...
— Ah! pourtant: tout cela c'est bien vieux pour finir!

— Va, lézard démodé! Faut passer, mon vieux type;
Il faut te voir t'éteindre et s'éteindre ta pipe ...
Passer, ta pipe et toi, parmi les vieux culots:
L'administration meurt, faute de ballots! ...

Telle que, sans rosée, une sombre pervenche
Se replie, en closant sa corolle qui penche ...
Telle, sans contrebande, on voit se replier
La capote gris-bleu, corolle du douanier! ...

. . . .

One day — it was your day — I saw you redoutable:
    Beneath your feverish arm the table rodeos
    And the crested paper swims — it's so scattered;
    In your ready hands the pen has sputtered
    And from your black brow your green spectacles
    Shoot flashes of lightning down your bucking nose ...

    We were drawing up! you were drawing up!
    A summons for two black sheep of Albion's dye:
    "Plus the two aforesaid ... one keg being dry ..."
    I had indited, you were polishing up ...

. . . .

— Vanished like a dream, the red-letter days you've spent!
Turn to good account now your right to retirement ...
— No, Sir, you won't be right without my proviso! ...
— No never-ending days scanning the horizon,
No siestas in the sun, no smokes by the moon,
No more evenings stalking rabbits from dune to dune ...
No more anything! ... but memories, gout and grog ...
— Ah well! all that's old hat, save a hair of the dog ...

— You're over the hill! This, *amigo,*'s where the path stops;
You have to see yourself go out like your pipe does ...
Racked, both pipe and you, among end-of-season briars:
The administration's dying, for lack of sops! ...

Just as, with no dew, a dark periwinkle
Folds upon itself, closes its drooping corolla ...
So, with no contraband, it can be seen to crinkle,
The slate-blue watch-coat, the tidesman's corolla! ...

Quel sera désormais le terme du problème:
— L'ennui contemplatif divisé par lui-même? —
Quel balancier rêveur fera donc les cent pas,
Poète, sans savoir qu'il ne s'en doute pas ...
Qui? sinon le douanier. — Hélas, qu'on me le rende!
Dussé-je pour cela faire la contrebande ...

. . . .

— Non: fini! ... réformé! Va, l'oreille fendue,
Rendre au gouvernement ta pauvre âme rendue ...
Rends ton gabion, rends tes *Procès-verbaux divers*;
Rends ton bancal, rends tout, rends ta chique! ...
Et mes vers.

Roscoff. — Novembre.

What will be the end of things now he's on the shelf:
— Contemplative boredom at variance with itself? —
And what dreary pendulum will do sentry-go,
Poet, and not know that he's not in the know ...
Who but the tidesman? — Heigh ho, let him be brought back!
Even if I have to carry contraband for that ...

. . . .

— No: too late! ... you're dismissed! Being their whipping post,
Hand over to the government your poor surrendered ghost ...
Your wicker-basket, your *Official Reports* — diverse —
Your rickety table, your all, your quid! ...
                                          And my verse.

Roscoff. — November.

Le Naufrageur

Si ce n'était pas vrai — Que je crève!
. . . .
J'ai vu dans mes yeux, dans mon rêve,
La NOTRE-DAME DES BRISANS
Qui jetait à ses pauvres gens
Un gros navire sur leur grève ...
Sur la grève des Kerlouans
Aussi goélands que les goélands.

Le sort est dans l'eau: le cormoran nage,
Le vent bat en côte, et c'est le *Mois Noir* ...
Oh! moi je sens bien de loin le naufrage!
Moi j'entends là-haut chasser le nuage!
Moi je vois profond dans la nuit, sans voir!

Moi je siffle quand la mer gronde,
Oiseau de malheur à poil roux! ...
J'ai promis aux douaniers de ronde,
Leur part, pour rester dans leurs trous ...
Que je sois seul! — oiseau d'épave
Sur les brisans que la mer lave ...
. . . .
Oiseau de malheur à poil roux!

— Et qu'il vente la peau du diable!
Je sens ça déjà sous ma peau.
La mer moutonne! ... Ho, mon troupeau!
— C'est moi le berger, sur le sable ...

L'enfer fait l'amour. — Je ris comme un mort —
Sautez sous le *Hû!* ... le *Hû* des rafales,
Sur les *noirs taureaux sourds, blanches cavales!*
Votre écume à moi, *cavales d'Armor!*
Et vos crins au vent! ... — Je ris comme un mort —

The Wrecker

If it weren't true — May I croak!
. . . .
I have seen in my eyes, in my dream,
Our BLESSED LADY OF THE BREAKERS
Toss up for her penniless folk
A huge vessel onto their shores ...
Onto the strand of the Kerlouans
As seagull-like as seagulls seem.

Fate is in the water: the cormorant's afloat,
The wind buffeting; it's *the Month of the Shroud* ...
Oh! I can sense the shipwreck from afar!
I can hear up there the driven cloud!
I can see deep into the night, O dark, dark ...!

Bird of ill omen with red locks,
I whistle when the sea is stormy!
I've promised the tidesmen due on watch
Their share to stay in their box ...
A lone bird of wrecks — let me be! —
On the sandbanks washed by the sea ...
. . . .
Bird of ill omen with red locks!

— And let it blow every outside in!
I feel it now beneath my skin.
Hey, white horses, my rearing band!
— I'm breaker-in, here on the sand ...

All hell is making love. — I laugh like a corpse —
Leap under the *Gee-up!* ... the *Giddy-up* of squalls,
On every *dull black bull* there's a *fine white horse!*
Your foam is for me, *pure-bred mares of Armor!*
And your manes for the wind! ... — I laugh like a corpse —

Mon père était un vieux *saltin**,
Ma mère une vieille *morgate*† ...
Une nuit, sonna le tocsin:
— Vite à la côte: une frégate! —
... Et dans la nuit, jusqu'au matin,
Ils ont tout rincé la frégate ...

— Mais il dort mort le vieux *saltin*,
Et morte la vieille *morgate* ...
Là-haut, dans le paradis saint,
Ils n'ont plus besoin de frégate.

Banc de Kerlouan. — Novembre.

* *Saltin:* pilleur d'épaves.
† *Morgate:* pieuvre.

My father was a *wrecker* old,
My mother an old *octopus* ...
One night, when the tocsin tolled:
— Quick to the coast: there's a frigate there! —
... And all night long, non-stop, tireless,
They stripped the frigate bare ...

— But he's dead asleep the *wrecker* old
And dead is the old *devil fish* ...
Up there on paradise's shoal
For frigates they've no further wish.

Kerlouan Reef. — November.

À Mon Cotre le Négrier

SOLD TO THE TUNE OF
"ADIEU, MON BEAU NAVIRE! …"

Allons file, mon cotre!
Adieu mon Négrier.
Va, file aux mains d'un autre
Qui pourra te noyer …

Nous n'irons plus sur la vague lascive
Nous gîter en fringuant!
Plus nous n'irons à la molle dérive
Nous rouler en rêvant …

— Adieu, rouleur de cotre,
Roule mon Négrier,
Sous les pieds plats de l'autre
Que tu pourras noyer.

Va! nous n'irons plus rouler notre bosse …
Tu cascadais fourbu;
Les coups de mer arrosaient notre noce,
Dis: en avons-nous bu! …

— Et va, noceur de cotre!
Noce, mon Négrier!
Que sur ton pont se vautre
Un noceur perruquier.

… Et, tous les crins au vent, nos chaloupeuses!
Ces vierges à sabords!
Te patinant dans nos courses mousseuses! …
Ah! c'étaient les bons bords! …

— Va, pourfendeur de lames,
Pourfendre, ô Négrier!
L'estomac à des dames
Qui *paîront leur loyer.*

364

To My Cutter Le Négrier

SOLD TO THE TUNE OF
"ADIEU, MON BEAU NAVIRE! ..."

Off you go, my cutter!
My *Négrier*, adieu.
Sail in the hands of another
Who may scuttle you ...

We'll go no more on the lascivious wave
   Still frisky when losing steam!
No more adrift above a watery grave
   Rolling along in a dream ...

   — Adieu, my rolling cutter,
   My *Négrier*, roll on,
   And you may even scuttle
   The flat-footed one.

We'll go no more a-rolling, stoned and free ...
   You'd go the pace washed-up;
And the heavy seas'd splash their *eau-de-vie*
   At our wakes: and did we sup! ...

   — Go, roistering cutter!
   My *Négrier*, live fast!
   Let an old fossil wassailer
   Wallow below your mast.

Once, port-holey virgins! well-launched floosies,
   Manes astream in the wind,
Came down on you in our frothy cruises! ...
   Ah! they were wild boardings!

   Go, cleaver of the waves,
   O *Négrier*! cleave in two
   The bellies of those jades
   Who *will pay their due.*

... Et sur le dos rapide de la houle,
   Sur le roc au dos dur,
À toc de toile allait ta coque soûle ...
   — Mais toujours d'un œil sûr! —

   — Va te soûler, mon cotre:
   À crever! Négrier.
   Et montre bien à l'autre
   Qu'on savait louvoyer.

... Il faisait beau quand nous mettions en panne,
   Vent-dedans, vent-dessus;
Comme on pêchait! ... Va: je suis dans la panne
   Où l'on ne pêche plus.

   — La mer jolie est belle
   Et les brisans sont blancs ...
   Penché, trempe ton aile
   Avec les goëlands! ...

Et cingle encor de ton fin mât-de-flèche,
   Le ciel qui court au loin.
Va! qu'en glissant, l'algue profonde lèche
   Ton ventre de marsouin!

   — Va, sans moi, sans ton âme;
   Et saille de l'avant! ...
   Plus ne battras ma flamme
   Qui chicanait le vent.

Que la risée enfle encor ta *Fortune**
   En bandant tes agrès!
— Moi: plus d'agrès, de lest, ni de fortune ...
   Ni de risée après!

---

* Large voile de beau temps.

... And on the spanking backside of the swell,
    Against the hard-backed rocky spur,
You, squiffy skiff, would crack on in your shell ...
    — But your eye didn't err! —

    — Go and get slewed, my cutter,
    My *Négrier*, till you burst.
    Let your new master splutter
    That we could tack from the first.

... Often the weather was fine when we hove to,
    The wind backing and filling;
What fishing we did! ... Now, there's no more to do
    As I'm on the rocks — and reeling!

    — The sea is quite ravishing
    And the breakers are white ...
    List, and dip your wing
    With seagulls in flight! ...

And steer a course so your sole mast whips
    The sky that scuds without yawing,
So, as you glide, the deep seaweed licks
    Your porpoise-belly awning.

    — Go without me: your soul;
    Make great headway, unpinned! ...
    No more will my pennon be blown
    Aflutter hugging the wind.

Let the flurry, by bracing your tackle,
    Not let your mains'l fall slack!
— For me: no more gaff, no ballast, no fores'l,
    No flaw — or guffaw — at my back!

... Va-t'en, humant la brume
Sans moi, prendre le frais,
Sur la vague de plume ...
Va — Moi j'ai trop de frais. —

Légère encor est pour toi la rafale
    Qui frisotte la mer!
Va ... — Pour moi seul, rafalé, la rafale
    Soulève un flot amer! ...

    Dans ton âme de cotre,
    Pense à ton matelot
    Quand, d'un bord ou de l'autre,
    Remontera le flot ...

— Tu peux encor échouer ta carène
    Sur l'humide varech;
Mais moi j'échoue aux côtes de la gêne,
    Faute de fond — à sec —

Roscoff. — Août.

... Sail on without me, taking
The air, inhaling sea-frets,
With featherwaves breaking ...
Sail off — I've too many debts. —

The blustery gale that is still mild to you
    Still frizzes the salt-race!
— I'm in dire straits and the squall I pass through
    Raises such bitter waves! ...

    — Deep in your cutter's heart
    Just think of your *matelot*
    When, to starboard or port,
    The tide slaps your bow ...

— You can still run your hull aground — I can't —
    On sea-wrack that's in soak;
As I am stranded on the shores of want
    For lack of reserves — stony broke —

Roscoff. — August.

Le Phare

Phœbus, de mauvais poil, se couche.
    Droit sur l'écueil:
S'allume le grand borgne louche,
    Clignant de l'œil.

Debout, Priape d'ouragan,
    En vain le lèche
La lame de rut écumant ...
    — Il tient sa mèche.

Il se mate et rit de sa rage,
    Bandant à bloc;
Fier bout de chandelle sauvage
    Plantée au roc!

— En vain, sur sa tête chenue,
    D'amont, d'aval,
Caracole et s'abat le nue,
    Comme un cheval ...

— Il tient le lampion au naufrage,
    Tout en rêvant,
Casse la mer, crève l'orage,
    Siffle le vent,

Ronfle et vibre comme une trompe,
    — Diapason
D'Éole — Il se peut bien qu'il rompe,
    Mais plier — non. —

Sait-il son Musset: À la brune
    Il est jauni
Et pose juste pour la lune
    Comme un grand I.

The Lighthouse

Phoebus, in a blazing temper, sets.
        Erect, lighting up the sky,
This shady, cragfast character whets
        And winks his one eye;

Stands, Priapus of the hurricane;
        Lascivious rollers lick
Him with their foaming crests in vain ...
        — He holds up his wick,

Braces himself, laughs at his trick
        Of tensing for tossing off;
It's proud, his untamed candlestick
        Stuck there on a rock!

— In vain the high clouds caracol
        Like wild grey mares and crash
Down on his hoary head; his poll
        Withstands the lightning's flash ...

He holds his lampion, in a dream,
        So no-one will be stranded,
Let sea break, waterspout steam,
        Wind whistle and,

Like a foghorn, vibrate and boom,
        — The diapason
Of Aeolus — He could well snap in two,
        But bending's not on.

Does he know his Musset? At dusk
        He's turned yellow
And poses like a capital I, just
        For the moon — so!

... Là, gît debout une vestale
　　　— C'est l'allumoir —
Vierge et martyre (sexe mâle)
　　　— C'est l'éteignoir. —

Comme un lézard à l'eau-de-vie
　　　Dans un bocal,
Il tirebouchonne sa vie
　　　Dans ce fanal.

Est-il philosophe ou poète? ...
　　　— Il n'en sait rien —
Lunatique ou simplement bête? ...
　　　— Ça se vaut bien —

Demandez-lui donc s'il chérit
　　　Sa solitude?
— S'il parle, il répondra qu'il vit ...
　　　Par habitude.

. . . .

— Oh! que je voudrais là, Madame,
　　　Tous deux! ... — veux-tu? —
Vivre, dent pour œil, corps pour âme! ...
　　　— Rêve pointu. —

Vous percheriez dans la lanterne:
　　　Je monterais ...
— Et moi: ci-gît, dans la citerne ...
　　　— Tu descendrais —

Dans le boyau de l'édifice
　　　Nous promenant,
Et, dans *le feu* — sans artifice —
　　　Nous rencontrant.

... There a vestal lies upended
        — She will ignite —
Virgin and martyr (male gender)
        — He snuffs the light. —

Like a lizard steeped in brandy
        In a flagon,
He corkscrews his life, going randy
        In this beacon.

Is he philosopher or poet?
        — He's no idea —
Complete lunatic or half-wit? ...
        — They're the same to my ear —

Now ask him if he cherishes
        His solitude?
— If he speaks, he'll say that he lives
        In a well-worn groove.

.   .   .   .

— Oh! how I'd like to live — would you,
        Madame, as a team,
Here, body for soul, eye for tooth! ...
        — A pointed dream. —

You'd be perching in the light-bell:
        I would climb up ...
— And I'd be lying in the well ...
        — Down you would drop —

We'd wend our way through the entrails
        Of the edifice,
Coming together in *the blaze* ...
        — Without artifice —

Joli ramonage ... et bizarre,
        Du haut en bas!
— Entre nous ... l'érection du phare
        N'y tiendrait pas ...

Les Triagots. — Mai.

Between ourselves, with brush and rod,
        We'd chimney-sweep so fast
The lighthouse's stiffness — how odd! —
        Could hardly last ...

Les Triagots. — May.

La Fin

Oh! combien de marins, combien de capitaines
Qui sont partis joyeux pour des courses lointaines
Dans ce morne horizon se sont évanouis! ...
. . . .

Combien de patrons morts avec leurs équipages!
L'Océan, de leur vie a pris toutes les pages,
Et, d'un souffle, il a tout dispersé sur les flots,
Nul ne saura leur fin dans l'abîme plongée ...
. . . .

Nul ne saura leurs noms, pas même l'humble pierre,
Dans l'étroit cimetière où l'écho nous répond,
Pas même un saule vert qui s'effeuille à l'automne,
Pas même la chanson plaintive et monotone
D'un aveugle qui chante à l'angle d'un vieux pont.

V. HUGO. — *Oceano nox.*

Eh bien, tous ces marins — matelots, capitaines,
Dans leur grand Océan à jamais engloutis ...
Partis insoucieux pour leurs courses lointaines
Sont morts — absolument comme ils étaient partis.

Allons! c'est leur métier; ils sont morts dans leurs bottes!
Leur *boujaron** au cœur, tout vifs dans leurs capotes ...
— *Morts* ... Merci: la *Camarde* a pas le pied marin;
Qu'elle couche avec vous: c'est votre bonne-femme ...
— Eux, allons donc: Entiers! enlevés par la lame!
　　　　Ou perdus dans un grain ...

Un grain ... est-ce la mort ça? la basse voilure
Battant à travers l'eau! — Ça se dit *encombrer* ...
Un coup de mer plombé, puis la haute mâture
Fouettant les flots ras — et ça se dit *sombrer*.

* *Boujaron*: ration d'eau-de-vie.

376

The End

Oh! many a sailor, many a captain too
Who's joyfully embarked to sail across the blue
Over the bleak horizon has passed away! ...
. . . .

Oh! many a skipper has gone down with his crew!
Of their lives the Ocean has taken every page,
And, with one breath, has scattered them over the waves,
None will know their end as they've plunged to wat'ry graves ...
. . . .

None will know their names, not even the humble stone
In the narrow graveyard where echoes are sole reply,
Not even a green willow shedding its autumn leaves,
Not even the plaintive song of a blind man who grieves
Monotonously on an old bridge close by.

V. HUGO. — *Oceano nox.*

Well now, all those sailors — ratings and captains too,
In their mighty Ocean engulfed eternally ...
Who heedlessly embarked to sail into the blue
Are dead — just as they were when they put out to sea.

So what! that's their job; they've died in their boots, alive
And kicking in their oilskins, their rum down the hatch!
— *Dead* ... No fear: *wan Death*'s not got sea-legs at all;
Let her bed down with you: she is your loving wife ...
— They've been swept off their feet by the tiderace! — despatched
                    Or lost in a squall ...

A squall ... is that your *death*, then? the low studding-sails
Slap-slapping through the water! — That's called *floundering* ...
A heavy leaden sea, and then the top mast flails
Lambasting the waves flat — and that's called *foundering.*

— Sombrer — Sondez ce mot. Votre *mort* est bien pâle
Et pas grand'chose à bord, sous la lourde rafale ...
Pas grand'chose devant le grand sourire amer
Du matelot qui lutte. — Allons donc, de la place! —
Vieux fantôme éventé, la Mort change de face:
　　　　　　　La Mer! ...

Noyés? — Eh allons donc! Les *noyés* sont d'eau douce.
— Coulés! corps et biens! Et, jusqu'au petit mousse,
Le défi dans les yeux, dans les dents le juron!
À l'écume crachant une chique râlée,
Buvant sans hauts-de-cœur *la grand'tasse salée* ...
　　　— Comme ils ont bu leur boujaron. —

. . . .

— Pas de fond de six pieds, ni rats de cimetière:
Eux ils vont aux requins! L'âme d'un matelot
Au lieu de suinter dans vos pommes de terre,
　　　　　Respire à chaque flot.

— Voyez à l'horizon se soulever la houle;
　　　　On dirait le ventre amoureux
D'une fille de joie en rut, à moitié soûle ...
　　　　Ils sont là! — La houle a du creux. —

— Écoutez, écoutez la tourmente qui beugle! ...
C'est leur anniversaire — Il revient bien souvent —
Ô poète, gardez pour vous vos chants d'aveugle;
— Eux: le *De profundis* que leur corne le vent.

... Qu'ils roulent infinis dans les espaces vierges! ...
　　　　Qu'ils roulent verts et nus,
Sans clous et sans sapin, sans couvercle, sans cierges ...
— Laissez-les donc rouler, *terriens* parvenus!

À bord. — 11 février.

378

— Foundering — Sound that word. Your *death* is very pale
And a mere fleabite on board in a stinging gale ...
A drop in the ocean beside the bitter grin
Of the battling sea-dog. — Give him leeway, make space! —
Old wind-swept spectre Death takes on another face:
                    The Drink! ...

Drowned? — Go tell the marines! The drowned are fresh-water.
— Sunk! with all their booty! From deck-hand to mate, dumb
Defiance in their eyes, an oath between their teeth!
Spitting chewed plug at the foam, they ask no quarter,
Down a schooner of brine — their stomachs do not heave —
Like they downed their rum.

. . . .

— No six-foot underground, no rats to dig God's acre:
For *they* go to the sharks! The soul of a sailor,
Instead of seeping up into your potatoes,
                    Breathes with every breaker.

— See, to the horizon, the swell before their prow:
                    Like the amorous belly of
A chorus girl on heat and half-seas over. Now
                    That's where they are! — The swell has its trough. —

It's their birthday again! — Listen; hear the blizzard
Raging, and you'll feel the strength they go on pitting ...
O poet, may your blind man's songs stick in your gizzard;
— Theirs: the *De profundis* of the wind's trumpeting.

... May they roll endlessly in the virgin expanses! ...
                    May they roll raw in their blubber,
With no nails and no coffin, no lid, no candles ...
— Let them go on rolling, you upstart landlubbers!

On board. — 11th February.

379

RONDELS POUR APRÈS

RONDELS FOR AFTERWARDS

Sonnet Posthume

Dors: ce lit est le tie ... Tu n'iras plus au nôtre.
— Qui dort dîne. — À tes dents viendra tout seul le foin.
Dors: on t'aimera bien — L'aimé c'est toujours l'Autre ...
Rêve: La plus aimée est toujours la plus loin ...

Dors: on t'appellera beau décrocheur d'étoiles!
Chevaucheur de rayons ! ... quand il fera bien noir;
Et l'ange du plafond, maigre araignée, au soir,
— Espoir — sur ton front vide ira filer ses toiles.

Museleur de voilette! un baiser sous le voile
T'attend ... on ne sait où: ferme les yeux pour voir.
Ris: Les premiers honneurs t'attendent sous le poêle.

On cassera ton nez d'un bon coup d'encensoir,
Doux fumet! ... pour la trogne en fleur, pleine de moelle
D'un sacristain très-bien, avec son éteignoir.

Posthumous Sonnet

Sleep: this bed is yours ... Time to leave father and mother.
— He who sleeps feasts. — It'll come on its own, will the hay.
Sleep: you'll be well loved — The loved one's always the Other ...
Dream: She who's loved best is always the furthest away ...

Sleep: smart unhooker of stars, as they'll call you now!
Bestrider of beams! ... in darkness each the last straw;
And the angel of ceilings, lean spider, will draw
His web at night — Delight? — across your empty brow.

Muzzler of veils! there's a kiss under the canopy
Or fall for you ... none knows where: close your eyes to see.
Laugh: The first honours await you under the pall.

By trumpeting your praises they'll give you great clout —
Sweet bouquet! ... for the full-blown snout, his all in all,
Of a respectable sexton, with his snuffer-out.

Rondel

Il fait noir, enfant, voleur d'étincelles!
Il n'est plus de nuits, il n'est plus de jours;
Dors... en attendant venir toutes celles
Qui disaient: Jamais! Qui disaient: Toujours!

Entends-tu leurs pas?... Ils ne sont pas lourds:
Oh! les pieds légers! — l'Amour a des ailes...
Il fait noir, enfant, voleur d'étincelles!

Entends-tu leurs voix?... Les caveaux sont sourds.
Dors: Il pèse peu, ton faix d'immortelles;
Ils ne viendront pas, tes amis les ours,
Jeter leur pavé sur tes demoiselles...
Il fait noir, enfant, voleur d'étincelles!

Rondel

The dark is here, child, stealer of sparkles!
There are no more nights, there are no more days:
Sleep ... waiting for them to come, all the girls
Who kept saying: Never! Who kept saying: Always!

You hear their footsteps? ... Oh! they scarcely graze
The ground: such gentle feet! — Love is aerial ...
The dark is here, child, stealer of sparkles!

You hear their voices? ... The ossuary remains
Stone deaf. Sleep: your burden of immortelles
Is not heavy. Your friends the bears won't craze
A paving on damselflies: your damsels.
The dark is here, child, stealer of sparkles!

Do, l'Enfant, Do ...

Buona vespre! *Dors: Ton bout de cierge ...*
On l'a posé là, puis on est parti.
Tu n'auras pas peur seul, pauvre petit? ...
C'est le chandelier de ton lit d'auberge.

Du fesse-cahier ne crains plus la verge,
Va! ... De t'éveiller point n'est si hardi.
Buona sera! *Dors: Ton bout de cierge ...*

Est mort. — Il n'est plus, ici, de concierge:
Seuls, le vent du nord, le vent du midi
Viendront balancer un fil-de-la-Vierge.
Chut! Pour les pieds-plats, ton sol est maudit.
— Buona nocte! Dors: Ton bout de cierge ...

Bye, Baby, Byes ...

Buona vespre! *Sleep: Your little candle-end ...*
They've stood it here then gone — out of your mind? —
Poor love, you won't be afraid left behind? ...
It's the candlestick from your bed at the inn.

The big stick need frighten you no more! Intend
To wake you — No-one could be so thick-skinned!
Buona sera! *Sleep: Your little candle-end ...*

Is dead. — The concierge, you can't depend
On her, has left. Only the north or south wind
Will float you out a gossamer line.
Hush now! For flat-feet, your ground is malign.
— Buona nocte! *Sleep: Your little candle-end ...*

Mirliton

Dors d'amour, méchant ferreur de cigales!
Dans le chiendent qui te couvrira
La cigale aussi pour toi chantera,
Joyeuse, avec ses petites cymbales.

La rosée aura des pleurs matinales;
Et le muguet blanc fait un joli drap ...
Dors d'amour, méchant ferreur de cigales.

Pleureuses en troupeau passeront les rafales ...

La Muse camarde ici posera,
Sur ta bouche noire encore elle aura
Ces rimes qui vont aux moelles des pâles ...
Dors d'amour, méchant ferreur de cigales.

Comb and Paper

Sleep for love, wicked shodder of cicadas!
In dog's tooth grass which will give you good hiding
For you too the cicada will be riding
His tiny cymbals, being joyous.

The dew will be your early morning tears;
With lilies of the valley as your bedding
Sleep for love, wicked shodder of cicadas.

Blustering squalls will pass like flocks of mourners ...

Here the death's-head Muse will come flitting.
Your still black lips will have rhymes at her bidding
That cut to the quick of the cadaverous ...
Sleep for love, wicked shodder of cicadas.

Petit Mort pour Rire

Va vite, léger peigneur de comètes!
Les herbes au vent seront tes cheveux;
De ton œil béant jailliront les feux
Follets, prisonniers dans les pauvres têtes ...

Les fleurs de tombeau qu'on nomme Amourettes
Foisonneront plein ton rire terreux ...
Et les myosotis, ces fleurs d'oubliettes ...

Ne fais pas le lourd: cercueils de poètes
Pour les croque-morts sont de simples jeux,
Boîtes à violon qui sonnent le creux ...
Ils te croiront mort — Les bourgeois sont bêtes —
Va vite, léger peigneur de comètes!

A Little Mock Corpse

Go quick, light-fingered comber of comets!
Grasses in the wind will be your hair;
Will o' the wisps, prisoners of the blank stare,
Will leap from your gaping eye-sockets ...

The flowers for graves called none-so-pretty
Will be teeming in your earthy laughter ...
And forget-me-nots, those flowers of oubliettes ...

Don't be a clodhopper: coffins for poets
Are simply pranks for the mute undertaker,
Violin cases that couldn't sound hollower ...
They'll think you're dead — The bourgeois are nit-wits —
Go quick, light-fingered comber of comets!

Male-Fleurette

Ici reviendra la fleurette blême
Dont les renouveaux sont toujours passés ...
Dans les cœurs ouverts, sur les os tassés,
Une folle brise, un beau jour, la sème ...

On crache dessus; on l'imite même,
Pour en effrayer les gens très-sensés ...
Ici reviendra la fleurette blême.

— Oh! ne craignez pas son humble anathème
Pour vos ventres mûrs, Cucurbitacés!
Elle connaît bien tous ses trépassés!
Et, quand elle tue, elle sait qu'on l'aime ...
— C'est la male-fleur, la fleur de bohème. —

Ici reviendra la fleurette blême.

Minature Flower of Evil

She'll come again, the deathly pale small flower;
Her Spring revivals are always passé ...
In open hearts, in charnel houses, a
Foolish breeze, one fine day, will sow her ...

She is spat at; she has her mimickers,
So very-sensible people are scared away ...
She'll come again, the deathly pale small flower.

— Oh! don't be afraid of her humble curse
On your ripe bellies, Great Gourd Gourmets!
With her dear departed she goes all the way!
And when she kills, she knows she has lovers ...
— She's the errant flower, the flower that errs. —

She'll come again, the deathly pale small flower.

À Marcelle

La Cigale et le Poète

Le poète ayant chanté,
            Déchanté,
Vit sa Muse, presque bue,
Rouler en bas de sa nue
De carton, sur des lambeaux
De papiers et d'oripeaux.
Il alla coller sa mine
Aux carreaux de sa voisine,
Pour lui peindre ses regrets
D'avoir fait — Oh: pas exprès! —
Son honteux monstre de livre! ...
— Mais: vous étiez donc bien ivre?
— Ivre de vous! ... Est-ce mal?
— Écrivain public banal!
Qui pouvait si bien le dire ...
Et, si bien ne pas l'écrire!
— J'y pensais, en revenant ...
On n'est pas parfait, Marcelle ...
— Oh! c'est tout comme, dit-elle,
Si vous chantiez, maintenant!

To Marcelle

The Cicada and the Poet

The poet, having lilted,
        Wilted,
Seeing his Muse, almost soused,
Roll to the bottom of her cloud
Of cardboard, onto shreds
Of paper and Lurex threads.
He ventured out to obtain
At his neighbour's window-pane
(Nose to the glass) forgiveness
For having made — Oh: not on purpose! —
His shameful monster of a book! ...
— It's really got a dog-eared look!
— The hair of your dog! ... Is that bad?
— Scribe of the poor man's Iliad!
Who might have used his wit ...
And, just not have written it!
— I was thinking, as I came, how
One is far from perfect, Marcelle ...
— Oh! said she, it sounds as if, well well,
You're going for a song right now!

NOTES: À l'Auteur du *Négrier*: Tristan's father, Edouard Corbière, wrote *le Négrier (the slave ship)*, a maritime adventure, published to acclaim in 1832. It was the revised 4th edition (1855) whose wording had such an effect on Tristan. He asked for copies which he kept in his desk at school (in the little yellow box where he put his prize possessions) to give away to favourite teachers. He proclaimed in a letter home: *'J'ai ... dans la tête que je serai un jour un grand homme, que je ferai un Négrier.'* It's possible he came to see himself as a slave-ship in the hands of his commander-father-author. He wrote in his father's copy of *Les Amours Jaunes: À l'auteur de l'auteur de ce livre.*

À MARCELLE

Le Poète et la Cigale: La Fontaine's first fable *La Cigale et la Fourmi*, of which this is a pastiche, has the cicada wanting to borrow from her neighbour the ant, but she is sent packing with a flea in her ear for singing instead of stocking the larder. La Fontaine preceded his fables with a life of Æsop who was hideous, even malformed and almost dumb until the gods loosened his tongue, so that what he couldn't achieve by beauty, power and wealth, he could by cleverness. He said: *Je ressemble à cette cigale, je n'ai que la voix.* Then La Fontaine chides the cicada for singing all the time! Whereas Trist-ant becomes indebted to his cicada. He was as unconcerned about entomological accuracy as La Fontaine — he needed his neighbour to be blond and female. The poet was so short of rhymes that he has retained over half of La Fontaine's and the new ones show that his Muse is naked, just needing rhymes to clothe her and keep her happy *(nue, rimer, faut, elle, heureuse)*!

ÇA

Ça?
Album? ... décousu: The sketch pad *(mon album)* he took out of his yellow box at school to make room for his new paintings was torn (by the *maître d'étude* who disapproved of caricatures he'd drawn), and *tout décousu*. (Details from a letter home 13 years earlier.)
Ce n'est poli ni repoli: an allusion to Boileau's dictum in *L'Art Poétique* (l.172-3), which every French schoolboy would have heard quoted again and again.
> Vingt fois sur le métier remettez votre ouvrage:
> Polissez-le sans cesse et le repolissez;

(Put your work back on the stocks twenty times over: Polish it ceaselessly and then polish it again*)*
chic, ficelles: for an artist *chic* can be a disparaging term: bad or insincere, but it's also to paint without a model, the hand of the artist having a memory. The sense of casual elegance is there too. *Ficelles* are the strings you pull, or for the artist the hidden tricks of the trade.
le huron: barbarous language. In Voltaire's novel *L'Ingénu* (1767), the hero is *le Huron*, whose misadventures result from him always saying what he thinks and

doing what he likes. The name is that of a North American tribe, from the Algonquin family, but came to mean a boor. In another Algonkian tribe, the Shahiyena (Cheyenne), the people were reputed to talk unintelligibly.

Gagne: Paulin Gagne (1808-76) imagined a universal language and called it Gagnemonopanglotte; stood in all elections as *candidat surnaturel, universel et perpétuel,* or as candidate for the mad; wrote a 3,000 line poem on suicide; and suggested that during the siege of Paris, to avoid famine, people over 60 (of whom he was one) should be eaten.

Musset: Alfred de Musset (1810-57) wrote sad Romantic love poems and confessions, lively drama and humorous verse, insouciant and witty, starting with *Contes d'Espagne et d'Italie.*

Préfecture de police: Tristan's places of composition are often pure fantasy. Here he has suffered an interrogation, where better?

20 mai 1873: 3 days *after* the printing of *Les Amours Jaunes* was begun.

Paris: Tristan spent over 2 years in Paris (1872-4).

i *Bâtard de Créole et Breton*: the hero in *Le Négrier*, Léonard, a *négrier (slave-trader)* himself, was born in a storm at sea to a young Creole woman, who'd been brought to France by a sailor from Brest. A Creole is normally a white West Indian, not a half-caste as the line suggests. For a chauvinist Parisian though he'd be expected to talk pidgin. And be illegitimate. Tristan thought highly of his father's novel and would have empathised with Léonard. And Tristan's home was in the part of Finistère called Léon.

Des seaux passent: Perhaps Tristan had in mind *Des sots passent (Fools pass)* too.

ii *passer, repasser...* Nothing being stable in Paris, *passer* keeps passing in slightly altered forms: it goes by, goes to court, goes harping on with the same old tune, goes past whoever's in the way and, going beyond itself, goes out like a light!

le paradis / Des mahomets et des houris: paradise for mahomets, in the plural! turns out to be a brothel, and a hard-hitting one at that! (I have kept the once popular spelling.)

iii The epigraph is the final couplet of *À la claire fontaine* with *Dondaine!* and *Dondé!* tacked on!

Le Parnasse en escalier takes up and distorts the phrase from manuals of rhetoric: *Gradus ad Parnassum* (the steps up Mount Parnassus, the dwelling of Apollo and the Muses). The Parnassians were French poets, born about the same time as Tristan, who gravitated round Leconte de Lisle. They tended to write on impersonal themes and were considerably influenced by the formal achievements of Théophile Gautier. The first Parnassian anthology appeared in 1866, the second in 1871, the third after Tristan's death.

la Chlorose: Chlorosis or green sickness is a kind of anaemia.

mancenillier: a tropical American tree whose latex is very poisonous and whose shade was considered mortal. Victor Hugo wrote in *Pleurs dans la Nuit: Et l'homme dort à l'ombre / De ce mancenillier.* (And man sleeps in the shade of this manchineel) *(Les Contemplations)*

iv *nuits blanches:* sleepless nights, the white remaining when the candle's gone! A sharp contrast with the reddened eyelids *(ta paupière rougie).*

tristes: the repetition of this word stresses how much sadness is part of him. He would have been affected by the words of Blanchefleur, Tristan's mother (in *Le Roman de Tristan et Yseult): Triste j'accouche, triste est la première fête que je te fais, à cause de toi j'ai tristesse à mourir. Et comme ainsi tu es venu sur terre par tristesse, tu auras nom Tristan.*

v *Les mornes:* a Creole word for small rounded mountains in the West Indies; or gloomy folk in the eyes of Parisians. *ta colonie:* there's a hint of backward savages here! *les bamboulas:* African dances.

vi *Évohé:* the frenzied Bacchic cry.

la veine: vein (whipping a vein could draw blood), luck, and poetic inspiration.

Voir les planches... instead of *See Naples and die.* This theatre is Paris. Your appearance is everything and once the play is over...

Cour des miracles: in the Middle Ages miracle plays were performed and beggars and crooks gathered in such a square.

vii *la tramontane:* tramontana: a north wind in the Mediterranean or the pole star — both could have risen; *perdre la t.* to lose one's wits, one's sense of direction.

Prométhée: Prometheus outwitted Jupiter, who had taken fire from the earth, by stealing it back from the chariot of the sun and bringing it down to earth at the end of a fennel stalk. Further provoked, Jupiter punished him by having him tied to a rock, where for 30,000 years a vulture was to peck out his liver which would keep renewing itself. This Prometheus, chained up like the first on Mount Caucasus, is hardly a heroic figure. We aren't told that after 30 years he is rescued by a contemporary Hercules killing the vulture.

Monsieur Vautour ou le Propriétaire sous le scellé was vaudeville, written by Désaugiers, George-Duval and Tournay (1805), which aimed at unscrupulous critics and members of the public as much as landlords. *Monsieur Vautour* featured in cartoons by Daumier and fellow cartoonists as the ruthless property speculator at the time of Haussmann's grand plan for Paris (in the 17 years from 1853 when he became Prefect of the Seine).

le four: as well as the village oven, it is a flop in the theatre.

banal has two senses too: communal and commonplace, run of the mill.

la curée: quarry or spoils.

le pélican is an allusion to the poet-pelican in Alfred de Musset's poem *La Nuit de Mai* offering the public his entrails and life to feast on. *Les plus désespérés sont les chants les plus beaux (The most despairing are the most beautiful of songs),* the Muse tells the Poet as a prelude to the pelican's appearance.

le chant du cygne: fable has it that the dying swan sings its finest song.

bec-jaune: a novice, a fool, an eyas, an unfledged hawk.

viii *absinthe: le feu vert (green fire),* a bitter liqueur containing extract of wormwood, a 70% proof concoction of crushed herbs diluted in sugar and water, i.e. brandy. The end of the 19th century saw widespread drinking of absinth in Paris cafés, it often acting as a drug. A French Temperance Society founded in 1871 deplored its use but to no effect. A law was eventually passed (on 16th March 1915) prohibiting it.

Ton poumon .... evokes pulmonary tuberculosis aka phthisis, a terrible wasting disease much feared at the time, which had attacked Tristan himself.

Épitaphe:

Epigraph: To mark the end of the beginning of the collection an invented quotation for an inventive inventory to vent the death of *corps bière (body bier)*. It reads just like a commentary on Hegel's view of the relationship between logic, nature and mind. (A.Véra, 1867); with the novel lack of punctuation to suit the endless round.

Il se tua... S'il vit... After saying how he may have died, he allows that he may be alive.

la musette: bagpipes or small oboe (hautbois pastoral) played at the local fête. Or a little muse? Henry Murger has a character called Musette, an artists' model. 'She was twenty years of age, and luxury was almost necessary to her health... Her life repeatedly alternated between blue broughams and omnibuses, mezzanine and fifth storey, silk and cotton' (*Scènes de la Vie de Bohème*). Murger's poem in the novel's epilogue: *La Chanson de Musette* was set to music by Alfred Vernet and became 'one of the best-loved of all French songs'.

palette: range of colours as well as an actual palette; could even be *(pop.)* a guitar!

LES AMOURS JAUNES: Yellow, when applied to love of woman, as it could be in most of the poems in this section, is the colour of betrayal and cuckoldry. *La sauce jaune / De chic et de mépris (*in *Bohème de Chic)* suggests that the colour applies to a cast of mind, a whole way of seeing the world: *voir jaune,* which with scorn could elicit *un rire jaune.* Lying on his sick-bed, fearful of death and turning to the wall, only to see his own image (in *Un Jeune Qui S'en Va*), Tristan has coloured the wall yellow for me. If only it could be transformed like the wallpaper in Emma Bovary's room at Léon's approaches: *le papier jaune de la muraille faisait comme un fond d'or derrière elle.*

À l'Éternel Madame: *l'Éternel* is masculine, Madame is therefore wished into eternity! She seems to be Woman in general. (Armida for one wasn't married, though she may have been a madam.) As it's the first of *Les Amours*, a title which brings Ronsard and the Troubadours to mind, Madame could be heard, if only briefly, before the instructions to do the ironing and then sit on his knee, as Ma Dame, my Lady to be sung with *amour courtois* vocabulary like *flamme* and *âme.*

Fille de marbre may refer to a successful play by Théodore Barrière and Lambert Thiboust: *Les Filles de Marbre* (1853) in which an artist of talent called Raphaël is destroyed by an insensitive courtesan.

Âme ... Key-rhymes in lyrical love poems, comically juxtaposed, made even more ridiculous by the preceding *brame* and the allusion to Hugo's poem *Les Djinns* (in *Les Orientales*):

Elle brame
Comme une âme
Qu'une flamme
Toujours suit!

Féminin Singulier: particularly *elle*. This poem includes significant *-elle* rhymes, important facets of woman in Tristan's eyes: beauty and cruelty.
Jocrisse: a stage Simpleton, a clumsy figure of fun.
le dix-cors: the seven year old stag whose antlers have developed to their maximum.
sache tomber! parodies Hugo's *Oh! n'insultez jamais une femme qui tombe (Oh! never insult a woman who falls) (Les Chants du Crépuscule XIV).*
gladiateur: the poem moves from theatre to circus to Roman arena and suggests the woman won't feel a thing for her victim or won't feel a thing falling or both. It's just part of the act.

Bohème de Chic: 'Bohemia is the probationary period of artistic life; it is the preface to the Academy, the Hôtel-Dieu (i.e.the general hospital) or the Morgue.' And Henry Murger goes on in his preface to *Scènes de la Vie de Bohème* to divide the citizens of Bohemia into (i) unknown Bohemians, poor artists condemned to perpetual obscurity because they cannot or will not find a means of advertising their artistic existence and of proving, by what they are already, what they might one day become. On the fringe of society, in isolation and inertia, they wait for the pedestals to come and place themselves under their feet. They usually suffer hardship and die of malnutrition; (ii) amateur Bohemians, those for whom going without dinner every day, sleeping out on rainy nights and wearing a nankeen suit in December represents the summit of human happiness. They soon tire of this and go home to marry their cousins, set up as solicitors, sit by the fire of an evening boasting of their poverty-stricken artist days with the exaggeration of travellers describing a tiger-hunt; (iii) official Bohemians, those who have drawn attention to their existence in the literary or artistic world, and their products, bearing their hallmark, are in circulation, albeit at moderate prices. To arrive at their destination, which is clearly determined, they will take any road and can even turn to their advantage the accidents that befall them on the way. The life they lead is a work of genius, a daily problem to be solved by bold mathematics, hunting from morning till night that wild animal known as the five-franc piece (say £1). Once they have arrived they can never turn back.
chic: (V. note under *Ça*)
les bottes vernies...: 'if you calmly explain (to unknown Bohemians) that the five-franc piece is the Empress of humanity, and that boots do not fall ready-polished from heaven, they turn their backs on you and call you a bourgeois.' Henry Murger (*op.cit.*)
vierge comme une / Pièce de cent sous! Virgo intacta because this coin had no hole through the middle.
à trois queues: For the Turks a 3 tailed pasha had the right to three horse tails in

front of him whenever he went out.

Ma Muse est grise: grey-haired and/or tipsy and/or surly.

Chair-de-poule: poule is a bird (but not a goose!), more a tart, a whore.

Jérusalem: An epidemic of leprosy swept through Europe after the Crusades. The Christian Church (hence Jerusalem?) instituted a rite of expulsion for lepers: *separatio leprosorum.* Or Tristan could possibly be thinking of *rue de Jérusalem,* which once ran from *Quai des Orfèvres* to *rue de Nazareth.* There were police cells *(le violon)* there.

Gente Dame: Gentle Lady, the ideal partner for a Gentle Man, or perhaps a Noble Lord.

La Tour de Nesle: a play by Alexandre Dumas père (1832). The Tour de Nesle itself, across the Seine from the Tour du Louvre, was where the scandalous daughters-in-law of Philippe IV le Bel (King of France from1285-1314) had their lovers thrown into the river for their pains! One of them, Marguerite de Bourgogne, calls out one wonderfully stormy night: *La belle nuit pour une orgie à la Tour!* which is quoted (almost) in *Le Poète Contumace.*

La Tour de Presle was also infamous at that time for the scandalous behaviour of certain members of the Presle family.

Frisette: Théodore de Banville (1823-91) in *Mascarades* in *Gaietés (Odes Funambulesques)* has Frisette as a Bohemian participant in a riotous carnival:

> Au son de la musette
> Suivez Ange et Frisette,
> Et ce joli poupon,
> Rose Pompon!

grisette: a young working girl, fairly free with her favours. The name came from the cheap grey dress material most of them wore. 'A girl who is neither immoral nor virtuous, who knows how to reconcile work and pleasure, who goes to church in the morning with her mother, and dancing in the evening with her lover' (as defined by an 1835 dictionary of popular terms).

Bradamante: warrior virago in white armour who rides on in pursuit of her beloved Rogero despite many setbacks (in Ariosto's *Orlando Furioso,* 1532).

Eschôlier en fortune: archaism: young elegant dare-devil student (at the University of Paris in Villon's day?).

1 Sonnet:

Pindus: Greek mountain, or rather mountain chain, sacred to Apollo, god of music and poetry, and the Muses.

Archimedes: Greek mathemaician who perfected the Greek numerical system.

Pegasus: the winged horse, favourite of the Muses.

Pic de la Maladetta: A peak (3,312m.) in the Spanish Pyrenees, one of the 3 in the Maladetta range, aka *montes Malditos (Maudits* like his music in *Elizir d'Amor),* where the River Garonne rises and the rock is granite and porphyry.

Sonnet à Sir Bob:
metempsychosis: when souls migrate to other bodies after death, not a Christian concept.
Britisch channel: Tristan's spelling is retained.
15 may is in the middle of an English spring, the season of love!

Steam-Boat:
ménélas: with a capital m, he would have been the deceived husband of Helen of Troy.
déchantait: a sense of disenchantment and poor singing combined. cf. *Un Juvénal de Lait* & *La Cigale et le Poète.*
10' long.O./ 40' lat.N. In open sea north-west of Lisbon! Perhaps where Candide, Pangloss and a brute of a sailor were the only survivors of a shipwreck in the worst of storms. (Voltaire: *Candide:* chapters 4 & 5)

Pudentiane: The title, usually thought to be a neologism based on the Latin *pudens*, with an ending suggesting a flower like *gentiane*, a modest flower *(pomme en fleur)* or a pious hypocrite, a *sainte n'y touche (fleur de péché)*, is in fact the name of a saint. Saint Pudentiana, Virgin, whose cultus is connected with the foundation of the titular church of the Pudens, one of the most ancient in Rome. The *ecclesia Pudentiana* (the station on the third Tuesday of Lent) is built on the site of the house of Pudens, a Roman senator who, according to tradition, acted as host to St Peter. The house could have been the residence of the Roman pontiffs in the second century. Pudentiana's day is May 19th and the Mass prescibed is one of the Masses of a Virgin not a Martyr. The Introit of the station in Lent, taken from Psalm 17 begins: *I have cried to Thee, for Thou, O God, hast heard me: incline Thine ear unto me and hear my words: keep me, O Lord, as the apple of Thy eye: protect me under the shadow of Thy wings.* The Collect exhorts to wholesome self-denial. The Gradual begins: *From my secret sins, cleanse me, O Lord: and from those of others spare Thy servant.* (Psalm 19 v.12-13)
Ni ne retient etc. The quotations are from and a slight corruption of The Commandments of God:

> Luxurieux point ne seras,
> > De corps ni de consentement.
> Le bien d'autrui tu ne prendras
> > Ni ne retiendras à ton escient.
> L'œuvre de chair ne désireras
> > Qu'en mariage seulement.   (from an 1882 missal)

and The Commandments of the Church of Rome:

> Tous tes péchés confesseras
> Vendredi chair ne mangeras   (from a 17th century text)

which were to be learnt by heart in the Catechism.
Pomme: The forbidden fruit of the tree of the knowledge of good and evil is often taken to be an apple.

40 ans: the siege of Troy lasted 40 years! Psalm 95 v.10 reads: *Forty years long was I grieved with this generation, and said, It is a people that do err in their heart, and they have not known my ways.*

Rome. — *15 août:* Feast of the Assumption of the Virgin. Although not a church dogma until 1950, the Cultus of the Assumption was in the liturgy in Rome in the 7th century. There were processions in Jerusalem, Constantinople and Rome and the scriptural texts used on August 15th included: God speaking to the serpent: woman's seed shall bruise thy head, i.e. there will be perpetual antagonism between the serpent and the seed of woman (Genesis 3 v 9-15); the woman clothed with the sun and the moon under her feet and upon her head a crown of twelve stars (Revelation 12 v.1).

Après la Pluie: and, to complete the saying: *le beau temps.*
une Cocotte: an 1869 Guide for the English and American Traveller names the expensive Café Anglais, Boulevard des Italiens, which is open all night, adding: Beware *cocottes.*
déjeuner de soleil: literally: lunch of sunshine, but a phrase applied to material whose colour is quick to fade, or, more generally, anything transient.
Le quartier des *Batignolles:* a part of Paris frequented by artists in the 19th century.
La *Marquise d'Amaëgui* is the beloved in Musset's *L'Andalouse.*
Frétillon: could be a *grisette*, the verb frétiller: to quiver, wriggle, wag (of tails), wiggle.
Doña Sabine: from Victor Hugo's *Guitare (Les Rayons et les Ombres)* where she is loved by Gastibelza, *l'homme à la carabine*, carabine: a rifle and in common parlance of the time, a student's mistress.
l'Odéon: then the theatre in the Latin Quarter.
Abeilard: Pierre Abélard (1079-1142), a native of Brittany, a brilliant scholar and rational theologian who lectured in Paris. His conceptualist views were considered heretical. He fell in love with his pupil, a woman of learning, Héloïse, whose uncle, a canon, insisted he be castrated. The letters exchanged between the lovers during their subsequent enforced separation may be recalled when the *Poète Contumace* writes his letter to *l'Absente.*
Juliette takes us to Shakespeare where the morning song of the lark (Act III scene 5) tells Romeo he must leave her.

À une Rose:
Papier-Joseph: could be slang for bank-notes.
Aï: a choice wine from the Champagne or the pudendal region or both.
BOCK: to go with skittles.

À la Mémoire de Zulma: Could Tristan have known of Zulma Carraud, wife of a major at the Military Academy of Saint-Cyr? She was one of Balzac's closest friends, not at all coquettish, and wrote rebuking him for his tempestuous life ('Like the alchemist, having squandered your gold, you will find nothing at the bottom of your crucible'); and for swearing allegiance to Louis-Philippe. She was a Republican. Édouard Viénot painted her with her son in 1827.

hors barrière: beyond the bounds of Paris and probity.

Bougival: quartier populaire, down in the world.

jeune de vingt francs: What with Zulma and the moon he was 20 francs lighter too!

la Commune: a provisional government from March to May 1871 of Socialist and left-wing Republicans elected after the right-wing National Assembly at Versailles tried to disarm the National Guard. It fell when the Versailles troops captured Paris and massacred about 20,000 people.

Saint-Cloud: quartier aristo, up in the world.

Bonne Fortune et Fortune:

La Passante: Tristan's encounter with his passer-by is closer than Baudelaire's in À une Passante, but all the more hurtful. Where Baudelaire has a full sonnet, he has what amounts to two sestets!

Rue des Martyrs: a street in Montmartre known then for prostitutes.

À une Camarade:

Qu'il s'ôte ...: The cynic Diogenes's words to Alexander.

lazzarone: a Neapolitan beggar, famous for lazing in the sun.

mal-aimée: predates Apollinaire's *Mal-Aimé* by at least 30 years.

Un Jeune Qui S'en Va:

J'entends le renard...: The refrains of *La Jument de Michao* (in *Kanomp Uhol! Chansons Bretonnes*) go

> C'est dans dix ans, je m'en irai
> J'entends le loup, le renard chanter (bis)
> J'entends le loup, le renard et la belette
> J'entends le loup, le renard chanter (bis)

Despite its nursery-rhyme cradle-song air, the verses tell how the mare and her foal have eaten all the hay and each winter that comes brings departure (by death through starvation?) one year closer. The end of Tristan's poem has death cradling him in his Muse's arms. In *Sonnet Posthume* (the first of the *Rondels pour Après*) there is hay, sustenance for the poet, only in sleep.

mourir pour la patrie: quotation from Rouget de Lisle's *La Marseillaise.*

mes épreuves: since the poet is addressing his Muse, *épreuves* are his proofs as well as his ordeals. To be a success, he has to die in his poetry like other (Romantic) poets have in theirs.

Myosotis...: from Millevoye's *La Chute des Feuilles* (*Élégies* 1811) where the Romantic hero, the *jeune malade,* says: *dans chaque feuille qui tombe/ Je lis un présage de mort (in every falling leaf I read an omen of death).*

Rolla: the hero of a poem by Musset, who decides to die as soon as he's spent his inheritance. He spends his last night with a 15 year old prostitute who tries, in vain, to dissuade him. Musset's election to the Academy came almost 20 years later, but

Tristan's juxtaposing of *Rolla* and *l'Académie* suggests it's one form of death after another.

Murger: Henry Murger (1822-61) famed for his *Scènes de la vie de Bohème* (1851), a novel based on his own life (and the inspiration for Puccini's opera *La Bohème*). The heroes, fraught with artistic and romantic setbacks, die young.

Baudelaire: Charles Baudelaire (1821-67) Poems in *Les Fleurs du Mal* (1857) were condemned as immoral, and had to be cut out, but not surgically.

Lamartine: Alphonse de Lamartine (1790-1869) author of *Harmonies Poétiques et Religieuses* (1830) which includes *Une Larme ou Consolation*. He lost his daughter Julia at Beyrouth in 1832 when she was 10 and wrote *Gethsemané, ou la mort de Julia*.

abonnés: would be the subscribers to Lamartine's monthly *Cours familier de littérature* (1856-59).

Moreau: Hégésippe Moreau (1810-37), who died of TB. Frequent stays in hospital, led to *Un souvenir à l'hôpital*.

Escousse: Victor Escousse, pen-name of Victor Lasserre (1813-32), who gassed himself at the age of 19, was consumed by pride rather than consumption, when his third play was a flop.

Gilbert: Nicolas Gilbert (1751-1780), poet, whose fate was recounted in *Stello* by Alfred de Vigny (1832), and who was generally seen as a precursor of the Romantics, saw himself as a martyr to his art:

> Au banquet de la vie, infortuné convive,
> J'apparus un jour, et je meurs...
> Nul ne viendra verser de pleurs.

(Adieux d'un jeune poète à la vie). Among his other writings were *Le Poète malheureux* and paraphrases of several Psalms.

à l'œil: by eye and for nothing.

Lacenaire: wrote (or probably wrote some of) *Mémoires, Révélations et Poésies de Lacenaire, écrits par lui-même à la Conciergerie*, where he was incarcerated for murder and executed in 1836. Maxime du Camp claimed to have had his mummified hand. Gautier saw it and wrote *Lacenaire*, the second of his *Étude de Mains* (*Émaux et Camées* 1852)

Sanson: Charles-Henri Sanson, executioner of Louis XVI and André Chénier among others.

Lord Byron: (1788-1824)

Hugo: Victor Hugo (1802-85). Most of his apocalytic works, e.g. *La Fin de Satan*, appeared after Tristan's death, but the first part of their forerunner: *La Légende des siècles* was published in 1859, with the sub-title: *Les Petites épopées*. *Pleine mer - Plein ciel* and *La Trompette du jugement* were apocalytic works from the *1ère série*.

Ceci tuera cela is the title of Book 5 chap.2 of *Notre Dame de Paris*. The sense is: the Press will kill the Church or printing will kill architecture.

gardenational: each citizen was obliged to don a uniform on particular days, a scheme which lasted about 40 years from the coming of Louis-Philippe to the start of the Third Republic. Certain artists refused. Running two words into one was probably a conscious decision and makes Hugo an epic bourgeois!

Il n'en reste qu'un... Taken from, and an ironical gloss on, the last line of *Ultima Verba* where Hugo stands up for *liberté* and against the coup d'état of 1852, even if it means accepting exile: *Et s'il n'en reste qu'un, je serai celui-là.* (*Les Châtiments* 1853).

J'en ai lus mourir! parodies Hugo's line: *Hélas! Que j'en ai vu mourir de jeunes filles!* in *Fantômes (Les Orientales* 1829).

Chénier: André Chénier (1762-94), poet who supported the Revolution, but was guillotined as an enemy of the people for trying to help save the king's life. Little of his work was published until 1819, when it made a great impact. Vigny saw him as another poet martyr in *Stello.*

Charenton: a town famous for its lunatic asylum.

Insomnie:

Tantale: son of Jupiter by a nymph, Tantalus was punished for his crimes with an insatiable thirst, and placed up to his chin in a pool of water which flows away at his every attempt to drink. Above his head is a bough laden with delicious fruit; at his every attempt to taste it a gust of wind blows it out of reach.

Belle-de-nuit: Lady of the night and Marvel of Peru.

Messaline: Messalina married the emperor Claudius and, being insatiable, prostituted herself in both palace and public brothels. Juvenal wrote of her: *Et lassata viris sed non satiata recessit* (Satire VI) and Tristan would also have known Baudelaire's *Sed non satiata.*

l'Hystérie: from the Greek for the womb; wild emotionalism was still supposed to be a sexual malady.

Buridan: Jean Buridan, a 14th century French scholastic philosopher, is supposed to have imagined an ass, bound to starve between two bundles of hay of exactly equal size and attractiveness, unable to decide which one to make for. Aristotle and Dante wrote of the same predicament.

fer rouge: red-hot iron.

La Pipe au Poète: A variation on Baudelaire's *La Pipe.* Pierre-Olivier Walzer considers Tristan's more successful than the original. The title could mean: The Pipe to the Poet.

Le Crapaud: Inverted sonnet, and even the octave is dislocated. He, as repulsive poet-toad, repulses his interlocutor. He is *sans aile,* which is, homophonically, *sans elle*; and just as the night is *sans air (sans oxygène),* so his song is *sans air, (sans mélodie,* or at least without an easily flowing tune). Tristan had pinned to his mantelpiece, if we are to believe René Martineau (Preface to the 1920 edition of *Les Amours Jaunes,* Crès), an old dried-out squashed toad.

Femme:

croquer: to sketch or to eat (la Pomme), even to seduce (from *jolie à croquer*).

feux: parody of classic language of gallantry.

dragée: sugared almond; *tenir la dragée haute:* to hold out on somebody, showing one's power over them. *dragée:* also a bullet, in soldiers' slang.

Duel aux Camélias: recalling *La Dame aux Camélias* by Alexandre Dumas fils (1848).

Veneris Dies 13: Venus's day. Day of unluck. The Ides of April.

Le Poète Contumace: not a contumacious poet, but one who doesn't appear before the tribunal when summoned.

son bail...: this jocular version of a lease recalls François Villon's:
> Que maistre Pierre Bobignon
> M'arenta, en faisant refaire
> L'uys et redrecier le pignon. *(Le Testament* ll 995-7)

Cerf de Saint-Hubert: Just as in the legend of St Eustace, a stag with a luminous crucifix between its antlers appeared to Hubert, a noble from Brabant, while he was out hunting one Good Friday in the 8th century, and he became religious, an active missionary in the forest of Ardenne, and a bishop.

les vers (line 63): worms briefly before the *enjambement* makes you realise they're lines of verse, or are there worms with six feet?

savoir-mourir is a neologism in French. Knowing how to die is crucial for an immortal poet.

je vis: I live (on?).

en rupture de ban: illegally returning from banishment; in defiance of the accepted code of conduct. Adding a c to make *banc* doesn't change the sound, but gives an oyster a bed.

Paul et Virginie: novel by Bernardin de Saint-Pierre (1787) in which the lovers, pure and innocent, live in a tropical paradise. Paul's dog is *Fidèle!*

le clair de la lune: not a far cry from the song: *Au clair de la lune,* whose final verse tells of the search for a pen, and a fire, but the door is closed on *mon ami Pierrot* and his companion.

Belles nuits... a quotation from *La Tour de Nesle* by Alexandre Dumas père. (V. *Gente Dame*)

Nuits à la Roméo / rossignols:
> *Juliet:* Wilt thou be gone? It is not yet near day.
> It was the nightingale, and not the lark,
> That pierced the fearful hollow of thine ear.
> *Romeo:* It was the lark, the herald of the morn;
> No nightingale.....
> Night's candles are burnt out and jocund day
> Stands tiptoe on the misty mountain tops.
> I must be gone and live, or stay and die. (Act 3, sc.5)

poinçons: gai comme un pinson (happy as a lark, or rather, chaffinch) is the known expression, *un poinçon* being a bradawl or bodkin, both piercing instruments!

saint Antoine / Suppôt: henchman, the capital S suggests he's thinking of the phrase *Suppôt de Satan:* hellhound, connecting it with Saint Anthony's temptations.

castagnoles: V. the note below on *Inès de Las Sierras.*

Folle-du-logis: imagination (literally: Madwoman at home); in the plural, probably the Muses.

Inès de Las Sierras: Spanish tale (1837) by Charles Nodier (1780-1844), retold in a poem by Théophile Gautier (1811-72) in *Émaux et Camées* (1852*),* both called *Inès de Las Sierras.* Three travellers, who have taken refuge from a storm in an old ruin, see at midnight the ghost of a woman who'd been killed by her lover. Dressed in a macabre and yet seductive way, she dances with *castagnettes:* ... Inès l'assassinée

> Dansant, un poignard dans le cœur!
> Sa rose, jaunie et fanée,
> S'effeuille dans ses noirs cheveux.
> ... on la suivrait même en enfer.

Could the Spanish for castanets: *castañuelas* be the reason for Tristan's spelling: *castagnoles?*

en pantenne: maritime term: in disorder.

Ma sœur Anne: French readers would know Charles Perrault's retelling of the folktale *La Barbe Bleue (Bluebeard)* (1697). Bluebeard's wife, threatened with death for disobedience, asked her sister Anne to climb the tower to call their brothers to hurry to the rescue. It was only on the fourth call of *Anne, ma sœur Anne, ne vois-tu rien venir?* that she saw them.

satin de brouette: la brouette could be Death's wheelbarrow, as in *Nature Morte,* making the bed a tomb with a dog couchant. Tristan's nickname was *Ankou,* the spectre of Death.

ma vielle: Tristan is known to have played the hurdy-gurdy.

Ma chandelle...: a quotation from *Au clair de la lune.*

Les petits morceaux blancs... recalls Hugo's *Vere Novo (On the return of Spring) (Contemplations* Bk.1 *Aurore,* 1856*),* where, in complete contrast to Tristan's Christmas Day, love letters from dreamy lovers are sent in April, torn up in May and fly to roses, jasmine and periwinkle *(pervenche)* like so many butterflies: *petits morceaux blancs... / De tous les billets doux, devenus papillons.* There is surely a reference also to the torn up letter tossed from the famous coach careering through the streets of Rouen in *Madame Bovary* (Part 3 chap.1). It was Emma's letter announcing the impossibility of adultery. *'Une main nue passa sous les petits rideaux de toile jaune et jeta des déchirures de papier, qui se dispersèrent au vent et s'abattirent plus loin, comme des papillons blancs, sur un champ de trèfles rouges tout en fleur.'* It is singularly appropriate that the blinds are yellow and the lover behind them is called Léon. To the astounded bourgeois this closed cab seemed like a rolling ship, which could account for the drawn blind and the *fiacre-corsaire* in *Gente Dame,* verse 5.

Penmarc'h: Breton for horse's head; a wild point, on the coast of Cornouaille s.w.of Quimper, where Tristan, on the point of death, waited for Yseut to cure his wounds.

SERENADE DES SERENADES: The religious words in this section: *cantique des cantiques, encense, Iscariote, Diable, martyre, litanie, mystiques, chapelet, Ascencion, Capucin,* etc. confirm that it is a burlesque of *The Song of Songs (Le Cantique des Cantiques).*

Sonnet de Nuit:
nemesis: from the goddess of vengeance, retributive justice.
Iscariote: The lover wants a kiss he knows will betray, like Judas's did.

Guitare:
Psyché: In the popular version of the legend (Apuleius: *The Golden Ass*), Cupid took Psyche to his secret palace when she incurred the wrath of Venus. He visited her constantly but always in darkness and unseen.
Mercure: As messenger of Jupiter, he was presented with winged sandals, winged cap and short sword, could make himself invisible and assume what shape he pleased. As god of thieves *(voleurs)* he stole, among other things, Venus's girdle and many of Vulcan's instruments. As Jupiter's confidant, he would learn of his master's theft of love in when disguised as a shower of gold, etc. He invented the lyre and offered it to Apollo in exchange for the *caduceus,* with which the god of poetry used to drive flocks of sheep. As he was the god of eloquence, the Greeks and Romans offered tongues to him by throwing them into the fire. Some statues of Mercury portrayed him with an erection, others with no arms, because the power of speech can prevail over everything without them.
Cendrillon: In Perrault's fairy-tale, Cinderella must make herself invisible to the prince before midnight in case he saw her in her everyday rags. The guests at the ball, seeing her in gold and silver finery and bejewelled exclaimed *"Qu'elle est belle!",* a view echoed by the Ugly Sisters to whom she had given oranges and lemons.
Je suis si laid!: recalls lines by the hugely popular writer of ballads Pierre-Jean de Béranger (1780-1857): *Je suis vilain et très vilain,* and *Qu'elle est jolie!*
fraîche / crèche: a rhyme common in ancient carols.

Rescousse:
Kriss: Malayan dagger with a long curved blade.
Bois de justice: the guillotine.

Toit:
Colique de miserere: a very painful intestinal obstruction, which often proved fatal.
peau d'âne: title of a Perrault verse tale. A princess, to avoid her father's amorous intentions covers herself with an ass's skin and goes into hiding. She works on a pig-farm. A prince spies her dressed in finery, which a fairy had granted her for wearing secretly, and is determined to wed Peau d'Âne, as she is called. If only Tristan's drum-skin could lead to such a fairy story ending.

Litanie: The Catholic *Litanie de la Vierge* has phrases which are brought to mind in

this devilish litany: *Rose mystique, Tour d'ivoire, Étoile du matin.*
Tour ivoirine recalls Vigny's ivory tower where poets would shut themselves up.
Gérard de Nerval (1805-55) wrote: *Il ne nous restait pour asile que cette tour d'ivoire des poètes, où nous montions toujours plus haut pour nous isoler de la foule.*
Nef sans voile could also be a ship without a sail and certainly no *Refuge for sinners* (another from the *Litanie*).
Vesper, amoris Aurora: Evening, Dawn of love. The Virgin Mary is Star of Morning, but it's time now for a serenade — a (piece for) performance in the open air by night, especially at a lady's window. Serenade: from the Latin *serenus (bright clear sky!)* influenced by *serus (late).*

Chapelet:

Perfeccion, Circoncicion, Crucificcion, Ascencion may seem Spanish, but are spelt incorrectly, possibly on purpose, perhaps derisively.
AVE: Hail, as in Hail Mary!
Navaja-Dolorès-y-Crucificcion: Knife-Pain-and-Crucifixion. Dolorès is a name for Mary, *Notre-Dame-des-Douleurs (Our Lady of Sorrows)*
absinthe: (V. Paris viii) Not exactly what the soldiers offered Jesus on the cross. They offered a sponge of vinegar.
Ascencion: Luke's Gospel has Jesus going up to Heaven 40 days after Easter. The Ascension of the Virgin Mary is celebrated by the Catholic Church but it is called the Assumption.
Isaac Laquedem is the Flemish name for the Wandering Jew, who was condemned, according to legend, to wander the earth for ever, for not allowing Jesus to rest in front of his door, for insulting him and perhaps even striking him, during the carrying of the cross.
Todas-las-Santas is a feminine All Saints Day prepared for by the female Saints in line 3. All Saints Day: November 1st (Blood month).
Secundum ordinem: According to the order (from Psalm 110 v.4: *Thou art a priest for ever / After the order of Melchizedek.)*
la Quasimodo is the first Sunday after Easter (the name coming from the introit of the mass for that day). There was an ancient rite in parts of Brittany (in Finistère and Morbihan for example) where the merry-making included the smashing of old pots to shouts of *"Quasimodo casse les pots!"*.Quasimodo, Hugo's monstrously deformed character with the gentle ways and humane feelings (*Notre Dame de Paris*) could be here — or rather not yet here — too.
mandore: a round-backed stringed instrument like a lute, sustained notes being played by repeated plucking; a large mandoline.
Se habla español: Spanish spoken: *Paraque...* could be: *Por qué?* What for? *raquando?* could be an abbreviated *para cuándo?: When for?* Other possibilities for *raquando*: could it be from the verb *raquear, raqueando:* stealing wrack, going after spoils, being a wharf-rat? *Raque* is beachcombing, *raquero* a pirate or stealer along the coast. *Rascar, rascando:* scratching (the head), rasping, scouring, and, last but not least, strumming. Then there's the Portuguese verb: *recuar, recuando:* retreating, giving ground, flinching.

Elizir d'amor: another spelling which would make a Spaniard wince — a love potion like the one taken by Tristan and Yseut. The elixir of love rather than life is his music, decidedly harsh, etc. All for love, the love of art!
pieux: pious (for piety?) as well as a stake or post.
borgne: shady as well as one-eyed.
viole d'amour: viola d'amore, a tenor viol with sympathetic strings under the finger-board.
Salamanque: the University of Salamanca in the West of Spain dates from the 13th century. The hero of Le Sage's novel *Le Bachelier de Salamanque* could obtain his degree in theology because the corrégidor of Salamanca died. *Ce fonds jamais ne me manque* takes up La Fontaine's line from *Le Laboureur et ses enfants* *"C'est le fonds qui manque le moins!"* which puns on *fonds:* resources, monetary and amatory.
castagnole: castagnette. cf. *Le Poète Contumace* l.137
Pur-Don-Juan-du-Commandeur: a strange linking. Don Juan, for his sexual exploits, is dragged to hell, where the statue of the Commander grasps his hand to exact the vengeance of Heaven. Unbridled love leading to catastrophe.
Abeilard: the lover in this poem doesn't want to be associated with a man who's been castrated.
Alcibiade: famous, not for his riches or brilliance, but for having cut off his dog's tail. Which is why he did it.

Vénerie: Venery is sexual indulgence (from Venus) as well as hunting.
Diane: The cult of Diana, Roman goddess of hunting, had cruel rites. She was also patroness of chastity, but granted favours to Pan, Orion and the shepherd Endymion on seeing him naked.
bête varie: a variant of *souvent femme varie, bien fol est qui s'y fie* — supposedly said by François 1st, reported by Brantôme in his *Vie des Dames Galantes*, popularised in Hugo's *Le Roi s'amuse* (1832) and Verdi's *Rigoletto* (1851).
Un pied de biche... a bell-pull; *biche:* hind or doe or mistress. I have omitted the street scene in this verse to retain the hunting and sexual double-entendres in keeping with the rest of the poem.
laie: forest-track (where a *pied de biche* could be picked up) and sow.

Heures: for the Church, hours can be set times of prayer, the offices so prescibed or a book containing them. *Horus:* Egyptian sun-god, whose symbol was the eye.
Pampelune: Pamplona, Spanish town in the Western Pyrenees.
Cafarde: hypocritical, two-faced. Hecate was called Luna in heaven, Diana on earth, Hecate or Proserpina in hell, a woman with three faces, who presided over enchantments.
plus de quatorze heures: Is it coincidence that the number of peasants (more than 14) who insulted Tristan of Léonois (dressed as *le fou Picous)* and whom he strikes with his crutch (other passers-by shed tears at his pitiable state) is the same as the number of hours struck like knells in this sonnet (and each hour is a tear) where he is *le fou de Pampelune?*

Chanson en *si*: si: if, *so* (B, the 5th note of the sol-fa), and taken homophonically as scie: a saw, painfully dissonant, sawing on and on. cf. the epigraph for *Litanie du Sommeil* & *À une Demoiselle* (l.2). Collections of folklore in the 19th century invariably included the song known as *des Transformations or des Métamorphoses*.

Donnez-vous l'un l'autre......un baiser: this verse is a sacrilegious yoking of Jesus's *Love one another* (John 15 v12) and Luke 22 v19-21 where Jesus offers bread as his body and predicts that he will be betrayed by one of those present.

ton petit cœur: cf. *J'ai donné mon petit cœur / À Jésus mon doux Sauveur (bis),* a hymn in the traditional catechism.

Rossinante: the ridiculous mare of that great Spanish lover, Don Quixote! The duenna who combs Tristan's beloved is called by the mare's name and is a mock version of Musset's duenna in Madrid who *n'ouvre sa fenêtre qu'à moi* (only opens her window to me). What is more: *Elle est jaune, comme une orange (Premières Poésies,* 1829)!

Portes et fenêtres:

À damner je n'ai plus d'alcades...... sérénades: an ironical reference to Musset's *L'Andalouse*, otherwise known as *la marquesa d'Amaëgui*. (V. *Après la pluie* & *Grand Opéra Act 3*). Je veux ce soir des sérénades/ À faire damner les alcades... (the first of *Chansons à Mettre en Musique* from *Premières Poésies.)*

Grand Opéra:
Ier acte (Vêpres)
Hostie: from Latin *hostia* = victim

Saint-Jacques de Compostelle: According to Spanish tradition Saint James visited Spain and preached the gospel there. After his martyrdom it was said that his body was brought from Jerusalem to Spain. In the later Middle Ages his shrine at Santiago de Compostela was and still is a great centre for pilgrimages. The faithful are given to touching the statues of saints. By retaining the French spelling I keep an *'elle'* (V. the Postface).

IIe acte (Sabbat) A witches' midnight meeting where the devil is worshipped, rather than a day of rest.

Beelzebub: prince of the evil spirits from the Hebrew: fly-lord.

truc: general word for a thingummy, but in theatrical slang, a transformation scene.

IIIe acte (Sereno) the nightwatch in Spain who sang out the time and the date in certain villages. *sereno* is also serene, clear (sky).

Sangre Dios: The blood of the Lord would be *Sangre de Dios.*

Cigaro, Gracia, Carambah are near misses again.

violon: violin and colloquially: police cells.

Je damne les alcades/ De Tolose au Guadaleté: almost a direct quotation from Musset's *L'Andalouse*, already adapted in Portes et Fenêtres.

Son page était en ambuscades: based on the same verse of *L'Andalouse.*

Caramba: By Jove!

Pièce à carreaux: could also be a piece of ordnance where *carreaux* are projectiles; or patchwork!

Tolède: famous for swords.

Cordoue: for leather.

vache espagnole: to speak French like a Spanish cow is to murder the language. In 1853 Louis Napoleon married Eugénie de Montijo and she was portrayed in a caricature by Zut as 'the Spanish cow', her fart alarming her useless little husband.

connaître le numéro: (pop.arg.) connaître sa valeur morale: to know one's moral value.

ZÉRO: allows the beloved no value at all! Zero-grazing: a system of dairy farming in which the cattle are kept indoors and cut grass is brought to them.

Cadix: a military port on the Atlantic, on a small island called Léon, in Andalucia, the Spain of operetta.

RACCROCS

Laisser-courre: a term from hunting, when the hounds are released. A sense of letting slide is present too.

Isaac Laquedem: the Wandering Jew (also in *Chapelet*). Eugène Sue wrote *Le Juif errant* (1844-5), Alexandre Dumas père *Isaac Laquedem* (1853), but the legend was popular as a story, transmitted orally at first and later brought round the villages as a booklet ending with a lament: *L'admirable histoire du juif errant qui depuis l'an 33 jusqu'à l'heure présente ne fait que marcher.* This poem adopts the 6 line hexasyllabic form and rhyme scheme of the most known lament dating from 1774.

tours, fours: tour is a medieval tower where the beloved is inaccessible, locked up; *four* could be a fiasco, erotic and/or artistic.

La Palisse: Jacques de Chabannes, seigneur de La Palisse, a captain born c.1470, distinguished himself in various battles and when he was killed at the battle of Pavie in 1525, his men composed a song in his honour, including this verse:

> Monsieur d'La Palice est mort
> Mort devant Pavie;
> Un quart d'heure avant sa mort
> Il était encore en vie.

Une vérité de La Palisse came to mean a painfully obvious truth.

À ma jument souris:

Souris could be the name of the mare, and by line 4, a woman of easy virtue.

faire la culbute: to come a cropper; *culbuter une femme:* to have sex with... *culbuter* to win over.

À mon chien Pope: Alexander Pope (1688-1744), author of virulent satire whose *Epigram engraved on the collar of a dog which I gave to his Royal Highness.*

> I am his Highness' dog at Kew;
> Pray tell me, sir, whose dog are you?

His Highness being Frederick, Prince of Wales.

Gentleman refers back to Pope as well as forward to the aristocratic dog.

New-land is a direct translation of Terre Neuve, Newfoundland in English, a Canadian island famous for a breed of dog of the same name, large, intelligent, and a strong swimmer (originally black). Hence Pope is a thoroughbred.

cynique: the Cynics, in the 4th century B.C., Diogenes for example, scorned riches, arts, science, amusement, was morose and pessimistic, the root of the name coming from the Greek for dog.

Île de Batz: just off Roscoff and almost visible from the Corbière summer residence, this island was said to be a refuge for the solitary poet (J. Vacher-Corbière, *Portrait de famille*).

À un Juvénal de lait: Juvenal (c.AD 60 - c.136) Roman satirist.

Incipe, parve puer, risu cognoscere matrem is the complete quotation from Virgil's 4th Eclogue, which in C.Day Lewis's version reads: Begin, dear babe, and smile at your mother to show you know her. Or in E.V.Rieu's version: Begin, then, little boy, to greet your mother with a smile. Mother is omitted.

À une Demoiselle:

Érard: a high quality grand piano, called after the original maker Sébastien Érard (1752-1831).

osanore: A rich dentist William Rogers wrote an immense didactic poem called *Osanores*. Every line had some weakness or other, but the editor of *Le Corsaire* advised him to pay to have it improved at 50 centimes a line. The poem became well-known, because Podevin the editor, who wouldn't pay his contributors more than 6 centimes a line, entrusted a certain number of osanorian lines to those whose work he accepted, in accordance with a fixed tariff. An interesting story would entitle the author to a bonus of 40 lines; a piece of scathing criticism 5 lines, etc. *Osanore* (from *os sans or*) is used of false teeth made from hippo ivory, that hold to the gums without metal hooks.

Plangorer: a neologism based on the Latin *plangere:* to lament loudly, to beat in grief.

Décourageux: another neologism, opposite of courageous.

Pur héros... This verse is not far from Musset's *Ballade à la Lune* and the address to the Muse in *La Nuit de Mai (brune, lune, blonde)*. When he speaks (verse 6 on) it is as though he's offering a corrupted version of Musset's Muse, contradicting her purity and faithfulness.

Rapsodie du Sourd: A former version was called *La Scie d'un Sourd, scie:* saw, catch-phrase, catchy tune, bore (i.e. someone boring) and something rasping.

Limonadière: Café proprietor.

Tantale: V.*Insomnie*.

coucou: bird or clock and in the sound close to cuckold *(cocu)*.

Saint Jean Chrysostome: bishop and doctor (c.347-407), his name means golden mouth. A whole-hearted, if rather tactless, reformer, who attacked misuse of wealth and was exiled. The fact that he was a fine preacher hardly goes with *Silence is golden!*

Frère et Sœur Jumeaux:
Tityre: Virgil borrowed the name from the Idylls of Theocritus for his lovesick shepherd nonchalantly stretched out beneath a tree playing his reed-pipe (1st Eclogue).

Litanie du Sommeil: Most of the poem is in *laisses*, typical of ancient *chansons de geste* and medieval epics: verses have a variable number of lines, each *laisse* having a single full rhyme. Therefore no alternation of masculine and feminine rhymes, so prevalent in French rhymed verse. Tristan has feminine rhymes from lines 17 to 83, masculine from 86 to 145. This poem was popular among Surrealists, though how surrealist is it? André Breton, including part of it in his *Anthologie de l'Humour Noir,* writes: *Corbière doit être le premier en date à s'être laissé porter par la vague des mots qui, en dehors de toute direction consciente, expire chaque seconde à notre oreille et à laquelle le commun des hommes oppose la digue du sens immédiat.*
The epigraph, supposedly from Macbeth, is based on Macbeth's words to his wife after he has stabbed Duncan to death:
> Methought I heard a voice cry, 'Sleep no more!
> Macbeth does murder sleep!'
There follows a brief list of the blessings of sleep, e.g. *balm of hurt minds,* a tiny foreshadowing of the definitions of Sleep in this Litany.
pot-au-noir: a dangerous situation, adopted by Tristan's time as a sailors' term for a zone of very bad weather with reduced visibility.
The *RUMINANT,* the bourgeois, doesn't experience real Sleep. Insomnia is full of anguish and yet marvellous. By the power of Insomnia he can record and celebrate the richness of Sleep.
Folle-brise: Edouard Corbière's novel *Folles-Brises* is recalled here, as *brises folles* is the normal word order.
Vaisseau fantôme: The Flying Dutchman is a black spectral ship with blood-red sails condemned to sail round the Cape of Good Hope for ever, and only allowed to dock once every seven years so its captain could search for true love.
Domino: masked ball costume, a long cloak of black silk with a hood, or its wearer.
Diables-bleus: creatures of dream; evil demons; apparitions seen in *delirium tremens.*
Le *TEMPS:* political daily founded in 1829, for the defence of the Republic.
Le *SIÈCLE:* political daily founded in 1836, of socialist Republican persuasion post-1848.
La *REVUE DES DEUX MONDES:* fortnightly periodical, founded in 1829: Liberal conservative party paper. SLEEP, evening paper, is all three together.
accord éolien: the aeolian harp is played by the wind, and loved by Romantics.
Larve: larva, spectre or ghost.
monsieur la Palisse: the proofs he offers need no conscious thought.

Peau d'Âne: Mother Goose. (V.*Toit.*)

Dame Malbrouck: Malbrouck s'en va-t-en guerre was the French equivalent of *Boney was a warrior, Malbrouck* being a French version of the Duke of Marlborough, famed for victories at Hochstædt, Ramillies and Malplaquet. His wife was maid of honour (*dame d'honneur*) and favourite of Queen Anne but fell out of favour, and both were in disgrace.

Psyché / l'Amour: Apuleius (fl.AD 155), in *The Golden Ass,* tells how Psyche (the soul) incurred the anger of Venus, was whisked off to his palace by Cupid/Eros, who visited her at night and told her he must remain unknown, unseen. Persuaded by her jealous sisters, she lit a lamp and saw her handsome adolescent lover... A drop of oil fell on him as he slept, he awoke and disappeared. She searched for him in vain. After her death, Cupid prevailed on Jupiter to make her immortal.

chibouck: a long straight-stemmed Turkish pipe.

Parque... The Parcae, the 3 Fates: Clotho, the youngest sister, holds the distaff and presides over birth, Lachesis spins the thread of life and Atropos cuts it off. They care nothing for the wishes of mankind.

le chant de l'alouette indicates the harsh ending of the amorous night for Romeo and Juliet.

Idylle coupée:

perruches: as *perroquet* was artists' slang for absinth (Delvau: *Dictionnaire de la Langue Verte*) and parakeets are often green... cf. toujours vert le jus de trique.

BON RETOUR... A liking for inn-signs is also apparent in *Cap'taine Ledoux* and *Le Novice en Partance et Sentimental.*

petit mort pour rire: V. the Rondel with this title.

C'est le fonds qui manque le moins parodies La Fontaine, by using his line from *Le laboureur et ses enfants* (Bk 5 ix) in another earthy context.

bitume: bitumen was used in oil-painting as a glaze; transparent and yellowy-brown, it could give a rich glow, but didn't completely harden and suffered craquelure.

Galimard (1813-80), pupil of Ingres, and *Ducornet* (1806-56), who painted with his feet, were highly thought of in the 1850s.

La Muse malade: Baudelaire, in his sonnet *La Muse malade,* wants her to stay healthy, with strong thoughts and flowing rhythms, and no more nightmare visions.

Le convoi du pauvre:

From 1870 the annual exhibition of paintings opened its doors on May 1st or 2nd. What the Salon jury selected was what up to 50,000 people a day would see. Napoleon III allowed the Salon des Refusés in 1863 and this is where Courbet set up his stall. Those refused would, if their painting was large, have to take it away on a stretcher (*un brancard*).

Rue Notre-Dame-de-Lorette goes up towards Montmartre, where Tristan lived among artists. Henry Murger got a sixth floor flat at No.48 in this street.

la Lorette: the Virgin Mary (Notre-Dame-de-Lorette) and a loose woman for hire in that very street!

la Cayenne was slang for a cemetery *extra-muros* (Delvau)

L'Élysée: Le Salon was held at Le Palais de l'Industrie on les Champs-Élysées; Elysium was the home of the gods.

martyrs: la Brasserie des Martyrs on the slopes of Montmartre was where Courbet and other artists would often meet!

courbet: Gustave Courbet was scornful of Italian painting, even going so far as to say: *Phidias et Raphaël nous ont mis le grappin dessus (they've got their claws into us).*

Déjeuner de soleil:

something (e.g. material) quick to fade; a sunny 'breakfast' or 'lunch', a Spring scene in the Bois de Boulogne, which Haussmann & Co had turned into a park in the early 1850s, where race-courses were added at Longchamp and Auteuil in 1870. The Bois itself became a fashionable   place to stroll and meet...

les lauriers...: Nous n'irons plus au bois, les lauriers sont coupés are lines from a popular round, already used in *Stalactites* by Théodore de Banville.

Persil: parsley! but here: *faire son persil:* to take an early walk in the Bois de Boulogne or well-frequented place to stroll; *aller au persil:* to walk the street (of prostitutes)

Serpolet: perhaps a name for a part of the Bois or a café *qui sert pot lait!*

Chère Madame: what one 'lady' calls to another.

Bibi: darling!.

Arthur: l'amant de cœur (Delvau)

Diane: Diana, huntress, dominates fearsome animals: *Son Tigre et les vieux beaux Lions.*

Veder Napoli poi mori: See Naples and die.

Corinne: heroine of a novel by Madame de Staël: *Corinne ou l'Italie* (1806)

Lasciate ogni speranza, voi ch'entrate: Abandon hope all ye who enter here: the inscription above the gates of Hell at the start of Dante's Divine Comedy.

Mignon: In Gœthe's *Wilhelm Meister* and his *Italian Journey*, Mignon feels nostalgia for her homeland Italy; she reappears in Mme de Staël's *De l'Allemagne;* and again in Ambroise Thomas's opera, *Mignon* (1866)

Phœbus: the sun-god.

mépris de Byron: Byron's *Childe Harold* sees Italy as a living ruin, a desert compared with what it used to be.

Mazanielli: the humble Neapolitan fisherman Masaniello led a revolt in the 17th century against the Spanish masters of the city. The *lazzaroni* are seen as his heirs.

Dolce Farniente! Sweet idleness!

è pur si muove: Galileo, having had to abjure his theories, particularly about the movement of the earth, is supposed to have cried out 'And yet, it moves!' (*Eppur, si muove!)*

ruolze: Count Henri de Ruolz invented electrodeposition: adding a layer of silver or gold by electrolysis.

Dogana del porto: port customs.

Vésuves et Cie:
Pompéïa: town in Campania buried beneath the ash from Vesuvius erupting in 79 A.D.
Le dernier jour de Pompeï: opera by Félix Victorin de Joncières performed in Paris in 1869.

Soneto a Napoli:
The Italianate subtitle reads: To the sun (or in sunshine), to the moon (or by moonlight), to Saturday (or on the witches' sabbath), to the canon, and all and sundry — with Mr Punch — *Commedia del arte* came originally from Naples.
Il n'est pas... The proverb runs: Il n'est si vilain samedi, que le soleil ne brille à midi.
L'Ombilic du jour: the Latin *umbilicus diei* means navel of the day, i.e. noon.
Lucia etc... Characters from operas by Auber: Fra Diavolo and La Muette de Portici (both set near Naples and both have tarentelas) and Donizetti: Lucia di Lammermoor and Pia di Tolomei. Tommaso Aniello, better known as Masaniello is the main character in *La Muette di Portici.* Portici is on the coast between Naples and Vesuvius. Corbière sanctifies Pia di Tolómei! She is wrongly suspected of adultery and killed by her husband.
Fra Diavolo: a Neapolitan bandit courts a lady; husband gets jealous, quarrel, etc
La Mergelina is a popular quarter of Naples which includes the harbour and the beach. In Lamartine's *Graziella* Graziella lives there as do *lazzaroni* who spend their days asleep or dancing the tarentela, the lively dance to the tambourine from Tarente.
Venerdì, aprile 15: Friday, the day of Venus, goddess of carnal love. April 15th, Spring is under way.

À l'Etna:
Sicelides... the first line of Virgil's 4th Bucolic/Eclogue: *Sicilian Muse, I would try now a somewhat grander theme.* (C.Day Lewis's translation)
August in Palermo, Sicily, a time of great heat!

Le fils de Lamartine et de Graziella: Alphonse de Lamartine (1790-1869) first published *Graziella* as part of his autobiographical *Confidences, Graziella, Raphaël* in 1849, then separately in 1852. Set largely in the Bay of Naples, it is a romantic Romantic work, ethereal and tearful. The quotation used as epigraph records the final lines. The abbreviation of *le volume* to *le vol* allows it to mean daylight robbery too.
L'Île de Procide is where Graziella was born, hence a sort of paradise on earth.
Lamartine's poem *Le premier regret,* which also figures at the end of the romance, includes these lines taken up by Tristan:

> *Sur la plage sonore où la mer de Sorrente*
> *Déroule ses flots bleus au pied de l'oranger...*
> *Laissons le vent gémir et le flot murmurer.*

Cygne-de-Saint-Point: Virgil, whose tomb is near Naples was known as the Swan of Mantua, and Lamartine had a château at Saint-Point, near Mâcon, where he is buried.

harmonieux: Lamartine wrote *Harmonies poétiques et religieuses,* and his style has often been described as harmonious.

Fornarine: la Fornarina was Raphaël's mistress.

Lesbienne: connoting lack of virility, transferred epithet which goes more with the author of *Graziella,* designated soprano in the following line.

Ischia: an island near Procida.

Jocelyn: the eponymous hero of an epic poem by Lamartine. The chaste narrator of *Graziella* resembles him in many ways.

picciola: poetic diminutive, little one.

Ton Orphelin, posthume... Graziella dies in 1812, aged 16. Therefore she was born in 1796. The Child of Nature, her son, or so he claims, is old. If he was 80 in 1872, the year of Tristan's second visit to Italy, he would have been born before his 'mother' and before the Lamartine of his romance, where he is 18.

Tu mourus à seize ans!... C'est bien tôt pour nourrir! is a corruption of a line from *Le premier regret: Elle avait seize ans: c'est bien tôt pour mourir!*

Isola di Capri: another island in the Gulf of Naples visited by Lamartine in *Graziella.*

Gennaio: January, too cold for eternal Spring and idealised love.

Libertà:

Gênes: chosen perhaps for the sense of constraint in the word *gêne?* Tristan wrote to his parents from Genoa playing on the word in this way: *Je ne dois pas vous dissimuler l'État de Gênes où je me trouve depuis deux jours.* Genoese authorities had the word *libertas* up on prison walls, probably from the Latin phrase *sub lege libertas.*

Lasciate ogni speranza (Abandon all hope) is from Dante's Divine Comedy.

Vanité, vanité: recalls Ecclesiastes: Vanity of vanities, all is vanity.

pigeons: dupes, suckers, and pigeons, of course.

Cerbère: the (at least) three-headed monster dog guarding the entrance to Hades to prevent the living from entering and the dead from escaping.

cruche: jug or imbecile cf. *oison:* gosling, who doesn't realise the charms of prison.

cloisonnée and *oison* helped choose themselves for internal rhyme.

Superba: proud as well as magnificent

nunc est bibendum: now is the time for drinking (Horace Ode Bk 1 xxxvii 1).

Hidalgo:

Hidalgo: a Spanish nobleman.

Le Cid: means chief or lord. Corneille based his successful play of that name (1637) on the 11th century Castilian champion Ruy Diaz. *Beau comme le cid* — phrase which came from the success of the play. cf. *laid comme un pou. V. Poux (fleas)* in line 1.

Cosas de España: a parody of titles like Gautier's *Tra los montes (Voyage en Espagne)* (1843)

Paria:
Le Moi humain est haïssable: Blaise Pascal (1623-62) in his *Pensées* Bk VII (455) wrote: *Le moi est haïssable.* Soon after he exhorts us to love only God, and hate only ourself.

ARMOR: the Celtic name for Brittany meaning 'on the sea'. It was the name given by the Gauls to the coastal region, the interior being called Argoat. Bretons, according to a proverb, 'are born with the waters of the sea flowing round their hearts'. Tristan, living in Roscoff, on the *Ceinture Dorée* (V. notes on *Au Vieux Roscoff*), wanting to be out at sea on *une mer jaune ou verte*, both of which are wild, was near, if not in, his element. A likely reason for the choice of Armor rather than Armorique was Tristan's love of puns: 'art mort' (dead art) being a vital side of his verse (this side and beyond!). The second poem in this group continues the idea: *Nature morte* is a still life (which an artist can endow with life) and dead nature (which an artist can endow with life)!

Paysage mauvais:
Palud (or *palus*): a Breton word from the Latin for marsh.
la lune, le soleil des loups (the wolves' sun) are one and the same, the moon; and in Breton folklore moon and wolves — the hare *(le lièvre)* too — are creatures of the devil.
Calme de peste... The ghost of a young girl still appears at the church of Brasparts, near *Yeun Ellez* or *Le Marais d'Enfer* (Hell Marsh). This *dame blanche* offered herself to be buried alive to deliver the parish from the plague. The plague stopped. But sometimes will o' the wisps *(les feux follets)* come up out of the peat and race between the hedges, setting fire to a tree here, a village there...
le follet damné: a demonic sprite out to persecute humans.
La Lavandière: les lavandières de nuit (kannerezed-noz or *maouès-noz):* these sinister figures of Breton legend and superstition are tall emaciated women who come to communal washing places at night to work hard for the remission of their sins by washing the shrouds of those about to die; they could wring out the life of the living as easily as clothes.*escabeaux:* Breton has the expression *skabellon tonsegad,* the exact equivalent of the English *toadstools.*
Marais de Guérande: on *la Côte Sauvage* in South Brittany near La Baule is the Guérande peninsula with its huge salt marshes. Inland from Guérande itself is extensive marshland as far as La Chapelle des Marais in what is now the Brière Regional Nature Park.

Nature morte:
les coucous, le chat-huant, la chouette, la corneille: all birds portending death in Breton lore. The screech owl was supposed to cry: 'the sign, the sign, the sign of death! Open for l'Ankou!'
la brouette de la Mort: Karriguel an Ankou or *Cariquel Ancou* (Death's wheelbarrow) draped in a white sheet, with unoiled axle, iron wheels, and an escort of funereal birds, pushed noisily along the cobbles at night to collect the dying.

Un riche en Bretagne:
O fortunatos nimium, sua si bona norint, / Agricolas! is the completed quotation from Virgil's 2nd Georgic (ll.458-9), meaning O how happy the country folk would be, could they but know their happiness.
Benedicite: prayer before a meal. Here it's come after *panem nostrum* (our daily bread) which can't be very filling. Then he's presented with manna from heaven as the Hebrews were: in his case, it's real bread.
cornandons: dwarves or pygmies.
la part du bon-dieu: beggars might well have used the phrase, demanding it as their due.
monsieur Delille: l'abbé Delille's academic translation of the Georgics was published in 1770 to great acclaim.
Saint-Thégonnec: a village 13 km. s.w.of Morlaix.

Saint Tupetu de Tu-pe-tu: Tu-pe-tu means, as Tristan says: On one side or the other. The correct spelling is Tu-pe-du, though in his time Breton was rarely written; for a long time the French authorities would not allow it to be taught in schoools. The expression about a sick man: *tu pe du ez aio,* typically Breton in its fatalistic attitude, means: he will live or die. There is no saint of this name among over 300 in the *Dictionnaire des Saints Bretons* (Sand, 1985). Nor is there a village of that name either. W.Branch Johnson (Folktales of Brittany,1927) claimed to have discovered the whereabouts of 'this popular saint', aka St Diboan, who helps the dying to die. Their friends would pray to the statue in the church of St Méen, before going to the nearby fountain dedicated to the saint. They empty the fountain and listen to the water returning. If it murmurs, the dying man will die; if it is silent, he will get better. I am informed by Mr Albert Le Goff, *recteur* of the church at St Méen, that there is no such statue and none of the villagers consulted has any knowledge of all this. He himself has been on the *pardon* in honour of St Diboan (aka Diboen, Thybon, Thibon, Abibon, Iboen and Yboiene according to the *Dictionnaire*) in south Finistère, presumably at Plevin on 28th January. Gwenc'hlan Le Scouëzec in *Le Guide de la Bretagne* (Beltan Breizh, 1989) is equally sure that a statue of St Diboan (saint Sans-Douleur) exists in the chapel Notre-Dame-des-Trois-Fontaines near Gouézec, and that he is a saint tu-pe-tu. Here there is a fountain, or rather, here are three. But there is no such statue, nor has there been in living memory, even though the booklet on the chapel mentions him, but it is in a photocopy of a Le Scouëzec article (from *Guide de la Bretagne Mystérieuse*

(Tchou, 1966) word for word the same as in the updated Beltan Breizh edition)! The *Dictionnaire* says that at one time there was a chapel dedicated to St Diboan at Gouézec. Whether this Notre-Dame-des-Trois-Fontaines is the chapel or not — it is 6 km from the village — it has been classed as a historic monument since 1927 and boasts interesting architecture, fine stained-glass windows and statues of other saints. Tristan would have enjoyed the striking gargoyles of the Seven Deadly Sins on the exterior walls. M^r Le Goff, at St Méen, thinks that Tu-pe-tu is probably a projection of a popular attitude in old-time worship of saints, because of the meaning of the words tu pe du: be cured or die. And the new incumbent at Gouézec thought it quite possible that Tupetus might exist here and there in Brittany offering a cure on this side of the grave, or heaven on the other. However, the whole tone of the poem suggests that Tristan's tongue is firmly in his cheek. But so was it with *Pudentiane* and she existed!

Léon: the n.w. tip of Brittany, the northern part of Finistère, with Brest in the south and Morlaix to the east. The chapel Notre-Dame-des-Trois-Fontaines is on the Roman road from Quimper to Morlaix, the route Tristan would have taken to boarding school in Nantes, but it isn't in Léon!

Cunégonde: appears in Voltaire's *Candide*, where she is hardly a saint. Cunégonde, Empress of Germany, wife of the Duke of Bavaria (then Holy Roman Emperor) Henri II. When accused of infidelity, she asked to prove her innocence before God, and walked across red-hot ploughshares. Died c.1033; canonised in 1200.

Cucugnan: Alphonse Daudet's tales were printed in *L'Événement* and then collected as *Lettres de mon Moulin* in1866. *Le Curé de Cucugnan* is one such. The good curé, l'abbé Martin, preaches a sermon that brings the villagers to God: he discovers all the dead souls from Cucugnan in Hell.

Quilbignon: a village so near Brest it is now incorporated in it.

quitte-ou-tout: quitte-ou-double (double or quits) is normal in gambling , all or quits is a bit extreme.

Rubicon: the crossing of this river is to take a decisive, irrevocable step, as Caesar did in 49.BC, thus virtually declaring war on Italia.

Petit Janus chair et poisson: The Roman god, having faces back and front, could see both ways at once. *Ni chair ni poisson* (neither fish nor fowl nor good red herring): a weak-willed or hypocritical fence-sitter, originally applied by Roman Catholics as a term of scorn for one whose faith was suspect. But Tristan takes the negatives out leaving Tu-pe-tu with flesh and fish.

à double fond: with a false bottom.

Ambigu patron....: the saint's response to candles offered by virgins may be ambiguous, but should the coin land tails up...

Jésuite: in its pejorative sense means wily and hypocritical.

La Rapsode Foraine et Le Pardon de Sainte-Anne: A very popular *pardon* in honour of the Virgin Mary's mother Anne, but dating back to the Celtic goddess Ana. A Bretonne, born in Cornouaille (south of Léon), brutalised by her husband on discovering she was pregnant, she is led by angels to Nazareth and gives birth to Mary. Returning to Brittany, she takes refuge in a hermitage in the bay *de la Palud*. She is *mamm goz* of Bretons and appealed to for all manner of things: protection of fishermen, thriving of crops, curing of ills and other more personal troubles. Sainte-Anne-la-Palud is just north of Douarnenez. Her *pardon* is on the last Sunday in August and led up to on the Saturday with merry-making, beggars camping out, gypsies selling goods to the huge crowd of pilgrims. The figure of Le or La Rapsode is traditional too, a beggar who sings and sells complaints. Edouard Corbière had written *(Voyage de trois jours dans le Finistère)* of a similar poverty-stricken, pipe-smoking vagrant woman.

Grand'tante (Great-aunt): inexplicable, but, according to René Martineau, Tristan sometimes called his own mother *ma femme,* and his sister's husband *mon gendre (my son-in-law)!*

Crésus: Croesus, the Rockerfeller of the ancient world, made extravagant gifts to the Temple at Delphi, and was patron to Aesop (6th century BC).

Angelus: Mary is waiting, not for the bell to summon the faithful to church at morning, noon and sunset, nor the prayer said at these times, but the original Angelus, the angel announcing the Incarnation *(Angelus domini nuntiavit Mariae).*

CANTIQUE: capital letters to emphasise the choral rejoicing of the religious ceremony and the unbridled fun of the fair and lusty drinking songs. Tristan may have got the idea for his poem from Gabriel de La Landelle's *À Sainte Anne, Cantique*, especially as he was a friend of the family, but that in no way detracts from the force and originality of this poem.

Arche de Joachim: in Christian tradition St Anne's husband and father of Mary was Joachim (incidentally one of Tristan's own names). As well as a large floating vessel at Deluge time, an Ark is a wooden coffer for the Tables of the Jewish Law. In the Litanies of the Virgin it is called *Arche d'alliance* and worshipped in its own right.

Médaille / Gui / Trèfle...: Talismans, lucky charms, superstitious beliefs are part and parcel of a *pardon*.

Mont d'Horeb: aka Mount Sinaï, where Yahweh dictated his Law to Moses. For Bretons all these come together in Anne.

Souche de Jessé: Pharez begat Hezron, and Hezron begat Ram, and Ram begat Amminadab, and Amminadab begat Nashon, and Nashon begat Salmon, and Salmon begat Boaz, and Boaz begat Obed, and Obed begat Jesse, and Jesse begat David, his seventh son. From this stem sprang Anne, Mary and Jesus.

cire-vierge jaune: special to the *pardon* of Saint Anne is this garland of wax wound round the outer walls of the church.

eau miraculeuse / les Job... Each *pardon* has its miraculous fountain for drinking from and washing face or even body at. Job was struck *'with sore boils from the sole of his foot to his crown.'*

la Foi vous a sauvé: Jesus to the woman who'd been twelve years haemorrhaging (Mk 5,34; Lk 8,48), to a blind beggar (Mk10 52), to the healed leper who thanked him (Lk 17,19).

Vide latus! (See my side!): Jesus appears to the disciple Thomas, who won't believe he is resurrected *'except I shall see in his hands the print of the nails, and put my finger into the print of the nails, and put my hand into his side'* (Jn 20, 25) .

Miserere: Have mercy (from the first word of the 51st Psalm).

Ankokrignets et Kakous: sick and crippled beings; *ankou - death, krignat - to gnaw: gnawed by death; kakou - leper;* pariahs who would at one time have worn a red cross on their clothing and only be allowed to work with hemp.

kyriè-éleison: Lord, have pity (from the Greek liturgy).

ex-voto: votive offerings

cimetière / calvaire; both cemetery and calvary (often elaborate in Brittany) are by the church, so the *pardon* procession would pass them on the way in.

Une forme humaine: The figure of the balladeer is not only on her last legs and named *Misère*, but, starting as Elle only because *forme humaine* and *rapsode humaine* are feminine, is referred to as *Ça* (It, That) until the not quite conclusive *Femme: on dirait*, and then *notre sœur*, which is almost as effective as Baudelaire's *mon semblable, — mon frère*, also addressed to the reader *(Au Lecteur)*. In *Le Cheval d'Orgueil* Pierre Jakez Hélias tells how sudden poverty could drive folk to begging or even to suicide, men by hanging, women by drowning. *Telle était la hantise de la misère qu'on s'attendait à la rencontrer, au détour d'un chemin, sous la forme d'une chienne efflanquée, hérissée, les babines retroussées sur des dents jaunes: la Chienne du Monde. Elle était muette, sournoise, et rien ne vous prévenait de son arrivée, voilà le malheur.* (Plon 1975, p.30)

Cris d'aveugle: The almost complete omission of punctuation here, as well as in the epigraph to *Épitaphe*, must be two of the earliest examples in literature.

Ann hini goz (the old woman): a well-known complaint, especially among beggars singing out for alms and exiled Bretons nostalgic for their homeland. Tristan suggests this poem be sung too. The hammering of masculine *-or* rhymes (*or* happens to mean gold, as in *cercle d'or*, which hammers light into the holes he has for eyes) could remind those who know the song that the heroine was chosen for her riches and the poor girl spurned..

Golgotha: mountain near Jerusalem where Jesus was crucified.

De profundis: Psalm 130 begins: *Out of the depths have I cried unto thee, O Lord!*

soufre: brimstone and fire rained on Sodom and Gomorrah (Genesis 19,24)

Menez-Arrez: Monts d'Arrée, near Huelgoat, the highest mountains in Brittany, but at their highest only 1,200ft. *Menez:* rounded hills, once sandstone or granite summits.

La Pastorale de Conlie: In October 1870, well over 40,000 Bretons (Tristan has 20,000), on the orders of Gambetta, and commanded by Count Émile de Kératry, were immobilised in the mud at Conlie, near Le Mans, stuck there, with little or no idea why, instead of going to reinforce the troops in Paris. The Republican leaders in Tours feared they might prove to be *'une armée de chouans'*, Royalist insurgents, and so Kératry couldn't get adequate arms. Awful weather, clayey soil, and the ground became a morass; provisions and munitions were not under shelter, tents were flooded, no-one could keep their footing or their morale. Gambetta refused to evacuate the camp. Six batallions from Ille et Vilaine went to join battle at Le Mans, but panicked as soon as they saw the enemy. Le Mans fell and they were the object of scorn.

Un mobilisé du Morbihan: Tristan's sister Lucie married Aimé Le Vacher, a volunteer with the troops at Conlie. Hearing that their daughter was born, he gave himself leave to return to Morlaix where Tristan joined them. The poem was clearly based on Aimé's report, although the speaker is deemed to be from the Morbihan *département,* south of Côtes du Nord.

Moral jeunes troupes excellent: Almost the words Gambetta used when he wished to advertise readiness for further action after the defeat of the army of the Loire and the loss of Orléans. An earlier version of this poem in *La Vie Parisienne* had a dedication and two sardonic verses addressed to *Maître Gambetta.*

Mois-noir / Mois-plus-noir: literal translations of *miz-du* and *miz-ker-zu.*

Vous du Quatre-Septembre! addresses those responsible for proclaiming the 3rd Republic on that day in 1870.

Citoyens-décréteurs...: Gambetta, advocate of full-scale war, escaped from Paris by balloon, took refuge in Tours, and then, because it was too close to the Prussian line, moved south to Bordeaux. With him went the *garde mobile,* the anti-riot police, who would now see little in the way of action. Gambetta resigned in January 1871, having had to accept the armistice.

La résurrection...: a dying sailor in *Le Négrier* can still make light of his fate: *'c'est dans ce hamac-là que je veux dormir jusqu'à la résurrection des boutons de guêtre (It's in that hammock that I want to sleep till the resurrection of gaiter buttons)'.*

Nos chefs...: Kératry packed his bags in November and the camp doctor in December.

parades: on 9th December a member of the government, Glais-Bizoin, came to review the troops and insisted on a salvo of cannon-balls.

ergot: a parasitic fungus that affects grasses, especially rye, wheat and barley. Infected bread causes ergotism, with gangrene or convulsions.

GENS DE MER:

Point n'ai fait ...
Messieurs d'Orléans: Sons, especially le prince de Joinville, and grandsons of Louis-Philippe went on many voyages.

Ulysse: in Homer's Odyssey, the hero Odysseus (Ulysses was his Roman name) took ten years to sail home after the Trojan war, encountering all manner of trials and hazards on the way.

Callot: Jacques Callot (c.1592-1635) talented engraver famous for his realistic portrayal of beggars and deformities. Tristan's uncle Edmond Puyo had an album of Callot's drawings.

oiseau... the halcyon (kingfisher) was once believed to nest on the sea, which stayed calm during hatching. Sindbad says: 'I saw a bird cometh out of a sea-shell, and layeth her eggs and hatcheth her chicks on the surface of the water'. *(The Arabian Nights)*

Matelots:

Opéra… comique: according to Édouard Corbière (*Des emprunts libres faits à la littérature maritime*), l'Opéra-Comique, along with other Parisian theatres, recruited, in a two-year period, more sailors than the navy.

Le *Vengeur:* the crew of this boat, sunk in 1794, was famed for their heroism in action against the English fleet.

quelle brusque et nerveuse saillie: one of the borrowings from his father's *Le Négrier*.

gauches et veules: Baudelaire (*L'Albatros*) applies these words to an albatross on deck, and censures the sailors for bringing him down for their amusement.

Île d'Ouessant: Ushant, a large rocky island off the coast of Finistère, famous among sailors for its fogs, reefs, wind and strong currents.

Le bossu Bitor:

gardiens du pur contour: a line, with the adjective transposed, from Gautier's *L'Art*, which was taken as a manifesto for Art for Art's sake, but its main argument is that strong, well shaped work will outlast even the gods. His keepers of pure contour are sculptures in Carrara and Parian marble!

Stella maris: the brothel light is literally star of the sea, and a name given to the Virgin Mary or, frequently, a sailing boat. cf. *Marie-Saloppe* for dredgers.

Lauzun: The duke of Lauzun (1633-1723), maréchal de France, was short and ugly, poor at first, but also witty and prepossessing, successful with women, especially king Louis XIV's cousin, Mademoiselle de Montpensier. He was imprisoned more than once for his indiscretions.

Triboulet: clown to Louis XII and François I, who died when about 30. He appears in Rabelais' *Pantagruel*. Also a deformed character in Hugo's play *Le Roi S'Amuse*, who, devastated by the seduction of his daughter, manages to disguise his suffering and plans for vegeance behind laughter and grimace.

Alain Chartier (c.1385-1433): secretary to kings and a poet, who wrote *La Belle Dame sans Merci*. While asleep on a bench, he was kissed on the mouth by Marguerite d'Écosse, first wife of the dauphin. Reproached for kissing someone so ugly, she replied: I did not kiss the man, but the precious mouth from which have come so many fine words (*tant de mots dorés*).

Lagardère: Le Chevalier de Lagardère, brave and handsome hero of Paul Féval's cloak and dagger novel: *Le Bossu ou le Petit Parisien* (1857) disguised himself as a hunchback to outwit his enemies and win his sweetheart.

Mayeux: this hugely humpbacked caricature of a bourgeois national guard, who did nothing but spout citizens' rights *ad nauseam*, was created after the 1830 revolution.

Tortillard: (pop.) a deformed cripple; and a character in the very popular *Les Mystères de Paris*, a novel (and later a play) by Eugène Sue (1842).

La Joliette: a dock built in the 1840s.

Le renégat: Edouard Corbière wrote (in *Les Pilotes de l'Iroise*) of the grim life of renegades aboard a foreign vessel, fleeing their native land, closed to them for ever, and enduring all sorts of daily ill treatment.

in partibus infidelium is the complete phrase and means 'in lands occupied by infidels'.

Ignace: St Ignatius of Loyola (1491-1556) Spanish soldier, wounded at Pamplona by the French, became a convert to Catholicism in 1521 and founded the Jesuits in 1540.

Cydalyse: Cydalise appears as the Bohemian girl in Gérard de Nerval's *Petits Châteaux de Bohême* (1853) and Théodore de Banville's *Les Cariatides* (1842) and *Nouvelles Odes Funambulesques* (1857)

Todos los santos: Spanish: all the saints.

T.F.: Travaux Forcés. The branding of convicts stopped in France in 1842.

Baléares: The ports of the Balearic Islands were stopping-off places or places of refuge for pirates of all nationalities in the Mediterranean, boats often being guided by a renegade.

Aurora:

The epigraph is from a successful operetta by François Bazin: *Le Voyage en Chine*.

corsairiens: a word from his father's *Les Pilotes de l'Iroise*: *des espèces de corsairiens, presque d'indomptables forbans*. Corsairs, as distinct from pirates or *forbans*, were commissioned (with *lettres de marque* which gave them the right in wartime) to seize and plunder enemy vessels. Corsairs were privateers like Duguay-Trouin, Surcouf and Jean Bart, but the quotation from Édouard Corbière shows that distinctions were not cut and dried.

C'est le grand foc... A passage from La Landelle throws light on these lines: *The main jib's halyard is a very bad subject, completely lacking a conscience, recognising none of the debts contracted on land, scorning hoteliers, innkeepers, tradesmen, money-lenders and tearful Ariadnes. — Cruel Theseus made no others!... This halyard is classic. "When we're out on the open sea, all our creditors will be paid; the main jib's halyard will let them have their money."*

Le novice en partance et sentimental:

Noukahiva: the main island of the Marquesas Islands, an archipelago in mid Pacific, where, under the Second Empire, political deportees were sent.

Recouvrance: an old word meaning recovery from ill health; a district in west Brest, on the right bank of the Penfeld estuary.

La goutte:

Lascar: the original sense of Hindu sailor, more or less shanghaied into service, had been overtaken by the sense of an adept and reliable if cunning seadog.

Bambine: Stendhal mentions a Captain Bambine in his *Mémoires d'un touriste*. He captained a passenger steamer around 1837.

L'OCÉAN!... recalls the repeated *THALASSA!* the joyful cry that went up when 10,000 Greeks led by Xenephon, exhausted after a 16 month retreat, saw the Pont-Euxin (the Black Sea).
Havre-de-Grâce: the original name of le Havre. *La Hève:* Le cap de la Hève bounds the north of the harbour.

Cap'taine Ledoux:
Saint-Mâlo-de-l'Isle: the privateers' encampment, once a granite island cut off from the mainland.

Lettre du Mexique:
Véra-Cruz: the port where troops would disembark for the indecisive war against Mexico begun by France, Spain and England in 1860 and continued by Napoleon III on his own from 1862-67.
Le zouave: a French (originally Algerian) infantryman of great dash, who wore quasi-Moorish dress.
Le Jardin Zoologique d'Acclimatation was five acres of the north corner of *Le Bois de Boulogne* for animals that could be acclimatised. By 1869 there had been success with only the llama and Tibetan ox.

Le mousse:
Baie des Trépassés: near the Pointe du Raz, said to be the bay for the embarcation of dead Druids for burial on the Île de Sein.
son sabot: the Breton song: *Les Marins de Groix* tells of 3 sailors: *Mon matelot, le mousse et moi.* One is swept overboard fixing a reef in terrible weather.

> Au jour j'ai revu son sabot
> Il flottait seul là-bas sur l'eau ...
> Plaignez d'mon pauvre matelot
> La femme avec ses trois petiots.

Au vieux Roscoff: Roscoff, where Tristan spent much of his writing life between 1863 and 1872, is living on its memories, its years of glory. When Tristan's father was 18 he was imprisoned on an English hulk for a year after a battle at sea just off the Île de Batz.
Les margats: Probably jackdaws (*margot* was a name for the magpie, but the jackdaw, a fellow member of the Corvidae family, is a bird of the cliffs like the cormorant). Shakespeare, in Midsummer Night's Dream iii 2, mistook choughs for what could have been jackdaws. I have used the English provincial name for magpie nearest to the French, the North country *cawdaw* being too euphonious.
une ceinture dorée: the sheltered rich alluvial coastal areas between St-Malo and the Loire, ideal for market gardening, are called la Ceinture Dorée (the Golden Belt) in the Michelin Guide, though elsewhere the name is only applied to a more restricted length of coastline: from the Pointe de Séhat, just east of the Bay of Lannion to well east of the Île de Batz, at the Anse de Kernic OR from Lambeur to la Pointe de

Saint Mathieu (just west of Brest), a coastline now known as Côte des Légendes or Côte des Abers. As in *Le Bossu Bitor*, la ceinture dorée is one worn by prostitutes to hold their earnings, setting the body off, the more decorative the more lucrative, perhaps.

friture: an episode in Le Négrier is enlightening: *Having disembarked in Roscoff, he begins by giving a dinner chez Rosalie. At the end of the meal the captain requests a frying pan and butter, fries some piastres on the open fire and then tosses them red-hot into the crowd , the most grasping burning their fingers and all my fellow corsairs laughing fit to burst.*

Le douanier:

Brantôme: Pierre de Bourdeilles, abbé and seigneur de Brantôme (c.1534-1614) famous for his racy *Mémoires*, particularly *Vie des Dames Galantes* with outspoken tales of court intrigues.

Anacréon: Greek poet (6th century B.C.) whose c.60 short lyrics on wine, women and song, known as the Anacreontics because of their metre (like that in Longfellow's *Hiawatha*), had a considerable influence on Ronsard and other poets of *La Pléiade*.

Barème: Bertrand-François Bar(r)ême (1640-1703), arithmetician, whose name came to be used for ready-reckoners. He wrote *Livre des comptes faits* etc.

le Portique: the Stoics, starting with Zeno c.300 B.C. taught their philosophy in the *Stoa* or Porch in Athens.

Homère-troubadour: To link the supposed author (perhaps 8th century B.C.) of *The Iliad* and *The Odyssey* and Provençal poets of the 12th and 13th centuries in Italy, Spain and France is a Hugo-like step through the centuries.

Curé voltairien: Voltaire (1694-1778) was decidedly anti-clerical and persecuted for satirising civil and ecclesiastical cruelty, obscurantism and humbug in such tales as *Zadig* and *Candide*.

Phœbé, Phœbus: Latin names for Diana (the Moon goddess) and Apollo (the Sun god).

Albion perfide: Albion was an ancient name for England; for the French *la perfide Albion!* is a joke name for England, but Bossuet wrote it with noble indignation which the deadly serious days of war between England and France perpetuated.

Brigadier... alludes to the chorus of a popular song by Gustave Nadaud (a 19th century chansonnier) called *Pandore ou Les deux gendarmes: Brigadier, répondit Pandore, / Brigadier, vous avez raison.*

gabion: a basket filled with earth and sand for use as protection.

Le naufrageur:

Notre-Dame des Brisans: Does Our Lady of the Breakers help sailors in distress or wreckers in crying need? In *La Mer et les Marins* by Édouard Corbière, pillager Bretons are delighted to see a boat wrecked and exclaim: *It's Holy Virgin Mary, mother of God, who's brought this result of the terrible weather just for us.*

la grève des Kerlouans: Kerlouan is in North Finistère, 35 kilometres from Brest.

le Mois Noir: As in *La pastorale de Conlie*, November.

à poil roux: red hair was associated with disaster. Didn't Judas have red hair?

saltin was an insult still heard in Brest early this century. A contraction of Salétin, a pirate from the Moroccan port of Salé on the Barbary Coast, it came to be applied, as Tristan indicates, to a plunderer of wrecks.

À mon cotre Le Négrier: Tristan sold his single masted cutter, called *Le Négrier* after his father's maritime adventure novel, in 1871. Catullus 4 has a fine fast yacht retiring from the sea and Alcaeus has a ship, weary of many voyages, described as if she were an old diseased courtesan at the end of her career.

Le phare:

Phœbus: Apollo, the sun-god.

Priape: son of Venus by Bacchus, at birth deformed by Juno in all his limbs and given an enormous penis. His mother ashamed of producing such a monster, ordered him to be exposed on the mountains. Shepherds took care of him and he became a favourite of the people of Lampsacus until he made too free with the wives. Greek god of generation, Roman symbol of virility. Imagine the statues.

Éole: island king of storms and winds, inventor of sails, great astronomer, Æolus tied all dangerous winds in a leathern bag and gave them to Ulysses for his voyage back to Ithaca. Ulysses' companions let them out and they were driven back to the island, but Æolus was too indignant to help them again.

Mais plier — non. — La Fontaine's head-in-the-air Oak is uprooted when Wind redoubles his efforts, but Reed bends *(le roseau plie)*. *(Le Chêne et le Roseau* Bk 1 xxii)

Musset... Tristan's verse is a part-quotation from this verse of Musset's *Ballade à la lune:*

> C'était, dans la nuit brune,
> Sur le clocher jauni,
> La lune
> Comme un point sur un i.

Musset was often referred to as the poet with the dot on the i. Note Tristan's capital I.

une vestale: in ancient Rome the priestesses of Vesta were young virgins whose task was to keep the sacred fire burning in the temple of the goddess.

ramonage: probably predating the alpinists' use of *ramoner:* to climb a chimney!

Les Triagots: the Triagoz lighthouse is 10 kilometres from la Côte de Granit, to the North-west of Trégastel.

La fin:

V.Hugo. — *Oceano nox:* (Night on the ocean: from Virgil's Aeneid Bk.2 line 250) There are several misquotations in these (misremembered?) lines from *Oceano nox* (*Les rayons et les ombres,*1840), the chief being:

> *L'Océan, de leur vie* for *L'ouragan de leur vie;*
> *Nul ne saura leurs noms* for *Rien ne sait plus vos noms;*

la chanson plaintive for *la chanson naïve;*
D'un aveugle qui chante for *Que chante un mendiant.*
De profundis: from Psalm cxxx: Out of the depths have I cried unto thee, O Lord.
La Camarde: grim Death.

RONDELS POUR APRÈS

The rondel form has not been as constant as the sonnet form. A normal rondel consists of 3 stanzas with only 2 rhymes, 13 lines including a 2 line refrain at lines 1-2 and 7-8, and the first line returning as the final line, the rhyme scheme being ABba abAB abbaA. Tristan's rondels are quite abnormal.

Rondel:

Qui disaient: Jamais!... Jacques Bridaine (1701-1767): preacher and missionary, in a sermon on Eternity, wrote: *Eh! savez-vous ce que c'est que l'éternité? C'est une pendule dont le balancier dit et redit sans cesse ces deux mots seulement dans le silence des tombeaux: Toujours, jamais! Jamais, toujours!...* The repeated lines return like a pendulum.
tes amis les ours: La Fontaine's fable *L'ours et l'amateur des jardins* has a lonely mountain bear befriending a lonely old man to a point where he even keeps the flies off him. But when one keeps landing on the sleeping man's nose, the bear takes a paving stone, crashes it down on the fly... *Demoiselles* are dragonflies as well as young ladies.

Do, l'enfant, do...: from a popular lullaby.
vespre, nocte approximate Italian.
Ton bout de cierge.../ est mort: is not a far cry from *Ma chandelle est morte* from *Au clair de la lune.* As in *Le Poète Contumace* where the same song is quoted, there is a similar theme: the lack of love.

Mirliton: a toy reed-pipe or kazoo; a hollowed out reed with onion-peel at either end. *Vers de mirliton* is doggerel, the sort of thing printed on bands of paper and put round *mirlitons.*
ferreur de cigales: to shoe cicadas (the old expression is *ferrer les cigales*) is to waste one's time doing something useless or absurd. Rabelais describing Gargantua's childhood (Gargantua ch.XI) has him ducking under water to avoid the rain, striking the iron while it was cold, putting the cart before the oxen, scratching where he didn't itch, shoeing cicadas *(il ferroyt les cigalles),* and tickling himself to make himself laugh. What's more: *il tiroit les vers du nez,* he would pull worms from his nose (i.e. worm information out), a play on words Tristan uses in *Laisser-Courre* ll.44-5. Marcelle, the cicada in the dedicatory poem, having lent him a rhyme, finds she has been shoed in Tristan's verse with clangings and kazooings.
Muse camarde: camard is snub-nosed, or of dogs: pug-nosed, or of ships: bluff-headed. With a big C it would be grim Death (fem!) as in *La Fin.*

Petit mort pour rire: the phrase *un petit mot* (word) *pour rire* is given a sinister twist.

peigneur de comètes (comber of comets): Tristan would have been well aware that *comète* is derived from the Greek *kometes:* long-haired.

Amourettes: London Pride aka Nancy-Pretty, none-so-pretty; quaking grass; as well as little love affairs, passing fancies. Also a common or garden name for lily of the valley *(muguet)*.

Male-fleurette: There's more than a hint of *Les fleurs du mal* (Baudelaire 1857) in this title.

Cucurbitacés: normally feminine and without a capital letter, they are members of the gourd family like melon, cucumber, pumpkin. Here they must be bourgeois with a capital B for Belly.

Ici reviendra....: In the first edition of *Les Amours Jaunes* the first lines of all the poems in the collection begin with a dropped initial. The only other line to do so is this final repeated line, which announces the return of the *male-fleurette*.

À MARCELLE

La cigale et le poète:

déchanté: no sooner has he said *chanté* (sung) than he changes the tone, revises the sense of what he's done, there is the song and the descant, there is the La Fontaine poem and in counterpoint him singing it down in a different key, corrupting it, which is how Marcelle will say she sees his book. He, the author, the poet, has lost his illusions *(déchanté)*, *un*sung his songs by singing flat, taken out any lyricism. What else can you do when your Muse is pissed? When La Fontaine was dying, he repented for having written his racy *Contes: J'ai eu le malheur de composer un livre de Contes, infâme.* The 10 year old Duke of Burgundy, grandson of Louis XIV, was delighted, agreeing that it was *un livre abominable,*and sent him a purse of 50 golden louis to tide him over.

en revenant: as well as going back to his neighbour's window-pane, the phrase has him going back as a ghost, a revenant (one who returns from the dead after a long absence). To live on, he needs to come back *après!* Although this poem is not one of the *Rondels pour après*, it's after after.

Henry Murger began his writing career with a short story called *Les Amours d'un Grillon et d'une Étincelle* (printed in *Le Corsaire* in 1845: the year of Tristan's birth). A cricket falls in love with a star. His hard-headed, earth-bound friend the beetle, tries in vain to cure him of his senseless passion. One Christmas night, taking refuge in a poor man's cottage, the cricket thinks he recognises the star in first one, then another of a succession of sparks coming from a log burning on the hearth. He serenades each spark with his best songs. Finally one spark lodges in a corner of the fireplace and the cricket, thinking his singing has at last had an effect, approaches, only to see his beloved go pale and turn to ash before his eyes.